WWJDWWJDWWJDWW
MW01122124

THIS BOOK
BELONGS TO:

_____

FROM:

_____

DATE:

_____

WWJDWWJDWWJDWWJDWWJDWWJDWWJWW

THIS BOOK
BELONGS TO:

FROM:

DATE:

What Would Jesus Do?

What Would Jesus Do?

366 DEVOTIONS IN THE FOOTSTEPS OF JESUS

JAN DE WET

CHRISTIAN ART
PUBLISHERS

Originally published by Christian Publishing Company
under the title *Wat sal Jesus doen?*

© 1998

First English edition © 1998
CHRISTIAN PUBLISHING COMPANY,
PO Box 1599, Vereeniging, 1930

Translated by San-Mari Mills

Second edition © 2000
CHRISTIAN ART PUBLISHERS

Cover designed by Christian Publishing Company

Scripture taken from the *Holy Bible*, New International Version.
Copyright © 1973, 1978, 1984 by International Bible Society. Used by
permission of Zondervan Publishing House. All rights reserved.

Set in 13 on 15 pt GoudySans Light
by Christian Art Publishers

Printed and bound by NBD, Drukkery Street,
Goodwood, Western Cape

ISBN 1-86852-708-5

© All rights reserved. No part of this book may be reproduced in any
form without permission in writing from the publisher, except in the
case of brief quotations embodied in critical articles or reviews.

00 01 02 03 04 05 06 07 08 09 – 10 9 8 7 6 5 4 3 2 1

Following in his footsteps ...

Someone lost his job as a labourer at a printing house. Six months later his wife died in wretched circumstances in New York. His daughter had nowhere to go, no one to turn to. For days on end he tried, without success, to find a job in Richmond, U.S.A.

One Sunday morning Henry Maxwell preached to a packed congregation from 1 Peter 2:21, *To this you were called, because Christ suffered for you, leaving you an example, that you should follow in his steps.*

Follow in the steps of Jesus in obedience, faith and love! was his urgent plea. Then a man went forward, a man who had been a hobo in Richmond, U.S.A. for the past ten months ...

What does it mean, he asked, to follow in Jesus' footsteps? Indeed. What would Jesus do if he should come across someone like this hobo?

Does this story sound familiar? Richmond, U.S.A., Johannesburg, R.S.A., London, U.K. Different places, same circumstances. And the same question. Charles Sheldon's well-known book, *In His Steps*, was written at a time when certain people undertook to ask what would Jesus do if He were in their place. They would do this before every decision they took for one year.

No, not what would Jesus have done, but what did He do? What would Jesus do? This is the question that Jan de Wet wants to answer in this diary. In this way he wants to help you, a youngster, to get into the habit of following in the footsteps of Jesus in every aspect of your life, so that it becomes a way of life for you.

To remind you of this, a bracelet has been bound in the diary with the question: What would Jesus do? Cut the bracelet loose and ask someone to help you burn off the ends so that they don't fray. Wear it as a symbol – it is what God tells us to do in Deuteronomy 6:8 – for following Jesus' example in specific circumstances.

– The Publisher –

The new year!

This is the day the Lord has made; let us rejoice and be glad in it. (Ps. 118:24)

At the beginning of this new year my wish for you is that it will be a wonderful year for you, and that you will be very happy.

It always feels good to start something new. It feels good to wear new shoes. It feels good to ride a new bicycle. You are most probably in a new grade this year with new challenges waiting for you.

If you put your hand in the hand of Jesus, then I know that He will lead you safely this new year, every step of the way. He says in his Word that every day is the day of the Lord and that it is a gift in your hand.

Come, let's be joyful and happy about every new day, and also about this new year that the Lord has given us. Join me now, and let's ask the Lord to bless us, and help us to do only what is important to him. With him to lead us this will be a wonderful year.

WWJD
On this day Jesus would pray, "Your will be done."

... only he who does the will of my Father ... (Mt. 7:21)

January 1

Winners

But thanks be to God, who always leads us in triumphal procession in Christ ... (2 Cor. 2:14)

It is always nice to be on the winning side. It is great to win a game. When your school's first team wins a rugby or cricket match, or an athletics meeting, you are very proud because it feels good to be on the winning side.

Just as there are winners on the sports fields, there are also winners in life. Paul writes that we are running the race of life. This means how we live will determine whether we win or lose. The Bible tells us if we live with Christ, that is, give our lives to him and belong to him, then we are in the winning team with him. We know Jesus is the great winner. He paid for our sins on the cross and He rose from the dead: He overcame death and the devil!

Decide to put your hand in the hand of the great winner, Jesus Christ, right now. Take on the rest of this day as a winner, with Jesus. And if something should happen today which is hurtful to you or becomes a problem, leave it in the hands of your great winner, Jesus Christ.

WWJD
Jesus would not give up, and He will win.

"Father, into your hands, I commit my spirit." (Lk. 23:46)

January 2

Is God dead?

The fool says in his heart, "There is no God." (Ps. 14:1)

Many people say God is dead. Some think He doesn't exist, some say He has retired, others that He is asleep, or is not interested in people. Maybe they say that because they cannot see him or touch him.

The Bible says someone who thinks this, is a fool. That is certainly not a compliment, is it? As we know, fools say and do foolish things.

The Bible says those who say God does not exist are really stupid. They are making a big mistake. One day a man also told someone that God does not exist. The answer was, "But that's impossible, just this morning I spoke to him and He to me!"

Yes, if one really believes in God you somehow just know, deep down: the Lord truly lives. He talks to you through his Word, and you can talk to him in prayer. Then you cannot doubt that He exists, and you just know that He lives in your heart.

Does God live in your heart?

WWJD
Jesus would live so that everybody
can see that his Father lives.

... Jesus Christ... who is at the Father's
side, has made him known. (Jn. 1:17, 18)

January 3

Starting all over again

[Paul says] (O)ne thing J do: Forgetting what is behind and straining toward what is ahead. (Phil. 3:13)

We all make mistakes. No one on earth has never had a problem of some kind, or made some or other mistake. Maybe you remember something you did that was a big mistake. The worst part is that we sometimes make the same mistake over and over again!

We get people who enjoy reminding us of this mistake that we made in the past. Then we hurt all over again. If we keep on thinking of past mistakes we can start feeling depressed.

But the Bible tells us if we have made a mistake and we are sorry about it, we must tell the Lord. The Bible calls it: to confess. And once we have confessed our sin, the Lord forgives us immediately. When the Lord forgives our sin, it means that He doesn't think about it again. So it is over and done with.

Paul says he will put everything that happened in the past behind him. He will look ahead and try to live the way he should. Tell the Lord that you are sorry about the mistakes you made in the past, thank him for forgiving you, and live to the full, every moment of this new day.

WWJD
Jesus would love and care for people, faults and all.

(Jesus) said ... "If any one of you is without sin, let him be the first to throw a stone at her." (Jn. 8:7)

January 4

Laugh and cry

Rejoice with those who rejoice; mourn with those who mourn. (Rom. 12:15)

I'm sure you have often had a good laugh about something that happened to you. But then again, you have also cried a lot about things that made you sad. All of us laugh sometimes, and sometimes we cry.

The Lord says we must laugh with those who laugh, and cry with those who cry. We must not laugh when others cry. If you do that, then you are really being nasty. Sometimes when others are laughing, their friends get fed up with them because they are in a bad mood and don't feel like laughing. This is also wrong. When people are happy, we must also be happy because we like people and we love them. If someone hurts and cries, we must cry with them, because surely, we don't like to see others hurting.

If the love of the Lord is in our hearts, we want to feel what others feel. Then we are happy when they are happy, and sad when they are sad.

If you know of a friend who is unhappy, go and tell him or her that you are sorry about it. If something good happens, tell him or her that you are happy for them.

WWJD
Jesus would laugh and cry with you and me.

 When Jesus saw her weeping
... Jesus wept. (Jn. 11:33, 35)

January 5

I'll show you

Do not take revenge, my friends, but leave room for God's wrath ... (Rom. 12:19)

Has anyone ever hurt you or upset you? Often people do things that make us very angry and we want to pay them back. We feel like saying, "I'll show you!" Some guys start fighting, using either their fists or their tongues. If we do that, it shows that we want to take revenge. We want to pay someone back because we hurt.

The Bible says that is not a wise thing to do. It is much better to forgive one another. And if we still feel in our hearts that the other person must be paid back, rather ask God to do it. The Bible tells us to let God decide. He is a fair Judge. And there is going to be a Judgement Day. At the end of our lives each one of us will stand before the great throne of God. Then God will pass judgement (cf. Rom. 2:3).

You must not judge. Leave that to God. Forgive any friend that hurt you. Do it right now, and then leave it in the hands of the Lord.

WWJD
Jesus would forgive his wrongdoers.

Father, forgive them ... (Lk. 23:34)

January 6

It's all right to go

... we have confidence to enter the Most Holy place by the blood of Jesus ... (L)et us draw near to God with a sincere heart in full assurance of faith ... (Heb. 10:19, 22)

Many people are afraid to go to God. Perhaps it is because they think the Lord will not understand how they feel. They think God is strict and just wants to judge them and punish them.

Surely this is not true! God loves us so much that He gave us his Son on the cross. Yes, He has proved his love for us, and that is exactly what today's scripture says. When Jesus died for us on the cross, the curtain of the temple tore from top to bottom and since then everybody can enter into God's presence. We can talk to him every day and anywhere and be with him. He is there with you on the sports field, or wherever you may be today.

You must not be self-conscious about speaking to God about your whole life. Everything you do and say, He knows about, and He is with you every moment of the day. You are in his presence. It's all right to take all your problems to him and to talk to him about everything that happens to you. He understands and He loves you.

WWJD
Jesus would talk to his Father.

... Jesus got up ... went off to a solitary place, where He prayed. (Mark. 1:35)

January 7

Every knee will bow

(T)hat in the name of Jesus every knee should bow ... and every tongue confess that Jesus Christ is Lord ... (Phil. 2:10, 11)

The Bible says everyone in heaven and on earth, and even under the earth will bend the knee before Jesus Christ. This means that everybody will confess that He is Jesus, the Savior, the only one who can free us from sin. Everyone wil also confess that He is the Christ: that He has been anointed by the Holy Spirit to bring you and me salvation.

But they will also confess that He is the Lord. The word "lord" means king, master, or someone with the highest authority.

In the olden days, subjects of the king bowed before him. In this way they confessed that the king was greater and more powerful than they were. That is why each and every one of us will also bow to King Jesus.

If you accept Jesus as your Savior, then you bow before him in your heart and you confess that He has become your King. Then you want to live for him and do what He wants you to. Have you gone down on your knees before him yet? Those of us who do not bow down before Jesus now, will have to do it in heaven one day, but then it will be too late.

WWJD
Jesus would confess that God is his Father.

(Jesus) looked toward heaven and prayed: "Father ... " (Jn. 17:1)

January 8

Work out the cost

"Suppose one of you wants to build a tower. Will he not first sit down and estimate the cost to see if he has enough money to complete it?" (Lk. 14:28)

Before you can buy something you want badly, you must first see if you have enough money. If you want to buy a rugby ball, or a skateboard or computer games, or anything that you would really like to have, you first have to work out if you have the money to buy it. Most things we want, we have to pay for.

The Bible says there is also a price to pay if we want to follow Jesus. Yes, it is true that Jesus loved us so much that He died on the cross for us. But it will cost us something very precious to know that we will be with him in heaven for ever: our hearts. We say to him, "Here is my heart, take it; I have decided to follow You." And if there are people who do not like it if I follow Jesus, or if some of my friends tease me because I say that I love Jesus, then that is the price I must pay for the joy of being his child.

But, do you know, it is always a bargain to follow Jesus.

WWJD
Jesus paid the price, so that we can be his children.

How great is the love the father has lavished on us, that we should be called children of God ... (1 Jn. 3:1)

January 9

Charge your battery

" ... He rested on the seventh day. Therefore the Lord blessed the Sabbath day and made it holy." (Ex. 20:11)

We all know that batteries get flat. New batteries make a torch shine brightly, and a car cannot go if the battery is flat. Just like a battery gets flat, we humans also get tired. That is why we must rest. That is why it is important that we get enough sleep. If our batteries are flat, it means we cannot do our work properly, and besides, we don't feel good.

Because God knows this, He set one day a week aside so that we can have a good rest. If we work hard every day of the week, do all our homework and go to sports practices, then we need to rest. Usually we rest over weekends. But we must also rest spiritually. Our hearts must be tuned in to hear the voice of the Lord and to do what He asks. One can enjoy resting in God's presence. That is why we go to church, listen to his Word, and sing songs with some of his other children – because we are glad that He loves us. In this way we charge the batteries of our lives, all over again.

WWJD
Jesus would be a regular churchgoer.

... they found him in the temple ... (Lk. 2:46)

January 10

The speck and the plank

" ... first take the plank out of your own eye, and then you will see clearly to remove the speck from your brother's eye." (Mt. 7:5)

A plank is a long flat piece of wood. It is quite thick and is used for making floors or to build things like wendy houses. Planks must be strong because a floor carries a lot of weight.

A speck is very tiny, so tiny that you can hardly see it. If a speck of dust gets into your eye, you will feel it, but if someone wants to take it out, they may have a problem finding it.

We all have our faults and sometimes these faults are so big that they are like a thick plank in one's eye. But we pretend not to notice, as if we have no faults. The worst part is that we then blame others, just as if we are without faults. We like telling others how big their sins and faults are, but we are not honest about our own.

Jesus says we should not blame others. It is much better to first see to our own faults and take the thick plank of sin out of our own lives. Even better than that, is not to find fault with others at all, just love them.

WWJD
Jesus would be tender and loving
with those who have faults.

... (Jesus) said to them, "If any one of you is without sin, let him be the first to throw a stone at her." (Jn. 8:7)

January 11

Train, train, train

... rather train yourself to be godly. (1 Tim. 4:7)

If you want to play the piano well, you have to practise a lot. Good athletes or rugby players must also train hard so that they can be fit, and learn the rules of their sport, so that they can be good at it.

It is not always easy to train or practise for something, but you do it anyway, because you know that it will help you do better. It is the same with school work: if you work hard, you get good marks in tests or exams.

The Bible says if we want to learn how to live successfully, we must also train ourselves in our relationship with the Lord. This means we have to read the Bible regularly, talk to the Lord, and do things that will help us in our relationship with him. But, just like an athlete, we must make time for God everyday and be busy with him.

Will you do this today?

WWJD
Jesus would make time to speak to his Father.

(P)ray continually. (1 Thes. 5:17)

January 12

The thirsty deer

As the deer pants for streams of water, so my soul pants for you, O God. (Ps. 42:1)

If you visit a game reserve, you will notice how far buck must walk to get to water.

They are usually so thirsty by the time they reach the waterhole that they spend a long time drinking, to quench their thirst. Especially in Bible times, the buck in the desert had to walk very long distances to get to water. By the time they got there, they were desperate for water.

This is the image the Bible uses to explain that human beings are actually also thirsty for the water that only God can give us. Jesus said He is the Fountain of Living Water, and his water will quench a person's spiritual thirst. The Lord's love is like a cool stream of water where we can stand and drink to quench the thirst in our hearts.

We drink the Lord's water as we listen when He speaks to us through his Word and we are filled with the Holy Spirit deep down. Why not tell the Lord right now, that you are drinking his Living Water, so that you may never be thirsty again.

WWJD
Jesus would give you water to quench your thirst.

"If anyone is thirsty, let him come to Me and drink." (Jn. 7:37)

January 13

Leave everything as it is

"Follow Me," he [Jesus] told him ... (Mt. 9:9)

Matthew was most probably a very rich man. He had a tax collector's booth where people had to pay tax money. Often the tax collectors took more money than they were supposed to and so they became very rich.

One day Jesus saw Matthew sitting at the tax collector's booth and Jesus said to him, "Follow Me!" Maybe Matthew was surprised at this invitation, but what is even more surprising is that he immediately left everything just there and started following Jesus. One can hardly believe this!

Perhaps the love in Jesus' eyes made up Matthew's mind for him. Perhaps Matthew had a longing for peace deep in his heart, that only Jesus could give. Perhaps Matthew realised that only Jesus could free him from sin.

If Jesus invites you to follow him, you would be foolish not to give him your whole life. Come, let's follow him!

WWJD
Jesus calls also you, to follow him.

"Come, follow Me ... " (Mt. 4:19)

January 14

Run away!

She [Potiphar's wife] caught him by his cloak and said, "Come to bed with me!" But he ... ran out of the house. (Gen. 39:12)

Joseph loved the Lord very much and He had a wonderful plan with Joseph's life. First Joseph's brothers were jealous of him because of his dreams that told him the Lord had a plan with his life. They first threw him into a dry well and then sold him to some merchants who took him to Egypt. But the Lord saw to it that nothing happened to him.

One day Joseph was in the home of the minister, Potiphar, an important man in the palace of the great Pharaoh. Potiphar had a bad wife. She had her eye on Joseph and wanted him to go to bed with her. But Joseph knew it would be wrong.

When Potiphar's wife told him a second time that she wanted to sleep with him, without her husband knowing about it, he refused again. When he ran away from her, out of her house, she grabbed hold of his coat. Later on she told lies about Joseph, but the Lord helped him.

It is always better to run away from people who want you to do something sinful. If your friends try to get you to do something and you know it is wrong, say "No", like Joseph did, and if they don't want to listen, it is better to walk or run away. Even if they think you're a coward, the Lord will be on your side.

WWJD
Jesus would not give in to temptation.

"Away fom Me, Satan..." (Mt. 4:10)

January 15

Seventy times seven!

"Lord, how many times shall I forgive my brother when he sins against me? Up to seven times?" Jesus answered, "I tell you, not seven times, but seventy times seven." (Mt. 18:21, 22)

Oh, sometimes it is so difficult to forgive. Especially if someone has hurt us or made us angry. We would much rather get them back than forgive them.

But the Bible says the best thing to do is to forgive someone for what he has done. Sometimes we say, "Yes, I'll forgive only this once, but not again." No, the Bible is quite clear about this. We must be prepared to forgive one another up to seventy times seven times. Wow, that's quite a lot. It is almost 500 times. Actually, the issue here is not really how many times, because seven is the perfect (complete or whole) number in the Bible. So what the Bible is really saying is that we must forgive perfectly or completely. Even if someone sins against me 3000 times, and the same sin every time, I must keep on forgiving.

Is there someone you need to forgive? Why not tell the Lord right now that you are sorry for wanting to pay him back in his own coin.

Tell Jesus now that you forgive that person.

WWJD
Jesus would forgive.

Who is a God like You, who pardons sin and forgives the transgression ... You do not stay angry forever... (Mic. 7:18)

January 16

Wonderfully made

I praise You because I am fearfully and wonderfully made ... (Ps. 139:14)

Just think how many people there are on this earth. Every person looks different and talks differently and every person acts in a different way. Isn't it wonderful? Not even twins have exactly the same characteristics.

Some people have black hair, others are blond; some are tall, others are short; some are fat and others are skinny. Every person is unique and special. You too! You are wonderfully made. Maybe you don't think you're very pretty, or maybe you can't run as fast as somebody you know. Maybe you can't sing. But it doesn't matter, because you are special, you are you. The Lord gave you something that nobody else has.

Don't try to be like someone else. God made you unique. Just be yourself. Then the Lord will be able to use you, and you will also be happy. Won't you thank him right now for making you so special and unique?

WWJD
Jesus would share his life with you and me.

You ... crowned him (the human being) with glory and honor. (Ps. 8:6)

January 17

Feeling miserable?

Hope deferred makes the heart sick ... (Prov. 13:12)

I remember well, when I was still small, our family planned a wonderful holiday at a good resort. We talked it over and dreamt about it and we were so excited when the holidays finally came. But then something came up and we couldn't go any more. My father cancelled the bookings and we had to stay home. I felt miserable.

It often happens that things don't work out the way we plan them. Sometimes everything seems to go wrong at the same time and we can't help feeling depressed. Fortunately the Lord knows everything, and if you are his child, you can trust him to help you. Through his Holy Spirit He helps and comforts us. Many times He assures us that there will be another opportunity to do what we would like to.

If you are feeling miserable about something, leave it in the hands of Jesus. He understands. Also, thank him for the things that you do have. And see, it will make you feel better.

WWJD
Jesus would cheer you up in difficult times.

"Come to Me ... and I will give you rest." (Mt. 11:28)

January 18

Mrs Lot loses everything

But Lot's wife looked back, and she became a pillar of salt.
(Gen. 19:26)

The Bible thinks so little of Lot's wife that her name is not even mentioned. Let's call her Mrs Lot. Lot and his wife lived in Sodom. The people there would not do what the Lord told them. So He decided to destroy Sodom. But because he loved Abraham, and Lot was family of Abraham's, the Lord warned Lot to flee. Mrs Lot, however, did not want to leave all her nice things behind. She did not really believe that the Lord would look after her. When she turned around to look back at Sodom, she was changed into a pillar of salt, and she lost her life and her possessions.

We must never love things better than God. He must be number one in our lives. He will look after us if we make him King in our lives. The Bible says when we give our lives to Jesus, we keep our lives.

Of course some things are very precious to us. But Jesus is much more precious than possessions. One day, when we go to him, we will have to leave everything behind anyway. Come, let's make Jesus number one in our lives right now.

WWJD
Jesus would store up treasures in heaven.

" ...the Son of Man has no place to lay his head." (Mt. 8:20)

January 19

Food without salt

"You are the salt of the earth ... " (Mt. 5:13)

There are large salt-pans in our country where salt is accumulated, and then it is ground, so that we can put it into a salt-cellar. When we eat an egg, or any other food that needs salt, we sprinkle salt from the salt-shaker on to the food. Salt gives food a better taste. When one is used to salt on food, it doesn't taste good without salt.

Jesus said we, his children, are the salt of the earth. Salt makes food taste better, and in the same way, we must flavour everything around us with our words and everything we do. People must enjoy having us around.

Today we use ointments and disinfectants to clean wounds. But in the olden days they used salt to disinfect wounds, in other words, to get germs out. They rubbed salt into wounds to make them heal quickly. We, as children of the Lord, must sometimes also be like salt in the wounds of others. With our words and our actions we must help heal people's wounds. If there is evil around us, me must overcome evil with good. For example, if someone swears, we should help them see it is wrong.

WWJD
Jesus would influence people
with his words and his deeds.

(A)nd He began to teach them... (Mt. 5:2)

January 20

Are you a tree?

They will be called oaks of righteousness ... (Is. 61:3)

An oak tree is a beautiful tree. Some towns in our country have beautiful oaks, like Sasolburg and also Stellenbosch which is called City of Oaks. An oak tree grows tall and wide. It is a lovely tree with many branches and bright green leaves. In summer one can take a rest in the shade of an oak tree. Birds also like building their nests in oak trees.

Isaiah says that you and I are also like these trees; oaks that stand tall and proud. When people look at us they must also be able to say, he or she is just as upright as an oak. What the Bible actually says is that you and I, because we are saved and belong to Jesus, stand up straight, like the oak: a tree of righteousness. As children of the Lord, we are like large, lush beautiful green oaks.

When people look at you today they must see an oak tree standing tall.

WWJD
Jesus would show He is proud to serve the Father.

" ... I know him because I am from him and He sent Me." (Jn. 7:29)

January 21

Light is stronger

The light shines in the darkness, but the darkness has not overcome it. (Jn. 1:5)

I'm sure you have walked in the dark before. As you know, it is very difficult to see where you are going. In the dark you can bump into chairs or other objects and hurt yourself. That is why we buy a torch, or switch on a light so that it can drive the darkness away. Light is stronger than darkness, we know that. The moment you switch on a light, the darkness disappears, because the light is so bright.

The Bible says that Jesus is the light that came into this world. The true light that gives light to every man was coming into the world (cf. Jn. 1:9). The true light is Jesus. He himself said, "I am the light of the world." Jesus is like a bright light that drives out the darkness. And what is the darkness? It is the devil's kingdom. The devil is also called the prince of darkness. The work of the devil is just as black as the darkest night. Jesus came to change the darkness of the devil into light.

WWJD
Jesus will shine in you, so that you will be a light to the world.

"I am the light of the world. Whoever walks in Me ... will have the light of life." (Jn. 8:12)

January 22

Love builds

... in humility consider others better than yourselves. (Phil. 2:3)

When we really love someone, then we do not want to hurt that person's feelings. When we love someone we want to make that person happy. Paul writes in 1 Corinthians 13 that love is not self-seeking, which means it does not always want its own way. This means we want to build, or uplift our loved ones and want what's best for them.

Uplifting someone is the opposite of running that person down. When we humiliate people, we make them feel small. All of us have, at some time or another, really felt like humiliating someone. But this is a very ugly characteristic. Let's try to uplift those around us with our actions and especially with our words and with our love. This will mean that you and I must encourage friends and other people and say something like, "Well done, that was good." Or, "You tried your best. If you carry on like this, you will be a winner."

Let's build one another in love.

WWJD
Jesus would never turn a person away but He will help in love.

"... I do not want to send them away hungry..." (Mt. 15:32)

January 23

Our Father

" ... Our Father in heaven ..." (Mt. 6:9)

Jesus taught us how to pray. When we pray, we talk to God. We open up our hearts to him and tell him everything that we think is important in our lives.

But before we can really pray, we need to have a personal relationship with the Lord. This means that we must not feel that God is far away, but that He is close to us, because Jesus introduced us to him. If we have worked out things between God and ourselves – because we accepted Jesus' offer on the cross – then the Almighty God becomes "our" Father.

"Our" shows that you own something. It is the same as "mine". When something belongs to you, you say it is "mine". The Bible also says he who has the Son has life; he who does not have the Son of God does not have life. If you have accepted Jesus, God is also your Father. Therefore you may call him "my Father". Then we pray together with all Christians, "Our Father in heaven ... "

WWJD
Jesus would help you speak to God the Father.

... in everything, by prayer ... present your requests to God. (Phil. 4:6)

January 24

Daddy-father

WWJD

" ... Our Father in heaven..." (Mt. 6:9)

Every person on earth has a father. Most people know their fathers. Unfortunately some children's daddies have died, or live somewhere far away, and some don't know who their daddy is.

Every person must have a father, otherwise no one can be born. To be born, every person must have a father.

God is the Father of Jesus Christ. But He also becomes our Father, our Dad, if we accept him in faith. The Lord wants us to be his children. But not everybody on earth is God's child; only those who accepted him. That is what we read in John 1:12, ... *to all who received him, to those who believed in his name, He gave the right to become children of God.* Are you God's child yet?

If you become God's child, you soon find out that He is a wonderful daddy or father. Because he loves us so much and wants only the best for us, we must feel free to speak to him, and he also talks to us through his Word. He comforts and helps us through the Holy Spirit that He gave us. Yes, He is a wonderful dad. Because he understands, and loves you, speak to him today.

WWJD
Jesus would talk to his Father regularly.

...to a solitary place, where He prayed. (Mk. 1:35)

January 25

Heaven

" ... Our Father in heaven ... " (Mt. 6:9)

God lives in heaven. Heaven is a perfect, wonderful place. There are no tears or heartache or pain or hurt. Everything in heaven is perfect and complete. God lives in heaven with his Son, Jesus, and also with millions of angels that praise and serve him all the time.

We don't really know where heaven is. We are also not sure what it looks like there. What we do know is that there are people who died and came back to life again. We say that they had a "seeming death", like a trance. They all say that heaven is a wonderful place. Most of these peole did not want to come back to earth at all because they enjoyed heaven so much. God rules in heaven and there is no sin to hurt people. Also, there isn't room for the devil. He lives in hell.

When God has become our Father, then we know for sure that there will be a place for us in heaven. Jesus went there to prepare our place. Do you also look forward to heaven? How about speaking to your Father in heaven right now?

WWJD
Jesus will be glad to see us in heaven one day.

" ... that you may also be where I am." (Jn. 14:3)

January 26

His name

" ... hallowed [holy] be your name ..." (Mt. 6:9)

The Lord has many names. He is sometimes called Father or Almighty or Immanuel or Jesus or King. All these names are just to tell us more about him, who He is and how he acts. Because the Lord can never sin, all his names are beautiful and show his holiness. To be holy is to be pure and without sin. God's name is holy. That is why it really is terrible when children or adults use his name just anyhow, and even as a swear word. Do you know anyone who uses his name like this? We must never do it. If you hear one of your friends doing it, you must, in a nice way, tell this friend that you love Jesus and that his name is holy.

When we pray, we say, "Hallowed be your name." What we really mean is, "May your name be just as wonderful and lovely as You, Lord." And when his name comes from our lips, then we speak with respect.

WWJD
Jesus would respect the name of his Father.

"You shall not misuse the name of the Lord your God ..." (Ex. 20:7)

January 27

The kingdom of the King

"(Y)our kingdom come ... " (Mt. 6:10)

Especially in the olden days, the king ruled over his land, and that was his kingdom, or as it is also called, his domain. Today there are many countries, and the leaders of these countries are state presidents or ministers. They also rule over a domain.

The most important kingdom that there is, is the kingdom of God. You might ask, "Where is the Lord's land?" Well, we could say it is in heaven, but it is also on earth. God does not have a piece of land like, say South Africa or Italy; no, his land or kingdom is everywhere that people accept his kingship. If you love the Lord and want to serve him, then He is your king. Then your heart becomes his kingdom. And wherever you might be, you take his kingdom with you: onto the sports field, into the class-room, or any other place. Come, let's make him King in South Africa and also of the whole world.

We pray, "Your kingdom come; be King here on earth."

WWJD
Jesus would build the kingdom of God.

Jesus went throughout Galilee ... preaching the good news of the kingdom ... (Mt. 4:23)

January 28

Your will or his will?

(Y)our will be done on earth ... (Mt. 6:10)

God rules in heaven and there his will is done. What He says, is done. His will is always best. He is like a good government that only wants what's best for citizens.

The devil also has a will, and he is so crooked that he always wants to get everybody to do his will. If we do what the devil wants, then we are asking for trouble. It is then that we get hurt and things start going wrong for us. On this earth there are many people that do the devil's will. Jesus teaches us to pray that the Lord's will be done on earth. You and I must choose to do the Lord's will, so that the earth can become a better place. I know I want to choose the Lord. What about you? Let's pray that the Lord's will be done, in our homes, and in our town.

WWJD
Jesus would do his Father's will.

" ... My Father... may your will be done." (Mt. 26:42)

January 29

Bread

"Give us today our daily bread." (Mt. 6:1)

Many people have only bread to eat. They live on bread. We all need bread or food to stay alive.

Mom and Dad work every day. The money they earn is used to buy food for the family. There are many poor people in countries all over the world. They are terribly hungry all the time, and don't even know if they will live till the next day. We must pray for them.

Because God is our Father, we trust him to take care of us. And we ask him to help us so that we will have bread to live on. The Lord promises in his Word that He will not allow his children to go hungry. He will look after us. If we really follow him and make him the king of our lives, He will take care of us. Let's thank him for everything He gives us, and let's give hungry people around us some of his bread.

WWJD
Jesus would take care of people who are having a difficult time.

Jesus then took the loaves... and distributed to... (the people) as much as they wanted ... (Jn. 6:11)

January 30

He forgives me

"Forgive us our debts [sins] ... " (Mt. 6:12)

Jesus came to stay on earth to die on a cross, so that God would forgive our sins. All of us are sinful. We are born with sin. Even when we are little, we do things that are wrong and that is why we all need to be forgiven.

If our sins are not forgiven, we have not made our peace with the Lord. That is why God wants our sins to be forgiven. Actually He is just waiting for us to say that we are sorry and then He forgives us immediately. We must never be too proud, or unwilling to tell the Lord that we are sorry about our sins.

That is why Jesus taught us to pray, "Forgive us our debts."

WWJD
Jesus would forgive sins.

If we confess our sins, He ...
will forgive us our sins... (1 Jn. 1:9)

January 31

I forgive you

" ... as we also have forgiven our debtors." (Mt. 6:12)

The Lord does not mind how often we have sinned against him; if we say we are sorry, He forgives us immediately. Sometimes we find it difficult to forgive others. But if the Lord forgives us so quickly, then we can also forgive a friend that has hurt us.

If a friend says, "I'm sorry," tell him or her straight away, "Never mind, I forgive you." Even if your friend does not say he's sorry, forgive him anyway in your heart. When you forgive someone there is peace in your heart and your life is clean before the Lord. It is the same when the Lord forgives you.

When you have done something that hurt your friend, you must also be prepared to say, "Please forgive me, I'm sorry I did this to you." If he forgives you then everything is forgotten. If he does not want to forgive you, you know you have done the right thing, and God is proud of you. Children of the Lord are called peacemakers. Be a peacemaker for Christ.

WWJD
Jesus would forgive someone who has hurt him.

Bear with each other ... Forgive as
the Lord forgave you. (Col. 3:13)

February 1

The spider web

"And lead us not into temptation ... " (Mt. 6:13)

A spider spins himself a web. This is his plan to catch insects so that he can eat them. The spider web is shiny when the sun catches it and it looks very nice, but if you are an insect and fly into it, you're finished.

The Lord taught us to pray that we must not be led into temptation. That means not doing things that can trap us like the insect in the spider web. The devil also spins a web for you and me. It looks very inviting, but once we are in his power, he destroys our lives. Sometimes we feel like taking part in things that seem such fun to do, but if doing this is not the will of the Lord, it cannot be good for us.

When we do something we must always ask the Lord if it is his will for us. Sometimes we are tempted to take someone else's things, or to tell a lie, or to talk behind someone's back. It is not good to do that.

Let's ask the Lord to help us so that we can tell when we are being tempted. He must also help us to be strong enough to say "no" to the devil who wants to catch us.

WWJD
Jesus would not give in to the devil's demands.

" ... Away from me, Satan ... " (Mt. 4:10)

February 2

The nasty old spider

" ... but deliver us from the evil one." (Mt. 6:13)

The spider spins a web to catch insects so that he can kill them. The devil wants to catch you and me so that he can kill us. The Bible also calls him the "enormous fiery-red dragon" or the "snake" or the "evil one". He is the one who fights against the Lord and his children and he makes war against us. He wants to destroy us.

Jesus taught us to pray that we may be delivered or saved from the evil one. There is only one way that we can be saved, and that is when the Great Savior protects us. His name is Jesus. Only He can save us from the evil one, and that is why we must be on his side. The devil wanted Jesus dead, but He is much stronger than the devil. Jesus rose from the dead and in this way, He overcame the devil.

We must also take sides with Jesus against the devil so that he cannot catch us. We do not belong to him, we belong to Jesus. Say "no" to the devil today, and "yes" to Jesus.

WWJD
Jesus would say "no" to the devil.

... count yourselves dead to sin
but alive to God ... (Rom. 6:11)

February 3

Amen

WWJD

... how can one [an ordinary person] ... say "Amen" to your thanksgiving ... ? (1 Cor. 14:16)

All our prayers usually end with the word "Amen". The real meaning of this word is "let it be so". It is almost like wishing that what I have just prayed will come true.

But we can only say "Amen" if that which we have prayed is the will of the Lord. God cannot give you and me what is bad for us.

He loves us and He wants only the best for us. That is why we must always ask if what we pray is his will. Many times we think we know what is good for us, but the Lord knows better. I have asked him for so many things that I did not get, and later on I saw that it was better that way. All the time God knew best. We can really trust him with our prayers.

By all means, pour your heart out to the Lord. It's all right to tell him what you would like to have. But then, just make sure in your heart, that what you are asking for is his will for you. Then you can safely end your prayer with "Amen".

WWJD
Jesus would always ask what the Father's will is.

"Father ... not my will, but yours be done." (Lk. 22:44)

February 4

Take his hand

" ... no one can snatch them out of my Father's hand." (Jn. 10:29)

Little children like taking their father or mother's hand. A child knows he is safe when his father takes his hand. Especially if he has to cross a busy road or walk in the dark.

He knows his daddy is big and strong and he is safe when his father is holding his hand.

The Lord asks us to put our hands in his big, strong hand. It is the best thing any person can do. We don't always know what tomorrow will bring. We need help. Apart from that, we often do not know what road to take. We must be led. That is why a Christian puts his or her hand in the big, strong hand of the Father. He will show us the right way. He will not let go of us. He will keep us safe. The Bible says if we put our hand in his, no one can snatch us out of his hand. The devil tries, but he won't be able to do it. When we hold on to the Father's hand, we are really safe.

Put your hand in his now. Ask him to lead you through this day. He will hold you tight.

WWJD
Jesus would take the Father's hand every day.

... your hand will guide me, your ...
hand will hold me fast. (Ps. 139:10)

February 5

It hurts!

I consider that our present sufferings are not worth comparing with the glory that will be revealed to us. (Rom. 8:18)

Now, at this moment, many children hurt. Some are in pain, maybe in hospital, dying. Others have been in a bad car accident and have cuts and bruises.

I'm sure at some or other time, you also fell and hurt yourself. Perhaps you are ill even as you read these words. Because we are not in heaven yet, we will sometimes suffer pain.

Jesus knew pain and suffering. He was hurt very badly when He was nailed to the cross for you and me. But one day all the hurt in our lives will be over. There is no pain and suffering in heaven. This is because Jesus paid for our sins. Because of his pain and suffering, a day will come when you and I will not hurt in any way any more.

Perhaps you are hurting now – your body or your heart. Give the hurt to Jesus. Ask him to comfort you. He knows pain, He understands how you feel.

WWJD
Jesus would always take my pain onto him.

Surely He ... carried our sorrows ... (Is. 53:4)

February 6

Good words

... the tongue of the wise brings healing. (Prov. 12:18)

Isn't it wonderful that we can talk to each other and understand each other? Words can heal or hurt. Words are very powerful.

The Bible says that one's tongue is very important, because it can have a great influence on people. If you encourage someone with your words, it can mean a great deal to that person. But with your words you can also run people down and hurt them.

The Bible says our tongues must be under God's control. We must ask the Lord to keep our tongues in check so that we don't hurt others. You get a nice feeling in your heart when you speak good words. Good, positive, uplifting words mean a lot to others. I hope you remember that when you speak to your friends.

Ask the Lord to help you speak only good, pleasant words to people today.

WWJD
Jesus would be honest and sincere and speak the truth.

"God is not a man that He should lie ..." (Num. 23:19)

February 7

The sulky minister

But Jonah was greatly displeased and became angry. (Jon. 4:1)

God had a plan with Jonah's life. He wanted to use Jonah. The Lord decided to send Jonah to a big city called Nineveh. But Jonah didn't want to go. He tried to run away from God. He went aboard a ship that was going to Tarshish. He was disobeying the Lord.

The Lord then decided that a fish must swallow Jonah. In a wonderful way the Lord saw to it that Jonah changed his mind and decided to go to Nineveh. But when Jonah saw that the Lord was not going to punish the people there, as He had threatened to do, he became very angry. He went and sat outside the city, sulking. Can you believe it! Instead of being thankful that the Lord was kind to the people of Nineveh, he wanted him to punish them. And all because Jonah didn't like them! He was a real old sourpuss.

You and I must not be like Jonah. We must be happy when the Lord's love changes people's lives, and we must also be willing to go if the Lord sends us to someone.

WWJD
Jesus would go wherever God sends him, right away.

"As the Father has sent me, I am sending you." (Jn. 20:21)

February 8

You must choose

" ... choose for yourselves this day whom you will serve ... "
(Jos. 24:15)

Many people choose not to serve the Lord. They want to have nothing to do with him, or they are afraid of him. Some do not believe that he exists. Perhaps they hope that they won't have to stand before him one day and account for their lives.

The Bible says we must choose whom we want to serve. If we want to serve the devil or even ourselves, then we must choose to do so. But if we want to serve the Lord, then we must choose him.

You and I choose the Lord because we know He is the true God, and because it is worth our while to serve him. We choose the Lord by saying "yes" to him: "Yes, Lord, here is my life, here is my heart, here is my everything. I want to follow You and I want to live for You." This is what Joshua and his family did. They decided to listen to the Lord and do what he said.

Have you made your choice for God yet? Do it now and tell him that you want to serve him.

WWJD
Jesus would always choose a life with God.

Now choose life, so that you ... may live. (Deut. 30:19)

February 9

The real God

For there is [only] one God ... (1 Tim. 2:5)

There are many religions in the world. Every religion has its own so-called god. The people who believe in that god, believe that theirs is the real god. We get Hindu gods, Buddha gods, some pray to their ancestors, and then there are people who worship the devil. They are called satanists.

The Bible tells us very clearly that there is only one real God. His name is God Almighty, the Father of our Lord Jesus. All the other gods will bow down before him one day. If we worship this God we are safe and we are fortunate. He is a God of love. He loved us so much that He sent his Son so that we could be washed clean from sin.

Also in South Africa there are many people that worship other gods. You and I must make it very clear that the only real God is the father of Jesus. He is also our God and our Father.

WWJD
Jesus would glorify only his Father.

" ...that your Son may glorify You." (Jn. 17:1)

February 10

Control yourself!

... the fruit of the Spirit is ... self-control ... (Gal. 5:22, 23)

Usually a metal bit is put into a horse's mouth. This helps to control him and we can lead him where we want, otherwise he runs just where he wants. A train runs on two rails. When it is on these two rails, it cannot overturn. A powerful motor car has brakes. Brakes slow a car down so that it does not get out of control and cause an accident.

People also need to be controlled. Some people are very silly and just break things. Others can't control themselves and take other people's things. Then there are also those who get so angry dat they hurt others. Yes, you and I also need to be under control.

The one that can really help us, is the Holy Spirit. When He is in our lives, He helps us to control our behaviour. This means that we won't fly off the handle, we will control ourselves. Actually, it's the Holy Spirit that takes control of our lives, and He helps us make the right decisions.

Open up your heart to the Holy Spirit. Ask him to fill you, so that you can be under his control.

WWJD
Jesus would be in control, because He is filled with the Holy Spirit.

He saw ... the Spirit descending on him like a dove ... (Mk. 1:10)

February 11

Stick to the rules

Everyone must submit himself to the governing authorities ... (Rom. 13:1)

When you play rugby or netball you have to play by the rules of the game. If you don't, the referee will blow the whistle. It is important to have rules, otherwise everyone would do just as he pleases.

Schools also have rules. If you don't obey them, you are in trouble. A country has rules. The authorities or the government of a country make the rules. For example, we have speed limits in our country. We are not allowed to take another's belongings. If we break the rules we can be found guilty and we must pay a fine, or even worse, go to jail.

Christians try to glorify the Lord in everything they do. They want to please the Lord. And the Lord tells us to obey the rules of a country. God likes to have order and he likes us to do things the right way. Let's keep the rules of our country and obey what they tell us, so that we can please the Lord. See that you stick to the rules today.

WWJD
Jesus would obey authorities.

... "Give to Caesar what is Caesar's ... " (Mt. 22:21)

February 12

Flat out for Jesus

Do you not know that in a race all the runners run, but only one gets the prize? Run in such a way as to get the prize. (1 Cor. 9:24)

Athletes taking part in a race, give their best. They run flat out because they hope to win. But there is also another, much more important race than an earthly race. The race of life.

The Bible says it is almost as if every human being on earth is running a race of life. We know there is a winning post, same as for athletes, and a prize. There is a difference, though. The prize at the end of our lives is not for winners, but for every one who believes in Jesus. Still, we must also do everything we can to finish the race, just like athletes. The Bible says the one who doesn't give up, will win the prize.

This means that we must keep the faith, even if we are having a hard time. We must believe the Lord is king and live for him. Read your Bible and talk to him. This will help that you won't get spiritually tired. Give your everything today to follow Jesus.

WWJD
Jesus would give everything to finish the race.

"It is finished." (Jn. 19:30)

February 13

Washing feet

After that, He poured water into a basin and began to wash his disciples' feet ... (Jn. 13:5)

In Jesus' time they didn't have tarred roads, and people didn't have motor cars. Most of them walked on foot from one place to another. The streets were dusty and sandy. So their feet got very dirty. When they reached the other side of the road, someone usually brought them water to wash their feet. Sometimes a servant washed their feet.

The Lord Jesus didn't think He was too important to wash the feet of his disciples. He went down on his knees and washed his friends' feet. This is our example. Today we don't need to wash a person's feet, because we don't have dirt roads. But we can follow Jesus' example and treat people well. We can make them feel at home when they visit us. We can be friendly. We can listen to them. We can give them food, or money, or love and pay attention to them. All of this is just another way of washing their feet.

Think of ways how you can "wash someone's feet" today.

WWJD
Jesus would serve everybody in love.

...serve one another in love. (Gal. 5:13)

February 14

He is calling you

Then the Lord called Samuel. Samuel answered, "Here I am." (1 Sam. 3:4)

In the Garden of Eden, Adam and Eve was with God. The Lord talked to them every day and they always knew He was there. But then they sinned and had to leave paradise. They hid from God, and the Bible says that He called them. Ever since that time God calls people to come to him. We read in the Old Testament that the Lord also called Isaiah and Jeremiah.

Samuel was just a little boy when God called him. The Lord wanted Samuel to follow him. When Samuel heard the Lord calling him, he answered, "Speak, Lord, for your servant is listening."

Even today the Lord calls people to come to him. He wants to forgive them their sins and use them. He also calls you. And He calls me. I have answered "yes". Have you said "yes" to him yet? Do it now.

WWJD
When the Father calls, Jesus would answer him immediately.

 "Here am I. Send me!" (Is. 6:8)

February 15

He knows everything

Everything is uncovered and laid bare before the eyes of him to Whom we must give account. (Heb. 4:13)

Have you ever done something that you kept quiet about? I think so. You didn't tell a soul anything about it. You thought nobody would ever find out. Sometimes we manage to hide things from people. But we can't hide anything from God.

God knows everything that happens on earth. He knows everything you and I do. He also knows what we think. Everything is laid bare before his eyes. That is why it is impossible to hide anything from him. The sooner we realise that, the sooner we can be honest about our sins.

Fortunately God is not a God that just wants to punish us all the time, otherwise we could never have peace in our hearts. He is a God of love. He wants to forgive us. When we have done something wrong, all we have to do is tell him we're sorry. He knows everything. He is just waiting for us to say we're sorry.

If we do not confess our sins, we will have to account for them one day, before the throne of God. It is better to say you're sorry now. He will forgive you straight away.

WWJD
Jesus will know and see everything you do.

O Lord ... you know me. (Ps. 139:1)

February 16

The Savior of the world

" ... we know that this man really is the Savior of the world." (Jn. 4:42)

Have you and your friends ever played a game where you tie up someone? When somebody's hands and feet are tied up, they can hardly move. And you cannot really untie yourself. You need someone else to free or save you.

The Bible says Jesus is called the Savior. He came to save us. From what? Sin, of course, and also from hell. Yes, and also from the devil. The name "Jesus" comes from the word Jesua, which means: to loose or loosen. Yes, Jesus was sent to untie the shackles and cords of the devil. Just He can free us, for He is the Strong Savior.

So many people are still bound tightly by their sins. We must tell them that Jesus is the Savior. I hope you have already asked the Lord to free you from sin and save you.

WWJD
Jesus would tell everybody that He is the only Savior.

" ...there is no other name ... by which we must be saved." (Acts 4:12)

February 17

Not rules, love

Love does no harm to its neighbor. Therefore love is the fulfillment of the law. (Rom. 13:10)

Some people think to follow the Lord means a lot of rules and regulations. They say, "You may not do this, or you may not do that." They think the Lord is like a strict teacher who watches you all the time, and the moment you break some or other rule, you are in trouble. This is not true. The Lord is not like that at all.

In the Old Testament the children of God (the people of Israel) had to obey certain rules and laws. But they couldn't, because they were sinners. That's why God sent Jesus to help us. Jesus proved his love for us when He died for us, to pay for our sins. Now we are so thankful that we want to show Jesus how much we love him, and that is why we do what He wants. Not because he orders us to, but because we would like to. We want to make him happy. We needn't worry about a lot of rules, but we must do what He would like us to do, because we love him.

WWJD
Jesus would do what God wants him to, because He loves God very much.

 "Love your neighbor as yourself." (Mt. 22:39)

February 18

I am afraid!

... in God I trust; I will not be afraid ... (Ps. 56:5)

Maybe you are afraid that something unpleasant will happen to you today. Maybe you didn't learn for a test, or someone may be cross with you and now you worry. Perhaps you are afraid of other things, like death. Many people are afraid of dying. Maybe you are afraid something terrible is going to happen to you. Everybody is afraid at some time or another.

When we are afraid we must give this fear to the Lord. This is what the writer of this psalm did. He calls on the name of the Lord. Another psalm says the name of the Lord is like a strong tower, and if we go in there, we will be safe. Give your fear to the Lord today. Tell him what scares you. Ask him to help you. I am sure He will, because he promises to do just that in his Word. The Lord likes us to trust him. We must thank him and praise him for that.

WWJD
Jesus will protect you, so you needn't be afraid.

"Fear not, for I have redeemed you ..." (Is. 43:1)

February 19

I am sending you

"Therefore go and make disciples of all nations ... " (Mt. 28:19)

The Lord decided to do his work here on earth, using not only angels (that we can't see), but especially human beings. People like you and me. Not only the minister, or pastor, or some or other important person in the church; just ordinary people like you and me.

We read in the Bible that the Lord called many men and women to do his work. He called Moses to lead his people, the Israelites, out of Egypt. He called Jonah and told him to go to Nineveh. He called Gideon to fight against the enemy. He called Samuel to serve him in the temple. He called Esther to save the people of Israel from ruin. He called Mary to raise the Child, Jesus. The Lord also calls you and me, because He has work to do, and He wants us to help him.

The Lord is calling you today. Go to the nations, or simply go to your class-mates, or your friends. All you have to do is to be willing. Tell him, "Yes, Lord, I am ready. Use me."

WWJD
Jesus would work for God.

"As the Father has sent Me,
I am sending you." (Jn. 20:21)

February 20

Just like an eagle

(L)ike an eagle that stirs up its nest ... that spreads it wings to catch [its young] ... (Deut. 32:11, 12)

Eagles are beautiful birds. They live high up in the mountains on rock-ledges. There they build their nests and hatch their eggs. Baby eagles live in these nests. But, the day comes when the mother eagle throws the baby out of the nest, so that it falls down the steep cliff. Can you imagine how scared the baby eagle is? I suppose it thinks it is falling to its death.

But the next moment the mother eagle spreads her wings and catches the baby. Then she carries it back to the nest. The next moment she does everything all over again. The baby falls, flaps its wings, and she catches it again. This is the way it learns to fly.

The Lord does the same to us. All the bad times in our lives teach us to fly and grow strong, spiritually. Thank the Lord, also for the bad times in your life. These will make you spiritually strong.

WWJD
Jesus would carry you through difficult times.

" ...the Lord your God carried you, as a father carries his son ... " (Deut. 1:31)

February 21

Bitter fruit

See to it that ... no bitter root grows up to cause trouble ...
(Heb. 12:15)

I'm sure you like delicious, sweet fruit. Some fruit trees give us the most delicious fruit. But there are also trees that give us bitter fruit. When you eat this fruit you feel like spitting it out, because it is certainly not nice to eat.

The Bible says you and I are also like a tree. We can bear good or bad fruit. We bear sweet fruit when we behave according to God's will. But there is something that makes our fruit taste really bad: bitterness.

Bitterness is when you are cross with someone and you are not prepared to forgive him. Then there is bitterness in your heart toward him. And this makes your whole life bitter. You become a grumpy, sour person, and others don't like being with you.

Are you perhaps not prepared to forgive someone today? Are you bitter? Tell the Lord now that you forgive that person and your bitterness will go away.

WWJD
Jesus would not be bitter.

"Father, forgive them ..." (Lk. 23:34)

February 22

Little becomes a lot

They all ate and were satisfied. Afterward the disciples picked up seven basketfuls of broken pieces that were left over. (Mt. 15:37)

When Jesus was on earth, he performed many miracles. He wanted to show that He was the true Savior and Lord. One of the miracles was when he made a little boy's fish and bread more. Do you remember there were thousands of people who became very hungry as they sat listening to Jesus? When he asked if anyone had food, a little boy brought him two small fish and five loaves of bread. How could thousands of people possibly eat this food? But Jesus turned it into much, much more!

When Jesus took the bread and fish and broke it, the disciples started handing the food out to the people, and right there in front of their eyes, it became more. There was even food left over! It was a miracle!

I think with this miracle Jesus wanted to show that even the little that we give him can become a lot in his hands. Don't you want to give what you have today – your talents, your beauty, your sport, whatever – to Jesus? He will use it and many people will be blessed by it. It's not how much you give that's important, but what you give him.

WWJD
Jesus would give what He has to God.

... offer your bodies as living
sacrifices ... to God ... (Rom. 12:1)

February 23

Wonderful!

He will be called Wonderful ... (Js. 9:6)

The Holy Spirit prophesied through Isaiah, that Jesus would be born for us and that his name would be "Wonderful". That means that no one is as fantastic as Jesus.

Everybody on earth has faults, and these faults make that we must forgive others. Sometimes we have to be patient with people. It's no fun being busy with the weaknesses of others all the time. But Jesus had no faults and He never sinned. It must have been wonderful to be with someone like him, to eat and drink and sleep and talk with him. Small wonder that thousands followed him just to be with him and listen to him.

Because Jesus is so wonderful, we praise and glorify him and tell others that it is worthwhile following him. Praise him, because you know He is wonderful and because you may love him and follow him. The greatest miracle is that He loves us, so much, that he died on a cross for us.

WWJD
Jesus would not sin.

God made him who had no sin ... (2 Cor. 5:21)

February 24

The lion that roars

Be ... alert ... the devil prowls around like a roaring lion ... (1 Pet. 5:8)

Lions are dangerous animals that prey on other animals and even gobble up humans sometimes. That's why we must stay as far away from them as possible.

The Bible tells us to be careful of the devil because he is just like a roaring lion. He wants to devour and destroy us. Many people's lives have been destroyed because they listened to the devil. Many things we see on television, or read about, seem so exciting. But everything that is not the Lord's will – no matter how much fun it seems to be – is not good for us. We must trust the Lord in this. His will is always best for us.

The best way to avoid the devil, is to follow the Lord. Tell Jesus, now, that you love him and that you want to do what He says. That will upset the devil. Read the Bible and talk to God every day. The devil hates it. Also tell the devil you want nothing to do with him, because the Bible says we must resist him, then he will stay away from us.

Choose against the devil today. Choose the Lord.

WWJD
Jesus would resist the devil.

"Away from me, Satan ... " (Mt. 4:10)

February 25

Peace for the world

" ... and on earth peace to men ... " (Lk. 2:14)

There is a lot of strife all over the world. There are men and women who fight with each other. There are families who fight a lot. There is also a lot of disagreement between friends; between countries and nations. There have been many wars in the world, just because nations could not live together in peace.

When Jesus was born, the angels sang that there was now a chance for peace on earth. Another name for Jesus is "Prince of peace". Jesus wants so badly for us to have peace in our hearts.

That is why He says, "Come and find peace with Me when I have forgiven your sins." When our sins have been taken away by Jesus we also find peace with God the Father.

Then we must still make peace with our fellow-humans. If you are in disagreement with someone, then you are not doing what the Lord wants. He says, "Blessed are the peacemakers, for they will be called children of God." Children of God don't want to make war. They want to make peace. Yes, we sometimes have arguments, but we want to say we're sorry afterwards and make peace.

Are you cross with someone today? Make peace. Be God's instrument of peace in your class, your school, your home, your town and even the whole world.

WWJD
Jesus would live in peace with everybody.

... live at peace with everyone. (Rom. 12:18)

February 26

Erased!

... He took it away, nailing it to the cross. (Col. 2:14)

What a good feeling it is to erase a mistake you have made in your school work. We always used an eraser, but these days you people use things like Tippex and other modern stuff. Then you can remove all mistakes easily and start again.

We all make mistakes, and this makes things a bit difficult. But the best part is that a mistake can be corrected. The greatest problem in a person's life is sin. Sin makes us miss God's purpose with our lives and we do the wrong thing. How can we be washed clean from sin? The Bible has good news: there is Someone who can erase our sins. His name is Jesus Christ.

When Jesus died on the cross, He paid for our sins with his blood. His death on the cross can erase our sins.

Give your life to the Lord today and ask him to erase all your sins. Then you can stand before him, clean.

WWJD
Jesus will forgive your sins.

... through his blood, the forgiveness of sins ... (Eph. 1:7)

February 27

Hallelujah

Give thanks to the Lord, for he is good ... (Ps. 118:1)

One of the best words in the Bible is "hallelujah". In some modern translations of the Bible the words "praise the Lord" are used instead of "hallelujah". To me this sounds more like an order, don't you think? It's almost as if the Bible tells us that we must praise the Lord. Naturally! After all, He is the Great King of heaven and earth. There is nobody like him. Of course we must tell everybody that He is great and wonderful. We also want to praise Jesus. He is our Savior. He gave his life for us. How can we keep quiet about this? It is impossible. All Christians want to praise and exalt the Lord.

We praise the Lord when we say that He is great and good. We can also sing this with all our heart. Singing songs of praise is exactly the same as telling people that the Lord is wonderful. The original meaning of the word "hallelujah" is actually to be proud of the Lord. Are you proud of the Lord? Let's tell others that He is great and wonderful.

WWJD
Jesus would glorify God.

" ...God is glorified in him ... " (Jn. 13:31)

February 28

The slot-machine God

He gives them [gifts] to each one, just as He determines. (1 Cor. 12:11)

I am sure every person who thinks that God lives, has asked him something at some stage. Many people have, in an emergency – when things have gone terribly wrong – quickly prayed to God and asked him to help. And often He does! Some people ask God to please give them something they want badly. They don't necessarily get what they ask for. God is not a slot-machine.

Do you know how a slot-machine works? One puts a coin in the machine and you get something out of it. Some vending-machines also work like that: you put a coin into the machine and you get a cold drink. You also get machines that sell cigarettes or sweets. When you have put your coin in, the machine spits out what you want. You ask, and the machine gives. But the Lord is not a slot-machine! He loves you and me, and he wants to give us what's best for us; that is why He won't give us everything we ask for.

We must ask according to his will, and then He will give as He wants. And we can accept what He gives us. It will always be what's best for us.

WWJD
Jesus would ask what the will of the Father is.

"For I have come down from heaven not to do my will but to do the will of him who sent Me." (Jn. 6:38)

February 29

Thankfulness

... being watchful and thankful. (Col. 4:2)

I'm sure you also know people who are always moaning and groaning. It's as though they always see the dark side of life and complain about it all the time. Just as if nothing is ever good enough for them.

Being unthankful is a very ugly characteristic. If you really sit down and think, you will find so many things to be thankful for. Think of the beauty of nature. What about the beautiful mountains, or flowers, or trees. Take a look at all the other things around us to be thankful for: friendly people, delicious food, a home, a warm bed, a motor car to take us places. There are too many to mention.

But the best of all to be thankful for, is that Jesus came and changed our lives with his love. When a heart is filled with his love, it overflows with thankfulness, and spills over also onto others. Then we can find something to be thankful for even in the most difficult circumstances. Start right now and get into the habit of looking on the bright side, and say thank you for it. The Bible says we must be thankful for everything. What can you thank the Lord for today?

WWJD
Jesus would be thankful in everything.

(A)lways giving thanks to God the
Father for everything ... (Eph. 5:20)

March 1

Like father, like son

... until Christ is formed in you. (Gal. 4:19)

You have most probably heard the expression, "Like father, like son." We can add to that, "Like mother, like daughter." What does this mean? One says this when someone acts in the same way as his or her mother or father, or looks like one of them. Some apple trees bear red apples. Others green apples. The kind of fruit they produce will depend a lot on what type of trees they are. It is the same with children. They often act just like their mother or their father.

The Lord wants us to look like him. When God becomes our heavenly Father, and we understand what He wants from us, and we hear him talk to us, then we will begin to think and act like him more and more. Paul wrote a letter to Christians and he encouraged them to look more and more like Jesus. They must have his stature. This difficult word simply means that they should act and think like Jesus, so that people will know they belong to him.

Ask the Lord to help you become more and more like him. When people see how you live, and what you do, and hear what you say, they must know you are a Christian. Yes, then they can also say, "Like Father, like son."

WWJD
Jesus would help people to be like him.

He must become greater;
I must become less. (Jn. 3:30)

March 2

Bless your enemy

Bless those who persecute you; bless and do not curse.'
(Rom. 12:14)

Enemies are people who do not like one another one bit. It can get so bad that they will even try to destroy one another. Perhaps there is someone that you don't like very much, and deep down you also think that person is your enemy. Although we don't have to like everybody, it doesn't mean they must be our enemies. It's true, sometimes a friend or someone can hurt us. Maybe there's a bully in your school who makes you unhappy. He or she is nearly like an enemy. But Christians should act differently.

The Bible says we must bless our enemies. It sounds nearly impossible to do. What does it mean? It means you must say, "I want the best for you in life. May the Lord pour his love out over you." But you must also say, "May the Lord work in your life so that you are also filled with love and goodness." Then you have blessed that person with only the best. Someone who comes closer to Jesus will have a change of heart. Then he doesn't want to be an enemy any more, but a friend, even a loved one. Ask the Lord now to bless your "enemy" and to draw him or her closer to Jesus. Then your enemy will become your friend.

WWJD
Jesus would pray for his enemies and bless them.

"Love your enemies and pray for those who persecute you." (Mt. 5:44)

March 3

How great are you?

" ... whoever wants to become great among you must be your servant." (Mk. 10:43)

We all know important people. There are sports stars who play very good rugby, or run very fast. They are great in the eyes of people because they have achieved success. You also get to know actors and actresses you see on television or in movies. They are also great in the eyes of people.

Jesus said very clearly if you want to be great or important, you must be prepared to serve others. So we see that greatness is not about being famous, but about helping and supporting others, or loving and serving them. Leaders who want to trample on others and always want their own way, and push others around as it suits them, are not great in the eyes of the Lord. A true leader is someone who works hard, someone who supports others, someone who wants to help.

How can you serve someone today? What can you do to help others? Perhaps a friend needs your help. Well, go and serve him, serve her. Then you will be great in the eyes of the Lord, and people will also respect you.

WWJD
Jesus would serve others.

"Now that I ... have washed your feet, you also should wash one another's feet." (Jn. 13:14)

March 4

The humble

"God opposes the proud but gives grace to the humble." (Jas. 4:6)

Haughty people are a real pain! They have this attitude that says, "I am much better than you." They think they are very important and want everybody to think so too. The Lord does not like this kind of pride. It is not good to have too much pride in your heart, because it makes that you look down your nose at others, and treat them without respect.

The Lord says in many places in the Bible that He will oppose the proud. One day every knee will bow before the King of kings and everyone will have to account for his or her life. Proud people should realise, while they are still on earth, that they are small in God's eyes, and they should treat others with respect.

A humble person admits to his own shortcomings and faults. If one is humble you don't think you are wonderful. You accept your talents and good points, but you don't think you are better than others. You also thank God for everything you have received. The Bible says God will give grace to the humble.

Thank the Lord that you are who you are, but also tell him you know you have faults and that you need him. Ask him to help you build others and enrich them.

WWJD
Jesus would be humble.

(He is) " ... gentle (lowly) and riding on a donkey ..." (Mt. 21:5)

March 5

Drink from a dirty cup?

If a man cleanses himself [from wickedness] ... he will be an instrument for noble purposes ... (2 Tim. 2:21)

In a large house there are not only utensils for everyday use; there are also things for special occasions. Mom doesn't use her best cups just every day. No, she uses the ordinary ones. But, when important guests visit, she brings out her best tea set. When we work in the garden we don't wear our best clothes. We wear just any old thing. Our best clothes we keep for special occasions.

The Bible says that we must be instruments that can be used for a specific purpose: *... there are articles not only of gold and silver, but also of wood and clay; some are for noble purposes and some for [everyday] ignoble* (2 Tim. 2:20). You and I can be a very special instrument for God if we keep ourselves pure. The Bible calls it sanctification. This means we must confess our sins, and obey the Lord.

Do you want the Lord to use you for a specific purpose? Then you must be clean before God. Ask him to wash you clean of sin. Do what He wants. In this way you will also become a precious instrument of gold or silver.

WWJD
Jesus will help you to be God's instrument.

"If a man remains in Me ... he will bear much fruit; apart from Me you can do nothing." (Jn. 15:5)

March 6

Believe and do

What good is it ... if a man claims to have faith but has no deeds? (Jas. 2:14)

So many people say they believe in the Lord. There are many people who go to church regularly and do all kinds of nice religious things, but one sometimes wonders if their faith is genuine. The Bible says quite clearly if we say we believe, then our deeds must show our faith.

This means that it is not enough to read the Bible and even know it well, but we must apply it to our lives. If the Lord tells us in his Word that we may not steal, we must say to ourselves, "I will not steal." If the Bible says we must not allow dirty words to come from our mouths, we must decide not to swear. If the Bible tells us to forgive others, we must not walk around with bitterness towards someone in our hearts. To follow Jesus is to believe in him, but also to do what He says. Faith without deeds means nothing.

I'm sure you want to do what the Lord asks you to do. I know it is not always easy. Let's try to follow the Lord properly. Let's ask him to help us today not only to believe in him, but also to do what He says.

WWJD
Jesus will help you turn your words into deeds.

... live by the Spirit ... (Gal. 5:16)

March 7

Don't kick me

... if someone is caught in a sin, you ... should restore him gently ... (Gal. 6:1)

Some people take pleasure in another's problems. Especially if a person should show some kind of weakness, it is so easy to point a finger at him. In this way the one pointing the finger, often feels good about himself. Some people enjoy gossiping about another's problems. Many don't stop at gossiping, they also pass judgement.

I'm sure you've heard the saying, "Don't kick a man when he's down." What we are really saying is, why keep on criticizing someone who has made a mistake? Forget it, so that he can get it behind him. This is also what the Bible says. The Bible admits that people sometimes sin, but it says that we must not keep running them down. Rather be gentle and help them. We should not be hard on someone who has made a mistake. We must be prepared to forgive, to be friendly, to help him work things out. Gentle people are people that don't like hurting others. Paul says in I Corinthians 13:4, 5: *Love ... keeps no record of wrongs.*

Don't take pleasure in someone's wrongs today. It is much better to help.

WWJD
Jesus would pick you up if you fall.

"Blessed are the meek ..." (Mt. 5:5)

March 8

Holidays!

He said to them, "Come with Me to a quiet place and get some rest." (Mk. 6:31)

Holidays are fun. When the schools are closed, we can relax at home, or visit friends, or go away to some or other holiday resort.

Holidays are necessary, because then we can do something other than just school work. We can rest, because we don't have to get up so early in the morning. We can get together with family or friends. Everyone needs time to rest. Even Jesus realised that He and his disciples had to rest, and that is why He called them to one side and said, "Let's just get away from the crowds for a while, and get some rest and relax in a peaceful, lonely place."

I hope you will enjoy the holidays, and that you will also have a good rest. Just see to it that you also make time for the Lord, read your Bible every day and take him with you wherever you go. Be his witness. Tell people about him. Fill your days with Jesus, and you will go back to school, re-freshed.

WWJD
Jesus would also make time to rest.

He withdrew privately to a solitary place ... (Mt. 14:13)

March 9

Samson's mistake

... [Samson] fell in love with a woman in the Valley of Sorek whose name was Delilah. (Judg. 16:4)

Samson was a very strong man. The Lord gave him very great strength. This was because God had a plan with Samson. He wanted Samson to defeat the enemies of the Lord's people.

Samson was an Israelite. God told the Israelites that they were not to marry anyone from outside. An Israelite was not allowed to marry a heathen man or a heathen woman. The Israelites believed in God and that is why they were forbidden to marry someone who didn't believe in the Lord.

Samson fell in love with Delilah. She was a Philistine girl and she did not believe in God. In spite of this, Samson decided to take Delilah for himself. It was against God's will; he had to pay for it. If we don't do what God wants, we are looking for trouble. In the end Samson's love for Delilah cost him his life. She cut his hair and he was overcome by the Philistines. Soon afterwards Samson died.

It is not too soon for you to start praying that the Lord must help you marry the right man or woman one day. Don't do what Samson did. Don't do what you want to.

WWJD
Jesus would help you marry the right person.

Commit to the Lord whatever you do,
and your plans will succeed. (Prov. 16:3)

March 10

Too young

"Ah Sovereign Lord ... I am only a child." (Jer. 1:6)

One of the most wonderful things is that the Lord uses people like you and me to do his work. He has a place and a task for each of us. Nobody is unimportant in his eyes. He uses some people when they are old, but He also uses young people, like Jeremiah.

Jeremiah was young when the Lord called him. The Lord told him to go and talk to the people of Israel about their sins and to bring them to him. Jeremiah's first reaction was that he was far too young. He would never be able to do it. They would not listen to him. But God said he was not too young. The Lord wanted to use him and no one else, even if he was young.

The Lord still does not use older people only. He also calls you, even if you are still a child. There may just be something He wants you to do. Tell him "yes". And see that you are willing to be used by him. Because Jeremiah was prepared to be used by God, he worked for the Lord for about fifty years as a minister. Not all of us need to become ministers, but this was the Lord's plan with Jeremiah. I don't know what the Lord's plan is with you; just tell him that you will be willing when He calls you.

WWJD
Jesus would answer when his Father calls.

"Here I am. Send me!" (Is. 6:8)

March 11

God's plan

... she got a papyrus basket ... Then she placed the child in it and put it among the reeds along the bank of the Nile. (Ex. 2:3)

At the time Moses was born, the pharaoh was worried about the many Israelites in Egypt. He ordered that all the baby Israelite boys had to be killed. Moses' mother loved him very much. She didn't want him to be killed. So she put him in a basket and hid him on the bank of the Nile river.

But God always has a plan with our lives. His plan was to use Moses to take the Israelites out of Egypt. That is why God saw to it that the pharaoh's daughter found the baby Moses in the basket, and took him to the palace with her. Here Moses grew up. He became a leader. And when he was older, the Lord told him to take the Israelites out of Egypt. God is truly wonderful! He has a plan with each of us. Even when Moses was in the basket the Lord already had a plan with his life. God also has a plan with your life. Follow him and trust him. Do what He asks you to. He can use you.

WWJD
Jesus will show you his plan with your life.

Trust in the lord with all your heart ... (Prov. 3:5)

March 12

What a surprise!

At this, she turned around and saw Jesus standing there ...
(Jn. 20:14)

A surprise is when something happens to you that you did not expect. This happened to Mary Magdalene.

Mary used to be a very bad lady. Then she met Jesus. He taught her about peace and forgiveness, and told her about his kingdom.

She believed him. This changed her life. She started loving Jesus as her Savior.

Then Jesus died on the cross. Mary's heart was broken. She loved Jesus so much and now He was dead. She must have cried a lot. Three days after Jesus' death she went to his grave. There a lovely surprise was waiting for her. She saw Jesus himself standing there. Jesus was alive! She couldn't believe her eyes. This was the nicest surprise of her life.

If we give our lives to Jesus, we find that He is just as wonderful towards us as He was to Mary. And He is alive in our hearts.

WWJD
Jesus would keep on surprising you with his love.

(may you) ... know this love that surpasses knowledge. (Eph. 3:19)

March 13

Treasure in your heart

... where your treasure is, there your heart will be also. (Lk. 12:34)

When you have been given something precious, you want to keep it close to you. If you have a shiny new bicycle, you won't leave it at school overnight. You want it near you, because you are so happy about it. And you want to look after it. You are proud of it. Also, when you love someone, you want to be with that person. Loved ones say they "treasure" one another.

The Bible tells us to keep the right treasures in our hearts. We all have something that we treasure. There is always something that is important to us. But we must keep the most important things in our hearts. The Bible calls these the things of the Lord's kingdom. The Lord, and our relationship with him are much more important than bicycles, motor bikes, TV games, or clothes or money. Of course it's nice to have these things, but they are not more important than our relationship with the Lord.

Make sure that Jesus is the most important one in your life. Your heart will be with your greatest treasure: the Lord of your life.

WWJD
Jesus would store up treasures in heaven.

For where your treasure is, there
your heart will be also. (Mt. 6:21)

March 14

Resist the devil!

Resist the devil, and he will flee from you ... (Jas. 4:7)

By this time you know the devil is your enemy. He wants to destroy you. He does not love you. He comes with all kinds of lies, like with Eve, and tries to lure you away from the Lord. I hope this is not happening to you.

How will we know when it is the devil talking to us? We will only know it if we know the Bible. The Bible tells us what God's will is, and that is always what's best for us. When other thoughts come into our minds, and they are not from the Bible, we can know for sure they are from the devil. He is trying to lead us astray. Then we must decide immediately not to do what is against the Lord's will. Then we obey the Bible: we tell ourselves loud and clear not to be disobedient to God. In this way we resist the devil, and when we do that he has no power over us.

We can never resist the devil in our own strength. He is too strong for us. But if we resist him in the name of the Lord, we will win. Is there something in your life that you know is not the Lord's will? Decide now to do God's will and resist the devil, then he can do nothing to you.

WWJD
Jesus would resist the devil with the Word.

... "Away from me, Satan ..." (Mt. 4:10)

March 15

Be honest

He who conceals his sins does not prosper, but whoever confesses and renounces them finds mercy. (Prov. 28:13)

Wanting to hide failure and sin is natural to all of humankind. If you have spilt something on Mom's new table-cloth, you quickly put a plate on the stain so that no one will notice it. If the teacher asks, "Who is using such bad language?" you are quick to answer, "I didn't, Teacher," but actually you are not telling the truth, you want to hide it.

When we sin, it always makes us feel a bit sheepish and we want to hide, but this is not the way to handle it. The Bible says if we hide our sin, we cannot be forgiven: If we confess our sin, then God is righteous and fair and He will forgive us (cf. I Jn. 1:9). The secret is to be honest about our sins, and to tell the Lord everything. I know it is very difficult, but truly, it's the best thing to do. The moment you know there is sin in your life, you must confess it to the Lord immediately. Tell him you are sorry; He will forgive you. You must also tell people you are sorry if you have treated them badly. We all appreciate a person who is honest about his or her sins and if they say they are sorry.

Do not hide your sins. Apologize and let go, and God will give you his grace. Grace means the Lord will forgive you and put his loving arms around you.

WWJD
Jesus would forgive you your sins.

 ... You forgave the guilt of my sin. (Ps. 32:5)

March 16

What is cool?

I consider everything a loss compared to the surpassing greatness of knowing Christ ... (Phil. 3:8)

A thing is cool when we like it a lot. Some things are obviously more cool than others. If you are really crazy about something you tell all your friends about it. This is what Paul did.

Everybody knew how clever Paul was, and he liked certain things very much. But then something wonderful happened in his life. He was on the road one day when a bright light fell on him. It was the Lord who had a special plan with Paul. This changed his whole life. He got to know the Lord, and from that day on, everything he thought was cool before, was not so cool any more.

He writes that the coolest thing on earth is to know the Lord, to love him and to follow him.

I know there are many things in your life that you enjoy. That's fine. The Lord wants you to enjoy yourself and to be excited about things that make you happy. Just make sure that the Lord is not pushed to one side in your life. Actually I pray that you will think the Lord is so wonderful that the coolest thing on earth for you will be to know and serve him, as it was with Paul.

WWJD
Jesus would love God and people.

" ...There is no commandment greater than these (two)." (Mk. 12:31)

March 17

Throw it away

Cast all your anxiety on him because He cares for you. (1 Pet. 5:7)

I'm sure you've seen someone who looks unhappy. If you should ask this person, "Why are you so unhappy?" the answer is often, "Oh, I have so many problems."

Problems are like a weight on our shoulders. They make us unhappy. And we worry.

If you are a Christian it is wonderful to know that the Lord knows about your problems. The Bible tells us to throw the weight of problems from our shoulders. Throw it away. "Cast all your anxiety ... " This means: throw away this thing that is making your heart heavy. Throw it into the hands of Jesus. Let him handle it. How does one do this?

In the first place, you must realise that you are worried about something. Ask yourself, "Why am I so worried?" When you have found the answer, tell the Lord about it. Pass it into his hands. In this way you throw it away from you.

Do it now. Throw away your problems. Give them to Jesus. I am sure He will help.

WWJD
Jesus would free you from your problems.

"Therefore do not worry about tomorrow ... " (Mt. 6:34)

March 18

The giant

A champion named Goliath ... was over nine feet tall. (1 Sam. 17:4)

I am sure you know the story of the giant, Goliath. He was a Philistine fighter, and an enormous man. The Philistines bargained on him in the fight against Israel. Everybody was afraid of this big giant and no one had the heart to fight against him. This made him boastful. Every day he came out and asked, "Who will fight me?" And nobody wanted to, because they were scared of him.

Only David was not scared. He was there because he had brought his brothers food so that they could be strong for the battle. He saw the giant challenging the Israelites. God then gave David courage. He was only a young boy, but he knew God was greater than Goliath and he was not afraid. He said to Goliath, "You come against me with sword and spear and javelin, but I come against you in the name of the Lord Almighty."

God helped David. He was happy about David's faith. So He helped David to defeat the big giant, Goliath.

Even if you are still young, you can also believe in God's great power, like David, and the Lord will also be able to use you to score a victory.

WWJD
Jesus will give you the strength to be a winner.

God arms me with strength ... (Ps. 18:33)

March 19

The king's sin

Then David said to Nathan, "I have sinned against the Lord." (2 Sam. 12:13)

David must have been the most important king Israel ever had. He was a good ruler and a brave soldier. What is more, David loved the Lord. The psalms in the Bible are songs he sang to the Lord.

Then David made a big mistake. He saw another man's wife and he thought she was very pretty. Her name was Bathsheba. In his heart David wished that she could be his wife. Then he had her fetched and just took her for himself. This was a sin in the eyes of the Lord, so the Lord sent a prophet to him to tell him that what he had done was wrong. David was very sorry and confessed his sin to the Lord. He realised it was wrong to take something that did not belong to him. It was stealing. And it was wrong to use his position as king to get hold of her.

There are also some things that we would like to have, same as David. Have you ever taken something that did not belong to you because you wanted it so badly? That was wrong, wasn't it? I hope you told the Lord that you are sorry.

God forgave David, and He will also forgive you and me if we are sorry about our sins.

WWJD
Jesus would forgive your sins.

...so far has He removed our transgressions (sins) from us. (Ps. 103:12)

March 20

Human Rights Day

... the law is paralyzed, and justice never prevails. The wicked hem in the righteous, so that justice is perverted. (Hab. 1:4)

In the book Habakkuk we hear the writer of this book pouring out his heart to the Lord. He wants to know why so much is so wrong in the world. He looks around him and sees misery. He sees people fighting and arguing, and the laws of the country have no power any more. Human rights are violated, because bad people have gained the upper hand over good ones.

We could almost think Habakkuk is living in our times. All over the world there is strife and fighting. The rights of many people are ignored. They are oppressed and hurt and their money is stolen. They suffer because they work all day and get paid very little.

Today is Human Rights Day. We must treat everybody with respect because that is what the Lord wants us to do. If we really love others as the Lord tells us to, then we will not oppress them or hurt them. Then we will do right by them, just as the Lord would.

Make an effort today to treat all people with respect.

WWJD
Jesus would respect all people.

Be devoted to one another in brotherly love ... (Rom. 12:10)

March 21

The secret is out!

(T)he mystery that has been kept hidden for ages and generations, but is now disclosed ... (Col. 1:26)

When something is a secret we know nothing about it. When somebody tells others a secret, then it is not a secret any more. Then the secret is out.

The wonderful message of Jesus was like a secret to some. No one in the Old Testament knew who Jesus was. Yes, the people of Israel did talk about the Messiah that would come, but they did not quite know who He was and what He would look like. But the secret came out!

Jesus was born in Bethlehem and while He was growing up there, He started telling people about his kingdom. Then the big secret was out! Jesus wanted to tell everybody that He came to this earth as a Savior. He also told the disciples to tell everybody this. They had to go to all the nations and tell them that only He is the Way and the Truth and the Life.

The secret is out. We know that Jesus is the Savior. This message must be told to everyone. There are still many people all over the world who have never even heard of Jesus. To them it is still a secret. What a shame! Let you and me tell everybody that Jesus is alive.

WWJD
Jesus would preach the message of heaven.

(T)hat is the mystery made known to me ... (Eph. 3:3)

March 22

A real pig

... get rid of all moral filth ... (Jas. 1:21)

"Sis, you're as dirty as a pig!" This is what we say when someone is very very dirty. A pig likes being dirty. A pig just loves rolling around in the blackest mud. It doesn't mind if the mud smells. A pig likes being dirty.

The Bible says sin is dirty. If you have not been washed clean of sin by Jesus, you are just as dirty as that pig rolling in the mud. The Bible invites us to have ourselves washed clean of sin. Only Jesus' sacrifice on the cross can wash you and me clean. I hope you have already asked the Lord to wash your dirty sins clean.

Because we are Christians it will worry us if we keep on sinning. We are not pigs any more, no more black mud for us; we are more like cats that cannot stand getting their feet dirty. You must have noticed how a cat hates stepping even into water. He immediately starts licking himself clean. Even if a pig has been washed clean, he will take the first chance he gets, to go and roll in the mud again. Not a cat. A cat doesn't like being dirty. Christians should be like that. If we have sinned, we must want to be washed clean as soon as possible. We tell the Lord we are sorry, and He forgives us.

WWJD
Jesus will wash you clean of all your sins.

"Though your sins are like scarlet, they shall be white as snow ..." (Is. 1:18)

March 23

The sweet book

... I ate it, and it tasted as sweet as honey in my mouth. (Ezek. 3:3)

I'm sure you have tasted honey before. It is vey sweet. One can spread it on bread, and some people even sweeten their tea or coffee with honey.

The Bible uses an image to tell us how good it is when you read the Word of God. Ezekiel saw in his imagination the Lord coming to him with a scroll on which the words of God were written. The Lord told Ezekiel to eat this scroll. To his surprise Ezekiel tasted that it was as sweet as honey. Of course Ezekiel did not really eat the scroll, the Lord just wanted to tell him something. The message of the image is that the Word of God is always good for us. It is as healthy as honey.

If you and I love the Lord we want to listen to his words. And hearing his words – which come from the Bible – is just as good for us as eating honey. It gives us just as much energy and is just as tasty. Yes, the Word of God is good for us.

You must make sure that you "eat" the Word of God every day. It is good for you; even better than honey.

WWJD
Jesus would read the Bible regularly.

Your word is ... a light for my path. (Ps. 119:105)

March 24

Joseph brings blessing

From that time ... the Lord blessed the household of the Egyptian because of Joseph ... (Gen. 39:5)

Joseph loved the Lord. And the Lord also loved Joseph. The Lord had a plan with Joseph's life. That is why He allowed that Joseph was taken to a far away country and thrown into jail. But the Lord looked after Joseph and saw to it that he was taken into service in the house of an important officer named Potiphar.

Because the Lord had blessed Joseph, He also blessed the house of Potiphar. And this just because Joseph brought the Lord with him to the house of Potiphar. It was good for Potiphar to have Joseph in his house, because the Lord himself was with Joseph.

When you and I serve God, we are his blessed children. Then the Lord walks with us. Wherever we go, He goes with us. In this way you and I can also be a blessing for the Lord, wherever we are. Be a blessing today to your class, or your school, or your friends, or on the sports field.

WWJD
Jesus would bless everybody.

... repay ... with blessing, because to this you were called. (1 Pet. 3:9)

March 25

Jesus forgives

And he [Peter] went outside and wept bitterly. (Lk. 22:62)

When Jesus was captured, his disciples got a fright and they ran away. Peter too, because he was afraid of what could happen to him. Yet he followed Jesus at a distance and saw the soldiers taking Jesus away. Then Jesus got to the big building where they were going to put him on trial. Peter stood in the courtyard while they were busy with Jesus. Two servant girls said they had seen Peter with Jesus before. But Peter denied it. He said they were making a mistake, because he was scared of what they would do to him. And so Peter disowned Jesus. He was being false, and denied that he had anything to do with Jesus. This means that Peter let Jesus down.

Jesus knew beforehand that Peter would disown him. He said a cock would crow to remind Peter that he let Jesus down. It happened just like that. When the cock crowed, Peter went outside and started crying bitterly. He was so sorry that he had turned his back on Jesus.

Because Jesus loved Peter very much and wanted to use him, He forgave him later on after He had risen from the dead. He appointed Peter to look after the disciples. The Lord forgives easily because He knows you and I are weak. Still, He wants to use us, in spite of our weaknesses.

WWJD
Jesus would forgive people.

... and remembers your sins no more ... (Is. 43:25)

March 26

Why worry?

"Therefore do not worry about tomorrow ... " (Mt. 6:34)

Worried people do not laugh easily. When we are worried about tomorrow, we don't look forward to it, we are actually not even keen that the new day must break.

In Proverbs 31:25 we read that a good woman who knows the Lord and loves him, *... can laugh at the days to come.* Yes, if you belong to the Lord, you learn to leave your worries in his hands and you can afford to laugh at tomorrow. This means being cheerful about what waits for us tomorrow. God is in control of my life, why should I fear tomorrow? I would rather laugh at tomorrow with joy in my heart, because my Lord is in control.

A cheerful, laughing person can handle all the problems of today and tomorrow best. Give your worries to the Lord right now, and be thankful that He is in control of your life. Then you will also laugh at tomorrow. This is a good laugh, because you know the Lord will be with you.

WWJD
Jesus would free you from worry.

Cast all your anxiety on *him* because He cares for you. (1 Pet. 5:7)

March 27

Wonderful things!

... Lord, how majestic is your name in all the earth! (Ps. 8:9)

Even if so many things are wrong on earth, and even if there are bad things like pollution, and certain animals, or plants or trees dying out, the earth is still a wonderful place. The Lord made heaven and the earth. He made everything very good and beautiful. Just think of all the wonderful things. There are so many different kinds of animals in the game reserves, and there are so many kinds of plants in gardens all over the world. Just think of the variety of fish in the sea. When a person makes a study of birds, you are amazed at the great variety we get.

Yes, the Lord made the earth wonderful. The Bible also says you and I are crowned with glory and honour (cf. Ps. 8:6). Of everything the Lord made, we are the best. Just think of all the millions of people ... and every one is different. The Lord also gave us a mind so that we can rule over the whole world.

Praise and glorify the Lord today for his wonderful creation. Praise him also for yourself. Let's tell everybody that the Lord's works are wonderful!

WWJD
Jesus would care for creation.

"Look at the birds ... your heavenly Father feeds them ... " (Mt. 6:26)

March 28

Ask, seek and find

" ... Ask, and it will be given to you; seek and you will find; knock and the door will be opened to you." (Lk. 11:9)

We all want answers to our questions, we want to find what we are looking for and see doors open for us when we knock. Unfortunately we often ask the wrong person or persons. We look in the wrong places. We knock at the wrong doors. That is why we do not really find what we are longing for deep in our hearts.

Jesus knows the plight of us humans, and that is why He invites us all to ask him. He would like to give us what we need. When we talk to him, we realise that we have a need in our hearts, not for earthly things, but for things that only He can give. Things like his redemption and his peace. Let's ask him, because He gives freely to those who ask.

He invites us to come to him for what we need. If we are looking for things with real meaning, Jesus will give them to us. Many people are looking for peace and quiet, but they do not find it, because they are looking in the wrong places.
Jesus invites everyone to knock at his door. He will open for everyone, and He invites us to join him in a feast. Yes, Jesus opens the right doors for us, so that we can live meaningful lives as winners. By all means, knock at his door, and He will welcome you.

WWJD
Jesus would give when you ask.

Then the Father will give you whatever you ask in my name. (Jn. 15:16)

March 29

A heavy or a light weight?

... let us throw off everything that hinders ... (Heb. 12:1)

There are many heavy loads that we can carry along with us. It can be anything, like a heavy suitcase with clothes, a friend that we piggy-back, or a bag of oranges that we carry on our shoulders. Whenever we carry a load, we need strength, and then we burn more energy.

A load can also be a weight that we carry in our spirit. This can be things like worries, or hurt deep inside. Sin is also a load that we carry around in our hearts.

The Lord wants us to travel light. This means that He wants us to feel free and not suffer unnecessary hardships. That is why Jesus came to free us from the heavy weight of sin in our hearts. Many people have so many other things that they have to attend to – like money or motor cars, or clothes or business problems – they are not free either.

Throw away the unnecessary baggage or load in your heart. Do it now. Give it to Jesus and see how free you feel.

WWJD
Jesus would carry your load.

For he bore the sins of many ... (Is. 53:12)

March 30

A gentle answer

A gentle answer turns away wrath ... (Prov. 15:1)

I'm sure someone has shouted at you at some stage. Or talked loudly to you, so that it sounded as if that person was angry with you. Perhaps it was your brother that shouted at you because he was cross with you. The first thing we want to do is shout back. But it is not the best thing to do.

The Bible says it is much better to give a gentle answer. When someone rages at you, and you are also furious, that can only mean war! This leads to strife. It is much better to react to angry words in a soft and gentle manner. This makes the other person cool off.

Let you and me give a gentle answer when someone has been nasty to us. Let's try it out together. A gentle answer helps that the devil doesn't win.

WWJD
Jesus would always give a gentle answer.

" ...neither do I condemn you ... Go now and leave your life of sin." (Jn. 8:11)

March 31

We all make mistakes

If we claim to be without sin, we deceive ourselves and the truth is not in us. (1 Jn. 1:8)

Some people pretend to have no faults. They always make excuses, even if they did make a mistake. The Bible says someone like this is misleading or cheating himself. Of course we all have faults! We all sometimes do something wrong.

If we realise that all of us make mistakes, we will be able to forgive more easily. Perhaps we won't be so impatient when someone makes a mistake with us. Because we also make mistakes!

But what should we do when someone has made a mistake? We must start praying for this person straight away, and forgive him in our hearts. We must say, "I forgive you." And if we have made a mistake, we must say as quickly as possible, "I am sorry! Please forgive me."

WWJD
Jesus would forgive you immediately.

... (forgive) each other, just as Christ in God forgave you. (Eph. 4:32)

April 1

Eyes on him

As the eyes of slaves look to the hand of their master, as the eyes of a maid look to the hand of her mistress, so our eyes look to the Lord our God ... (Ps. 123:2)

In the time of the Bible there were many slaves. These were boys and girls bought by rich people. Servants were always ready to serve their masters. Any time the master called them they had to be ready. They had to find out what the master wanted and carry out his orders. In exchange for their services the master took care of them.

The servant girl or boy was close by when the master sat at table, having a meal. Right through the meal the servant kept his or her eyes on the owner. If the owner wanted more salt, he lifted his hand and the servant would come immediately to serve him.

Psalm 23 says that in the same way, our eyes must be on the hand of the Lord. We must always be ready to serve him and please him. What He asks us to do, we must do. We must keep our eyes open and not leave his side. We must be available and notice it immediately when He indicates with his hand that we are needed. In this way we are of service to him and we please him.

Keep your eyes on the Lord today.

WWJD
Jesus would do what the Father tells him to.

" ... I have come ...not to do my will but to do the will of him who sent me ..." (Jn. 6:38)

April 2

The violent wind

Suddenly a sound like the blowing of a violent wind came from heaven ... All of them were filled with the Holy Spirit ... (Acts 2:2, 4)

When the wind blows, you hear its sound through the trees, but you cannot see the wind itself. You hear its sound, and clever people tell us from which direction it is blowing, but the wind itself has no body or shape.

When the Holy Spirit came to fill the hearts of people on earth, He came in the form of a violent wind. While the disciples were together, waiting for the Holy Spirit to come, they heard something which sounded like a violent wind blowing. I'm sure you've heard the wind pulling and tugging at your house before. Earthly winds are very strong and can lift the roofs from buildings. Hurricanes have blown whole houses away in countries like America and Japan.

The image of the wind tells you and me that the Holy Spirit is also very powerful. Just like the wind can blow into a room and blow things over, the Holy Spirit can come into you and me and change our lives. Don't be afraid of the Holy Spirit. He will never hurt us. Ask him to blow into your life and to fill your heart with his power.

WWJD
Jesus will fill you with the Holy Spirit.

"But you will receive power when the Holy Spirit comes on you ..." (Acts 1:8)

April 3

The Helper

... the Spirit helps us in our weakness ... (Rom. 8:26)

Another name for the Holy Spirit is the "Helper". It means that He has come to help us. Jesus sent him to earth for that purpose. He saw that we needed help urgently. The Holy Spirit likes helping us.

Sometimes we are really in need of help when we feel weak or are in some kind of trouble. This is when the Holy Spirit helps. He pleads for us with the Father, the moment that He notices we are in trouble, and inside our spirit He gives us hope and strength. The Holy Spirit is a wonderful Person. He is our Helper. No matter what difficult situation we get into, He is also in that situation, because He lives in us. If someone tries to hurt us, He feels it too. He shares everything with us, and He is the one that gives us strength when we are weak.

Thank the Holy Spirit, now, that He is also your Helper; today and for the rest of your life.

WWJD
Jesus will help you through the Holy Spirit.

" ... the Holy Spirit, whom the Father will send ... will teach you all things ... " (Jn. 14:26)

April 4

The Advocate

... the Spirit himself intercedes for us with groans that words cannot express. (Rom. 8:26)

An advocate's job is to defend people's cases in court. If you have to go to court there is usually a charge against you. Then you must say if you have done something wrong or not. An advocate helps prove that you are not guilty, or if you are, helps that you perhaps get a lighter sentence. Advocates are important to people who have been charged with some or other offence.

A charge is brought in against each and every one of us. The one who brings the charges against us is called the devil. In Revelation 12:10 he is called "the accuser of our brothers". These are the people who believe in God. He enjoys accusing us. He loves telling the Lord that you and I are not good enough, because, see there, we have sinned again! He is always busy accusing us.

Fortunately the Holy Spirit is our Advocate. He speaks for us and defends our case. He pleads for us with the Father. He helps us in difficult times. The Holy Spirit is our heavenly Advocate.

WWJD
Jesus would speak to the Father in our defence.

... we have one who speaks to the Father in our defence – Jesus Christ ... (1 Jn. 2:1)

April 5

My bosom friend

... Jonathan became one with David, and he loved him as himself. (1 Sam. 18:1)

I'm sure you have a friend you like very much. You like visiting your friend, and being with him or her. One can say you are bosom friends. One's bosom is your breast or your chest. Bosom friends can hold one another to their bosoms. It's like giving your mom or dad a hug. Bosom friends also show that they love one another.

The young man, David, met Jonathan. Jonathan was king Saul's son. Soon David and Jonathan saw that they liked each other very much, and they became so close that they were bosom friends. They could tell each other their deepest secrets. When one was in trouble, the other stood by him.

You must not be afraid to have friends. I hope you have a very special friend. And even more so, I hope you are also a very special friend to someone. To have a bosom friend you must also be a good friend. You must accept your friend just the way he or she is, be loving and prove to that person that you can be trusted. If the Lord is your best friend, you can also mean a lot to your friends on earth. Ask the Lord to help you be a good friend to someone.

WWJD
Jesus would be your friend.

"You are my friends if you do what I command." (Jn. 15:14)

April 6

All alone

"My God, my God, why have you forsaken Me?" (Mt. 27:46)

No one has ever been as alone as Jesus. Sometimes you and I are also alone, and perhaps you are lonely. One does not always feel lonely when one is alone. Lonely is when you feel forsaken and very alone in your heart. This is how Jesus felt when He was hanging on the cross.

Jesus had to go through the worst of the worst, for our sakes. That is why there was a moment on the cross that the Father had to, in a way, turn his back on his Son. At that moment Jesus knew that He was completely alone. There was not even an angel to make him feel better. The Father did not give him hope or strength. It felt to him as if He were the loneliest person on earth. He was also in pain and He was suffering. The nails hurt his hands, and the wounds the soldiers gave him were bleeding and painful.

When Jesus asked why the Father had forsaken him, He felt very lonely and deserted. He suffered this because of you and me. If we believe in him, we need never be lonely any more. Not even on the day that we die. He promised that He will always be with us.

WWJD
Jesus will always be with you.

"Never will I leave you; never will I forsake you." (Heb. 13:5)

April 7

Mocked

The men who were guarding Jesus began mocking and beating him. (Lk. 22:63)

While Jesus was on earth, people did not only praise him for the miracles He performed, they also mocked him. When He was captured, there were people who turned against him. Also the soldiers that guarded him, hit him and mocked him and said ugly things to him. Even when Jesus was nailed to the cross and suffering a lot of pain, they did not stop tormenting and mocking him. It was so bad that Jesus said, "Father, forgive them, for they do not know what they are doing."

Because the devil does not like Jesus at all, he will do everything he can to destroy the work and message of Jesus. One of his methods is to get people to make fun of Jesus and his kingdom, and also of Christians. Christians, as you know, are the followers of Jesus. The devil does not like us to follow Jesus. That is why he keeps on egging people on to make fun of us, because we are Christians and follow Jesus.

Perhaps there is someone who teases you because you pray, or because you read your Bible. Don't let it get to you. You just carry on. Even if people make fun of you, you know that they will stand before God's big, white throne one day. In the meantime you must pray for those people and love them. Jesus loved people even if they made fun of him.

WWJD
Jesus would bear the scorn of people.

The arrogant mock me ... (Ps. 119:51)

April 8

Good Friday

Carrying his own cross ... to the place of the skull ... Here they crucified him ... (Jn. 19:17,18)

Good Friday is the most important day in any Christian's life. It is even more important than Christmas. This is the day we remember Jesus' death on the cross, at the place of the skull. Another name for it is Golgotha.

Jesus was completely innocent, yet the crowds captured him, beat him and led him to this place for murderers, outside Jerusalem. This is where crooks were executed in a very cruel manner. Jesus was not a crook; He was innocent when He was nailed to a cross. A crown made of thorns was pushed hard into his head and He was bleeding. He had no strength left. He suffered terribly before He died. Why?

The heavenly Father knew that Someone had to die for our sins (yours and mine). Someone who was perfect, without sin. That is why Jesus died on the cross. He gave his life, so that you and I wouldn't have to die because of our sins.

Tell the Lord Jesus how thankful you are that He was prepared to die on a cross for you. Also, decide now to give him your life as He gave his to you. Praise him, serve him, tell others that you have a wonderful Savior. Without him we would all have died in sin.

WWJD
Jesus would lay down his life for you.

Greater love has no one than this, that he lay down his life for his friends. (Jn. 15:13)

April 9

Soap and blood

... and the blood of Jesus, his Son, purifies us from all sin. (1 Jn. 1:7)

One day a man explained why he did not believe in Jesus. He said Jesus died on the cross for us, two thousand years ago and yet the world has not changed much. So many people around him are dirty with sin. Just look how many crimes are committed. How many people do nasty things to others. If Jesus really came to forgive people their sins and to take the sins away, why is there so much sin in this world today?

Another man answered him. He said there must be millions of cakes of soap on shelves in shops all over the world. In spite of this there are still billions of dirty people. Why are they not clean? Because they do not take the soap and wash themselves. Soap washes away dirt only if you use it.

It works exactly the same way with the blood of Jesus. Jesus' blood was shed for our sins. Yet there are many people who do not believe this and don't accept it. They reject his death on the cross, his blood, because they do not believe. That is why they are dirty.

Everyone who accepts, in faith, the death of Jesus on the cross, is washed clean of sin.

WWJD
Jesus will wash you clean.

"Though your sins are like scarlet, they shall be white as snow ..." (Is. 1:18)

April 10

Already rolled away

... they were on their way to the tomb and they asked each other, "Who will roll the stone away from the entrance of the tomb?" (Mk. 16:2, 3)

After the death of Jesus the women who knew him and followed him went to his grave, because they wanted to embalm him. While they were on their way there, they wondered how they would roll the big stone away from the entrance to the grave. In those days people were buried in graves that looked like small rooms. Each "room" had a door, and a stone was placed in front of the door. The women were not strong enough to roll away the heavy stone. How would they get to the body of Jesus?

You can imagine how surprised they were when they got to the grave and saw that someone had already rolled the stone away. An angel did this, because by then Jesus had already risen from the dead.

You and I are often just like these women. We worry about how something can be done. The task ahead looks impossible. But when we get to the stage where we have to do something about it, we find that Jesus has already seen to it. Ask the Lord, in time, to help you. You needn't worry about what you must do later. He will see to it that you will be able to do the work.

WWJD
Jesus would not worry about tomorrow.

"Therefore do not worry about tomorrow ..." (Mt. 6:34)

April 11

God in your house

He has remembered his ... faithfulness to the house of Israel ... (Ps. 98:3)

Homes are wonderful places. People live in homes. Inside a house there are wall-hangings, furniture, eating utensils, beds to sleep on, and lots of other things. Some houses have many of these things, others few.

More important in a house than things, are people. A house can have beautiful furniture, but without people there is no life. I trust your house has a nice atmosphere so that you and your family can enjoy living in it together.

There are many houses with a bad atmosphere. There are arguments and unhappiness but no peace. There is no love. A home like this needs the Lord.

The Lord wants to reconfirm his love and faithfulness to every house in Israel (cf. Ps. 98). And to your house as well. If you love the Lord, pray that his love and faithfulness will reign in your house. Pray for your mom and dad and for all the family members. Pray that the Holy Spirit will be in your house. Pray for love that comes from God. Just keep on praying, even if it doesn't seem to be working. Keep on praying that the Lord will be king in your house.

WWJD
Jesus would pray for everyone in your house.

And this is my prayer; that your love may abound more and more in knowledge and depth of insight. (Phil. 1:9)

April 12

Light in the darkness

"You are the light of the world ... " (Mt. 5:14)

Most towns and cities have street lights that shine brightly, so that people who move in the dark can see where they are going. Maybe you also have a light at your front door or in the garden. Then one can see where to go.

The Bible says it is as if the world is dark with all the sin in people's lives. Even if the sun is shining, it is still spiritually dark in the hearts of many people and in their homes. They are just like people stumbling around in the dark. Their lives are without any purpose, empty and without direction. They are actually looking for light. Jesus said He is the light of the world. When one believes in him, it is like receiving the light, so that one can live a meaningful life.

But Jesus also said that you and I, his children, must be like a shining light. If he, who is light, lives in our hearts, then his light is inside us, and we shine brightly in a dark world. We must not hide this light of Jesus shining in us. We must be like lamp-posts that give light in the darkness around us. I hope you are like a lamp-post with a light on top, that shines in your street, or in your neighbourhood, or in your town. Let's ask the Lord that his light will burn in us today, brightly and clearly.

WWJD
Jesus would shine like a bright light.

The light shines in the darkness, and the darkness has not overcome it. (Jn. 1:5)

April 13

Sitting or moving?

... he spoke with great fervor and taught about Jesus accurately ... (Acts 18:25)

Some Christians seem to be sitting comfortably and relaxed in the armchair of their faith. They don't really seem excited about Jesus. They don't seem enthusiastic about the things of the Lord. Enthusiasm means that you are excited and glad about something and want to share it with others. The word comes from two Greek words which mean, "God is in you." If the Lord really lives in us, we are enthusiastic. Why? About him, of course, and about his kingdom.

I hope you are not someone who does nothing. I hope you want to move about and excitedly talk about Jesus and his kingdom. A Christian like this is on fire in his or her spirit. Someone even called it "boiling for the King". In the original language being "aglow and burning with the Spirit", means to be a few degrees below boiling-point for the Lord.

Let's ask the Holy Spirit to fill us with enthusiasm for the kingdom of the Lord.

WWJD
Jesus will fill you with the Spirit so
that you can witness with enthusiasm.

"But you will receive power when the Holy spirit
comes on you; and ... be my witnesses ..." (Acts 1:8)

April 14

Take off the handcuffs

... to proclaim freedom for the captives ... (Js. 61:1).

Isaiah prophesied many years ago that Jesus would come to do important work. The Spirit of God would equip him for the task and anoint him. He would become the important Savior of the world. He would proclaim freedom for everyone in captivity. This is an image the Bible uses to say that anyone who does not have the Lord in his life, is like a prisoner. Humanity's prison is sin. Jesus came to free you from this prison.

A prison is a place where people are locked up and guarded by wardens. People cannot do what they want in prison. One day they can be set free. Then the prison gate is unlocked and they can walk out, because they are free again.

Jesus the Savior came so that we could be freed from prison.

When Jesus unlocks the door for us, the devil cannot keep us inside his prison any longer. Then we are really free.

When you accept Jesus as your Savior and Redeemer, the doors of your prison open for you. I hope you have already been freed.

WWJD
Jesus will be your Redeemer.

(A)nd free those who all their lives
were held in slavery ... (Heb. 2:15)

April 15

Two are better

Two are better than one ... If one falls down, his friend can help him up ... (Ecc. 4:9, 10)

People were not made to be alone. People need people. There are billions of people on earth, and without one another there is not much purpose in our lives.

It's nice to know that when you are in trouble, there is someone who will understand and who will not let you down. The Bible says in Ecclesiastes that two are better than one. If you struggle to pick up something heavy, it becomes lighter when you have someone to help you. Two people find it easier to carry something. There are many things you cannot do alone. If you don't understand your school work, it helps if one of your friends can explain it to you. On the sports field we can encourage one another. Especially if you take part in a team sport like rugby or netball, it is so important for team-mates to support and help one another.

Do not isolate yourself from others. Make friends with everyone who crosses your path. Then you will have friends that can support you. You can also mean a lot to them. It makes our lives meaningful. Thank the Lord now for your friends and try to be a good friend to someone.

WWJD
Jesus would be your friend.

"You are my friends if you do what I command." (Jn. 15:14)

April 16

Think the right thoughts

... set your hearts on things above ... (Col. 3:2)

Someone said, one is what one thinks. When we think nice thoughts, we become nice people. You are beautiful, not only if you are good-looking on the outside, but when you are beautiful inside. On the other hand, if you think dirty and ugly thoughts, you become ugly in your actions also. One's thoughts are very important.

Every day thousands of thoughts come into our heads, even without us knowing about it. Often we don't even know that we are thinking of something, but our brain is working. We need help. We must ask the Lord to help us think the right thoughts. Often bad thoughts just come up by themselves, we didn't want to think them. When the Holy Spirit lives in us He can help us. The Bible says we must think of things above. This means we must think about good and clean and noble things. This is what God thinks about. We must learn to have some of his thoughts.

If you catch yourself thinking something ugly, try to get a better thought immediately. Ask the Lord to help you. I'm sure He will. May you have beautiful thoughts today.

WWJD
Jesus would think the right thoughts.

May the Lord direct your hearts
into God's love ... (2 Thes. 3:5)

April 17

Pets

... which you formed to frolic [play with] there. (Ps. 104:26)

How God must have enjoyed making all the different animals on earth. When I see how cute and interesting some of the animals are that He made, I cannot help thinking that the Lord is wonderful. Perhaps the Lord also played with the animals. In Psalm 104 we read that the Lord played with an animal called a Leviathan. This animal lived in the sea.

Do you have a pet? There are different kinds of pets like cats, or dogs, or budgies, even mice and rats! People keep pets so that they can have a special animal to love and care for. So we learn that the animal kingdom is very important, and can also mean a lot to us humans.

When we have a pet we must thank the Lord for it. We must take care of it with the love Jesus taught us. The love that Jesus puts in our hearts for humans and animals, will be seen in the way we treat our pets. Glorify God, also through your pet.

WWJD
Jesus would love animals.

"Look at the birds of the air ... your heavenly Father feeds them." (Mt. 6:26)

April 18

The beautiful grave

"You are like whitewashed tombs, which look beautiful on the outside but on the inside are full of dead men's bones ... " (Mt. 23:27)

I don't know if you have ever been in a graveyard. Actually it is a nice place. There are usually beautiful flowers on the graves and also in gardens around the graves. Many graves are beautifully decorated in expensive marble. On the marble slabs all kinds of nice things are written, and also the name of the person buried there. It is a good thing that our graveyards are made attractive, because then we think nice thoughts about our loved ones that have died. But we also know that a person's body decays in that grave under the ground. Later on only bones are left.

Jesus warned that our lives must not look like graves. Outside someone can look beautiful while he or she is stone-dead inside. By this the Bible means that we must live for Christ, and our hearts must be alive in this relationship with him. When you invite Jesus into your life, He lives inside you and then you are not like a grave. Let's live for Jesus!

WWJD
In Jesus everyone would have eternal life.

... count yourselves dead to sin but alive to God ... (Rom. 6:11)

April 19

Who hurts you?

... the men ... came after me and surrounded the house, intending to kill me ... (Judg. 20:5)

One of the saddest things is when someone keeps on hurting you. Many children in the world are sometimes hurt by people who are very close to them. I'm not talking about an ordinary hiding or discipline. No, I'm talking about someone who is hurting you very very much, and who does things that no one knows about.

There are children who are ill-treated and are almost beaten to death every day. Others have an uncle, or cousin, or brother or even a daddy who touches them in a way which is not right and they do bad things with them. We call this molestation. It is a very bad thing to do, and children who experience this are very unhappy.

Perhaps someone is hurting you in this way, or maybe you know of a friend who is being molested. What can you do? Apart from telling the Lord about your hurt, you must also get help. There is a number you can phone and it won't cost you anything. When you phone this number, someone who understands will talk to you and help you. If someone is doing this to you, phone this number. The number is 0800 123 321. It is better to get help than to keep on hurting.

WWJD
Jesus would protect you from harm.

Put on the full armor of God ... (Eph. 6:11)

April 20

A miracle in a crisis

And He touched the man's ear and healed him. (Lk. 22:52)

Jesus went to Gethsemane to pray for strength. He needed strength for the terrible time that lay ahead of him. His Father had sent him to die on the cross. That is why He prayed and asked God to help him. His disciples also had to pray, but they were so tired that they fell asleep. Jesus felt so alone. Luckily an angel came from heaven to be with him.

While Jesus was in Gethsemane with his disciples a lot of people arrived there to capture him. Judas, his friend, had betrayed him. But Peter pulled out his sword and cut off a man's ear.

Although Jesus was in a crisis situation, He stretched out his hand and, with love in his heart, touched the man's ear. There, in front of all the soldiers, a miracle was performed: the man's ear was healed. Isn't it wonderful that Jesus, in this moment of great crisis, still showed so much love, and even thought of others instead of his own problems.

Jesus is never too busy with his own life, or with his kingdom, to touch you with his love. Allow him to show you his love today.

WWJD
Jesus would help you in a crisis.

"Never will I leave you; never will I forsake you." (Heb. 13:5)

April 21

The back door

... [Sarai] said to Abram ... "Go, sleep with my maid-servant; perhaps I can build a family through her." Abram agreed to what Sarai said. (Gen. 16:2)

One night the Lord made Abram look at the stars in the sky, and told him to try and count them. The Lord then promised Abram that he would have just as many children as the stars in the sky. What God meant was that everybody who had a good relationship with him, would be Abram's descendants. In a way, even you and I are children of Abram.

Abram and Sarai, his wife, were already old, and still they had no children. So Sarai made this plan. She told her husband to sleep with her maidservant, Hagar, and if she had a baby, then at least they would have a child. Sarai didn't think that she would ever have a child. After all those years they didn't believe God's promise any more. They were making a big mistake!

When Abram and Sarai thought God's promise was not coming true, they kept a back door open (made their own plans). Our plans always make trouble if they are not God's will. Later on Abram and Sarai cried many tears about this plan of theirs.

We must learn from each other that making our own plans, without first talking to God, does not work.

WWJD
Jesus would always do the will of God.

"Father if you are willing ... not my will, but yours be done." (Lk. 22:42)

April 22

Joseph chooses God

"How then could I do such a wicked thing and sin against God?" (Gen. 39:9)

When Joseph was in a difficult situation there in Potiphar's house, he had to make a choice. Potiphar's wife wanted Joseph to sleep with her, but he knew if he did this, he would be sinning against God. So he had to make a choice. He did not choose Potiphar's wife, but God. That was the right choice.

You and I are often in situations where we must choose. You can choose to swear or not to. You can choose to steal or not. You can choose if you want to gossip or not. Yes, every day you and I can choose for right or wrong, good or bad. We must just ask the Lord to help us make the right choices. We cannot make the right choice if we do not know what God's will is. That is why it is important to read his Word. We must also listen to his voice in our hearts. The Holy Spirit will help us make the right choices.

Tell God today that you want to choose him. Ask his help to always make the right choices.

WWJD
Jesus would choose to do the will of his Father.

" ... your will be done on earth ... " (Mt. 6:1)

April 23

The angel next to you

... He will command his angels ... to guard you in all your ways. (Ps. 91:11)

Is there an angel next to me? I don't see him! Yes, of course you can't see him. But the Bible says that he is there. God sends his angels to guard his children. I find this very exciting, because I need God to be with me. Because Jesus is in heaven, He sent his Holy Spirit to be with us (cf. Jn. 14:16). But God also uses angels to be with people. Angels are heavenly beings, created to praise and glorify the Lord and to carry out his instructions.

Because we can't see angels, we do not always realise how they help us. Some people think angels are babies with wings. This is not true! Angels are like strong winds or flames. Angels are big and strong and powerful. They can be with us in seconds, like they were with Daniel when they helped him in the lions' den.

You can be sure there is an angel guarding you today, and who will be with you on the road. Thank God for his angels.

WWJD
Jesus will send his angels to help you.

Are not angels ministering spirits
sent to serve ... ? (Heb. 1:14)

April 24

Jesus is life

"(T)he bread of God is He who comes down from heaven and gives life to the world." (Jn. 6:33)

Many people have only bread to eat. But it keeps them alive. You probably also like a sandwich with nice jam or cheese on it. Although we like all kinds of tasty food, there is bread on the table just about every day. You and I cannot survive without food.

The Bible says one cannot live on bread alone, but on that which comes from the hand of God: life which He gives himself. God sent us his Son. He is the bread from heaven. He came so that we could have life. The Bible tells us to eat this bread. This doesn't mean that we must eat Jesus! That is not possible. It means we must accept him as the one who came to give us real life. If we accept Jesus and believe in him, and if we follow and serve him, He is our bread that gives life.

You can eat delicious earthly food and still be hungry in your heart. Only God can satisfy that hunger. Make sure that Jesus lives in you, and He will satisfy your hunger. He is the bread who gives life.

WWJD
Jesus would satisfy your hunger with the bread of life.

"I am the bread of life ... (you) will never go hungry ... " (Jn. 6:35)

April 25

Don't keep a record

Love ... keeps no record of wrongs. (1 Cor. 13:4)

When we want to remember something, we often write it in a book, type it into a computer, or make a note of it in our diaries. If you want to remember how much money you have spent, you also keep a record.

When we love someone, we would not like writing down all this person's faults and sins. You don't keep a record of his faults. Love wants to forget wrongs as quickly as possible.

Love does not make a list of someone's sins, to take out at a later stage and use against that person. Love forgives and forgets.

Maybe there is someone who wronged you. I hope you have forgotten about it. It is better to forgive and forget than to keep a record of everything others have done against you.

The best news is that Jesus does not keep a record of our sins. When we accepted him, He washed us clean from sin. He forgets about our sins and He doesn't want to think about them any more.

But, yes, the devil remembers our sins and he wants to use them against us all the time. Jesus frees us. He forgives. He forgets. Let's forgive others just as Jesus forgave us.

WWJD
Jesus wiped our sins clean with his blood.

(Y)ou will tread our sins underfoot ... (Mic. 7:9)

April 26

Freedom Day

"So if the Son sets you free, you will be free indeed." (Jn. 8:36)

Today is Freedom Day, and we celebrate the liberation of people. In many countries all over the world there was strife between people or groups. After a long struggle, freedom or peace was achieved. It is the same in our country. We celebrate Freedom Day because we are glad that people can be free in our country.

The Bible, however, says that one is not free simply because one lives in a free country. Even if there is not war or a struggle in a country, there can be many bonds that bind people. It does not have to be political bonds, but bonds of hatred and bad relationships between people. There are also all kinds of other ugly things that keep a person from being free. For example, people who are addicted to liquor can say they live in a free country, and yet they are the slaves of alcohol.

Jesus said very clearly that a person is never really free if he is not free from sin. Jesus is the great Liberator. He likes to free you and me free from the burden of sin. He helps us rid ourselves of any addiction.

Spread this message on Freedom Day: Jesus is the Person who really frees us; free from sin, from the devil, and also from ourselves.

WWJD
Jesus will free you.

Since we have now been
justified by his blood ... (Rom. 5:9)

April 27

Being faithful

... the fruit of the Spirit is ... faithfulness. (Gal. 5:22)

Faithfulness means that we can rely on something or someone. Faithfulness is very important in life. When you sit on a
chair, you trust that it will not collapse under you. Otherwise
you can hurt yourself! If the doctor gives you medicine when
you are ill, you trust that it is the right medicine and not poison
that will kill you. Without faith, life will not be easy on this
earth. If you cannot trust someone, you will always be sus-
picious that he or she might do something you won't like.

Often people tell us they will do something and we trust
that they will. But unfortunately they don't do it. Then they
have not been worthy of our trust. This is not a nice thing to
happen. The Holy Spirit wants to help us to be trustworthy in
everything we do. He wants to help us keep promises we have
made. Even when no one sees, we must still be faithful because
the Holy Spirit encourages us to do the right thing.

Ask the Holy Spirit to fill you today and to make you faithful
in everything you do.

WWJD
Jesus would be faithful to the truth.

*... you are a man of integrity ... in
accordance with the truth ... (Mt. 12:14)*

April 28

To sharpen hurts

... one man sharpens another. (Prov. 27:17)

Have you ever seen someone sharpen a knife? Most people hold it against a grindstone. A grindstone is a hard stone used to sharpen knives (or other tools). I'm sure if a knife or a grindstone could talk, both would say, "Ouch!" It must be sore to be rubbed so hard. Luckily a knife and a grindstone can't feel a thing.

Humans feel. We get hurt easily. Just like a knife rubs against a grindstone, people also sometimes rub against one another. I'm sure you've seen the smooth round stones one gets in a river. Those stones were not that shape to start off with. As the water rolled the stone around, it became rounder and rounder. It is the pushing and bumping of one stone against another that makes a stone take on a certain shape.

The Bible says you and I sharpen or polish one another in the same way. We shape one another. We don't always like it when people differ from us. When we humans sometimes clash, we shape one another. Another person's ideas can shape your ideas. What others say and think of you, can sometimes hurt, but once the truth is out, we can just give it a better shape.

Don't be afraid to be shaped by friends or other people. Above all, allow the Lord to shape you the way He wants to.

WWJD
Jesus would change your life.

" ... unless you change and become like little children ... " (Mt. 18:3)

April 29

You are a toe or a pinkie

... you are the body of Christ, and each one of you is a part of it. (1 Cor. 12:27)

When you belong to Jesus, you are part of his wonderful body. Not his body of flesh and blood, but the body which has many members.

You and I have wonderful bodies. We have many body parts: a nose, eyes, ears, legs, arms, toes and many, many more. Every body part has a function. With your hands to take something. You use the muscles in your body when you walk or run. You see with your eyes, and hear with your ears. Each body part has its own function, yet all the body parts need one another. The eye cannot say it doesn't need the ear, and the pinkie cannot say it doesn't need the kneecap. Together all the body parts form a lovely whole.

Every Christian has a place in the large body of Jesus. We need one another. Each of us also has a task. God has a plan with each and every one of us, so that his whole body can work together wonderfully well. Never think you are not valuable. The Lord wants to use you, He needs you. Say thank you right now that you can be part of his body, and ask him to use you just as He pleases.

WWJD
Jesus would use you, no matter what you are like.

Now to each one the manifestation of the Spirit is given ... (1 Cor. 12:7)

April 30

Smoke in your eyes

As ... smoke to the eyes, so is a sluggard to those who send him. (Prov. 10:26)

Have you ever sat at a fire somewhere in the open? It creates a cosy atmosphere. But if you sit on the wrong side of the fire, the smoke gets in your eyes. It burns your eyes. Soon your eyes water and you can't see much. It is very unpleasant when smoke gets in your eyes.

This is the image the Bible uses to tell us how it feels to work with a lazy person. Lazy is the opposite of diligent. A diligent person is hard-working and zealous. A diligent child is not afraid of work. A diligent child enjoys helping others. When you give a diligent child something to do, he or she does it with a smile, because it is no trouble to them. Lazy children or grown-ups get one down. They are like smoke in the eyes.

I hope you are diligent, and that you enjoy doing something for someone.

WWJD
Jesus would work diligently.

... always be zealous ... (Prov. 23:17)

May 1

Carrying a cross?

"And anyone who does not carry his cross and follow Me cannot be my disciple." (Lk. 14:27)

There are people who think to carry a cross, means to have a hard time and to suffer. They are thinking of the saying, "No house but has its cross." Jesus carried his cross. He had a very rough time and suffered a great deal, because He loves us very much.

When Jesus tells us, his disciples, to take up our cross, it does not mean we must carry a cross in the way that He did. It simply means that we must be prepared to follow him. To follow Jesus is to do what He asks us and to obey what He says. If people tease us or humiliate us because we follow him, it is hard on us, but we do not suffer half as much as Jesus did.

In Jesus' time the cross was a sign of disgrace. Only bad people were nailed to a cross. But to you and me the cross is a wonderful symbol or sign, because it is on the cross that Jesus died for our sins. Let's tell him that we are very happy, and let's tell others that we are prepared to follow him. When we do this, we also take up our cross like He did, and we are his disciples.

WWJD
Jesus would carry the shame of the cross for us.

"Cursed is everyone who is hung on a tree." (Gal. 3:13)

May 2

Call the doctor!

"It is not the healthy who need a doctor, but the sick." (Mk. 2:17)

When we are sick our parents watch us closely, and if we don't seem to get better, they quickly phone the doctor, or take us to his rooms. Doctors study a long time to help sick people get better. We can thank the Lord for doctors and pray for them.

Luke was a doctor. Jesus used the image of a doctor to tell people why He came to live on earth. Jesus came to heal sick people. Not only illness of the body, but especially of the soul. Everyone who lives far away from God is sick in his relationship with the Lord. Jesus was prepared to come down to earth for these lost, sinful people. The Bible says through his wounds we are healed. The wounds that He was given on the cross can be seen as medicine to make us spiritually well.

Some people think they do not need the Lord. The scribes in Jesus' time thought so. But Jesus says He came for the sick. Anyone who realises that he needs the Lord to be spiritually healed, experiences that the Word of God is true. Jesus really makes us well.

Be honest about your spiritual illness and ask the Lord to heal you now so that you can also be well.

WWJD
Jesus will heal you from sin.

Who will rescue me from this body of death?
Thanks be to God – through Jesus Christ ... (Rom. 7:24, 25)

May 3

The most important

(S)o that you will be able to discern what is best ... (Phil. 1:10)

Something we have to learn in life, is to know what is the most important. If you are writing a test tomorrow, then you know that it is important that you must see to it that you learn your work today. If you think it is more important to do other things today, like playing with friends, you may just do very badly in the test. Then you did not know what was important today.

To know what is important, more important, and even most important, needs the ability to discern. This means we must be able to tell one thing from another. The Lord helps us to sense things, so that we are able to tell the important from the more important in our spiritual lives. There are many important things that can mean a lot to us, but there are more important things that we should do. It is more important to have a good relationship with Jesus Christ than to have a good relationship with people. Maybe the most important is to know that your sins have been forgiven.

May the Lord teach you through the Holy Spirit and through his Word, which things are the most important.

WWJD
Jesus would teach you what is most important.

... be transformed ...Then you will be able to test and approve what God's will is. (Rom. 12:2)

May 4

The apple of his eye

... for whoever touches you touches the apple of his eye.
(Zech. 2:8)

Some people think they are not good enough for the Lord. They see their own faults, and think the Lord will never be satisfied with them. And yet the Lord redeemed them and calls them his children. When we are the Lord's children, He loves us so much that we can say we are the apple of his eye.

The Lord also said this about the people of Israel, his people. He said He loved them so, that if anyone should touch them, it would be like touching the apple of the Lord's eye. One's eye is a very sensitive organ. When something gets into your eye, you feel it immediately and try to get it out as soon as possible. Also, one cannot touch a person's eye, because it is very, very sensitive. Our eyes are very precious because we see with them. That is why we take very good care of our eyes. If the Lord says that we are the apple of his eye, it means that we are very precious to him.

You must know that you are precious to the Lord. You are just like the apple of his eye. He wants to protect and keep you. When someone hurts you, it is like hurting the Lord. Isn't it wonderful? Remember today that you are very special and that you are the apple of the Lord's eye.

WWJD
Jesus would shower you with love.

(A)nd to know this love which
surpasses knowledge ... (Eph. 3:19)

May 5

Open arms!

"Let the little children come to me, and do not hinder them ... " (Mt. 19:14)

When Jesus was on earth, some people thought He was so important and so busy that He did not have time for children. Fortunately this is not true. The Lord loves children very, very much. To tell the truth, He said if we don't become like children we will never enter the kingdom of heaven. The Lord's heart beats warmly for children. He loves them very much. He wants to be with them. He understands how they feel. He wants to guide them, and teach them and show them how to become happy grown-ups, and how to be happy children!

When the disciples wanted to stop the mommies from bringing their children to Jesus, Jesus said that He welcomed the children. Jesus worked very hard, but He was never too tired to have children around him. He put his arms around them. I'm sure He hugged them and blessed them. This shows us that He wanted just the best for them. I think that all the children who were with him, just knew straight off that they were welcome and that He loved them and understood them.

The Lord also loves you, even if you are not a grown-up. He understands you and cares for you. You will always feel welcome with Jesus.

WWJD
Jesus would always make time for you.

Don't let anyone look down on you because you are young ... (1 Tim. 4:12)

May 6

Heart transplant

"I will give you a new heart and put a new spirit in you ... "
(Ezek. 36:26)

Some babies are born with bad hearts. They need medical help urgently. There are also grown-ups that develop heart problems at a later stage in their lives. Some develop such a bad heart that they must get a new one. It was in our country that a doctor transplanted a heart for the first time. This means that they put a healthy heart into a person with a sick heart. There was new hope for the sick patient. The Lord is also like a doctor who does heart transplants.

You and I also have bad hearts. Our hearts are full of sin and we need to get new hearts. Only Jesus can give you a new heart. He wants to take the old one out of our lives and give us a completely new one. The new heart that He gives us will be clean and healthy, washed by his blood. We can live with this heart for ever.

It is very important that we must exchange our old heart for a new one. We don't have to lie on an operating table; the Lord does the operation quietly and without fuss when we tell him that we need a new heart. Have you asked him for a new heart? You can live with him, for ever, with this new heart.

WWJD
Jesus would give you a new heart.

" ... and get a new heart and a new spirit ..." (Ezek. 18:31)

May 7

Stone or flesh?

"I will remove from them their heart of stone and give them a heart of flesh." (Ezek. 11:19)

The Bible says we must get a new heart because sin has made our hearts as hard as stone. Sin makes one look at things differently than what the Lord would like you to. This makes that we can't be happy people and we can hurt others very easily.

The Lord tells us to give out hearts of stone to him, and He will exchange them for hearts of flesh. Flesh can be cut with a knife, but a stone can't. The Lord asks you and me to give our hearts to him. He will make our hearts soft, so that we can live better lives, can act better, and just be nicer people. Before I gave my life to the Lord I was hard on others. But the longer I serve him and know him, the more He helps me to become softer. Of course I still, like you, make mistakes. But a heart of flesh that is flexible and can adapt, is a heart that is prepared to learn.

Have you asked for a heart of flesh yet? Let's ask the Lord to help us even more to become soft-hearted.

WWJD
Jesus would give you a heart of love.

I will give you a new heart and put a new spirit in you ... (Ezek. 36:26)

May 8

The house collapsed

" ... and beat against that house, and it fell with a great crash." (Mt. 7:27)

The Lord told many parables. A parable is a story with a message. The parable that Jesus is telling here, is about a man that built a house. But this house he built on sand. The storms and the rain came and the lightning and thunder, and the house collapsed completely.

Another man also built a house. He made sure that his house was not built on stone, but on a firm foundation (a rock). When the storms came, his house was strong and safe. He could sit inside his nice, warm and cosy house while it was cold and stormy outside. The lesson of this parable is that every person's life, yours too, is like a house. There are many storms in this world that can hurt us and destroy our lives. But if we build on the right Foundation, on the right Rock, that is Jesus Christ, then the house which is our life, will remain standing in the face of all the storms of life. His Word is like a foundation which helps us build our lives the right way.

Tell the Lord, right now, that you would like to build a house on a rock. Tell him that you believe his Word, and that you want to build everything in your life on that Word.

WWJD
Jesus will always be your Rock.

As you come to him, the living Stone ... (1 Pet. 2:4)

May 9

Talk to the Lord

If you have anything to say ... speak up, for I want you to be cleared. (Job 33:32)

Sometimes we do not feel like speaking to someone. Especially when we are feeling sad and we think no one will understand, we don't want to talk. Perhaps your mother sees that you are unhappy and then says to you, "Tell me what is wrong. Talk to me!" Yes, it is better to talk about it. It is better to say how we feel. When we have talked about it we start feeling better. To bottle up all our feelings and say nothing, is not a good thing at all.

Because the Lord knows this, He wants us to talk to him. It is better to open up your heart to Jesus and tell him everything. Don't bluff yourself that He doesn't know about your problem, and then keep quiet about it. The Lord told Job that it is better to talk to him about everything that makes him unhappy.

Is there something you want to tell the Lord? Are there things in your heart that no one knows about? Talk to God about it – now.

WWJD
Jesus would talk to the Father about his problems.

"Father, if you are willing ... not my will, but yours be done." (Lk. 22:42)

May 10

He listens

... his ear [is not] too dull to hear. (Is. 59:1)

Some people can't hear because they are deaf. Something is wrong with their ears, they can't catch up sounds. Then you get those who do not want to hear. They can, but they don't want to. Sometimes when you speak to people they are thinking of other things, and they don't hear you. Or they pretend not to hear you, because they are ignoring you.

The Lord invites us to speak to him. He wants us to open up our hearts to him and tell him everything that is going on in our lives, and what we are keeping ourselves busy with. He invites us to speak to him and He will listen to us; He wants to. It is almost as if He pricks up his ears when we speak. He listens to everything we say or think. He is never too busy. He never ignores you. His thoughts are never some place else. Isn't it wonderful! He is listening to you only.

If you want to speak to the Lord now, you can be sure that He will definitely listen.

WWJD
Jesus would listen to you when you speak.

... while they are still speaking I will hear. (Is. 65:24)

May 11

The short arm

Surely the arm of the Lord is not too short to save ... (Is. 59:1)

People in time of the Old Testament thought that God was far away. He was there somewhere in the clouds of heaven. He was not yet Immanuel, God with you. Jesus had not come down to earth yet. That is why they always prayed that God must help them. Maybe they thought, "How can God help us if He is so far away? Maybe He has a long arm, so that He can help us here on earth even if He lives in heaven."

Of course they were making a mistake. God is not in heaven only. He is everywhere. He can help anyone on earth in a second. That is to say, if He wants to.

I can assure you that I know for sure that the Lord can and will help help us; we are his children, we believe in Christ. He has come very close to us, through Jesus and the Holy Spirit. His arm doesn't have to be long to be able to help. He is here, with us. His arms are powerful and strong enough to help us straight away.

If you need help, ask the Lord right now to help you.

WWJD
Jesus would help you.

 My help comes from the Lord ... (Ps. 121:2)

May 12

Bad spirits

For our struggle is not against flesh and blood, but ... the spiritual forces of evil in the heavenly realms. (Eph. 6:12)

The Holy Spirit is here with us. He is the Helper and the Comforter. The Lord also has other spirits in his service: angels that help us on earth. But there are also bad spirits: evil spirits.

The devil managed to get a lot of angels on his side, and he took them with him when he left heaven. They became very bad. These evil spirits are the servants of the devil and they attack people and want to destroy them. When Jesus was on earth He drove a lot of evil spirits out of people's hearts. Some of them screamed as they left a person, because they were afraid of Jesus. Jesus came to put an end to the work of the devil.

Evil spirits do the devil's work and they pester us. But if we belong to Jesus, the Holy Spirit lives in us and we do not have to be afraid of evil spirits. The best thing to do, really, is to ignore them. A heart that is full of the Holy Spirit and Jesus, has nothing to be afraid of.

Give your heart and life over in the hands of the Lord and ask the Holy Spirit to fill you so that there won't be room for the evil spirits, and they will leave you alone.

WWJD
Jesus would destroy the works of evil.

Do not tremble, do not be afraid ... (Is. 44:8)

May 13

Goodbye, Jesus!

After he said this, he was taken up before their very eyes, and a cloud hid him ... (Acts 1:9)

Today is Ascension Day. Christians want to remember this day. What does it mean to us that Jesus went to heaven?

When Jesus' work on earth was finished, He went to his Father in heaven, who was very pleased to see him again. It was like the day the Springboks won the World Cup and got a heroes' welcome in all the cities they visited. All over people cheered them. The angels and the Father also cheered Jesus when He got to heaven after working so hard for us, and after suffering for us. He conquered death. He is the Winner and that is why everyone in heaven received him with such joy. He then got a name above all other names.

Now Jesus is in heaven, to plead with God for you and me. He prays for us when we are in trouble. He sends the angels to help us. He also went to prepare a place for us. When we get to heaven one day, we will have our own place where we can live, with him. Jesus also promised that He would send the Holy Spirit as a Helper, so that He can be with us every day.

Thank Jesus that he went to prepare a place for us. Luckily we know that He will come and fetch us and then we will be with him.

WWJD
Jesus will come back again.

"This same Jesus ... will come back in the same way you have seen him go to heaven." (Acts 1:11)

May 14

The voice behind you

Whether you turn to the right or to the left, your ears will hear a voice behind you, saying, "This is the way; walk in it." (Is. 30:21)

Have you ever been in a situation where you didn't know which road to take? When you are on your way somewhere and you are not sure of the road, you sometimes take a wrong decision and you lose the way. When one travels by car to places far away, there are sometimes forks in the road (one road turns left and the other to the right). How do you know which one to take? There are road maps to help us, or someone will show you the way.

The Lord wants to direct us and show us the right way. The Bible says we will hear a voice behind us that will tell us if we should turn left or right. Of course it will not be the same as hearing one another's voices. The Lord's voice cannot be heard, he speaks through his Word and his Spirit. When we sometimes take the wrong decision and we go into a wrong and sinful direction, the Holy Spirit will guide us in our hearts. It is like a voice speaking behind us. That is why we must be quiet enough before the Lord so that we can hear him. When we focus our hearts on his voice, we will know which way to take. We will know to do something or not to.

Listen to the voice of the Lord, He will direct you.

WWJD
Jesus would be quiet and listen to the Father.

...Jesus got up ...and went off to a solitary place, where he prayed. (Mk. 1:35)

May 15

Milk or sausage?

I gave you milk, not solid food, for you were not ready for it ... (1 Cor. 3:2)

Three-day old babies can definitely not eat a sausage. I don't know any mommy that will even think of giving a baby a sausage, because he cannot digest it yet. Little babies can only drink milk, because they have not learnt to eat solids yet.

When you have given your life to Jesus you are like a little baby in faith. You must still be helped like a baby. You don't understand enough of what is written in the Bible. Someone must teach you about God's Word.

As a baby grows, he gets stronger. Quite soon this baby needs more than milk. Then his mommy gives him veggies and meat, and when he is older, he can even eat grilled meat or sausage when you have a braai. The same goes for you and me. First we were babies in our faith, but we learnt more and more about the Word of God. We have even become clever about the things of the Lord. It's not your age which makes you ready for the solid food of God's Word. There are young children who know a lot about these things. They know more about God's will than some grown-ups.

I hope you have finished with milk and are now eating the delicious, grilled sausage of God's Word.

WWJD
Jesus would help you grow.

Anyone who lives on milk ... is not acquainted with the teaching about righteousness. (Heb. 5:13)

May 16

Ten golden rules

And God spoke all these words ... (Ex. 20:1)

When the people of the Lord were taken out of Egypt, the Lord gave them the ten commandments. He did this to help them, so that they would know how He wanted them to live. If they kept these commandments all would be well and they would be happy. God's ten commandments were like ten golden rules that helped them love one another and do things the right way.

Because we are sinners and make mistakes, the Lord must teach us how to live. We can read the ten commandments, because they will help us do the right thing. If the Lord says we are not allowed to steal, then we must not steal. If the Lord tells us to rest, it is good that we rest on a Sunday, so that we can work hard again on the Monday. If the Lord says we are not allowed to kill, of course we must not kill. In this way the Lord helps us with his ten commandments.

Because Jesus came, we find it easier to do what he wants us to do. The Holy Spirit, that lives in our hearts, makes us willing to keep God's commandments. Let's do what the Lord wants. Just a fool will think what He says is not important.

WWJD
Jesus would help you live the way you should.

... let us keep in step with the Spirit. (Gal. 5:25)

May 17

Enjoy life!

Be happy, young man, while you are young, and let your heart give you joy in the days of your youth. (Ecc. 11:9)

I am not a young man any more, but I can still remember so many nice things that I enjoyed as a young boy. There were so many things that I did alone or with my friends that was great fun. You're only young once, and when you are young, there are so many things that are important to you; as well as things you can enjoy.

The Lord wants you to enjoy your youth. I wonder what things you like best. We all have different interests. There are things that you enjoy more than someone else would. Maybe you like TV games, or sport, or fishing. Perhaps you like riding your skateboard or going to the movies, or visiting friends. Maybe you like going to parties. Perhaps you like nothing better than playing rugby. Whatever you like, or whatever you want to do, the Bible says to enjoy it.

The Bible thinks that you and I can really enjoy our lives only if we do things the way Jesus will. That is why we ask in this book, "What will Jesus do?" Yes, we must try to keep sin out of everything we do. The Lord will help us and his Holy Spirit will show us how. By all means, enjoy your life. I hope that also this day, will be a good one.

WWJD
Jesus would enjoy life.

 Follow the ways of your heart ... (Ecc. 11:9)

May 18

God works with few

"With the three hundred men ... I will save you ... " (Judg. 7:7)

God wanted to save his people from a very powerful enemy. The enemies were the Midianites. They had a very strong army. The Bible says they were as many as a swarm of locusts.

The Lord told Gideon to get the Israelites together to fight against Midian. They got together twenty-two thousand very brave Israelite soldiers. But God said He did not want that many. Too many? Against the many soldiers of Midian they were just a handful. How could God say there were too many of them!

The reason for using so few men against Midian is that the Lord wanted to show very clearly that it was not the power of Israel which would bring them victory, but the power of God. The Lord knew that the Israelites would get swollen heads if they won the battle against the Midianites. That is why He made the impossible happen. If God wants to win, He uses anything. How much you and I have is not important. It all depends on his great strength. This is how he made Israel win.

Maybe you have a big problem in your life. Perhaps you feel small and unimportant. But with God on your side, you come out on top. Ask him to help you.

WWJD
Jesus would help you get the better of your problems.

...blessed is the man who takes refuge in him (the Lord). (Ps. 34:9)

May 19

Who do you trust?

He did not need man's testimony about man, for He knew what was in a man. (Jn. 2:25)

People often disappoint us. We put our trust in someone, and then that person does not do what he said he would. It would be a pity if we feel we can never trust anyone ever again, because we all need one another in life. Jesus didn't trust just anybody. We read in the Bible that when Jesus was in Jerusalem for the Feast of the Passover, many people started believing in him when they saw the miracles He did. The Bible also says that He didn't put his trust in them, because he knew all about people (cf. v. 24). Yes, Jesus knew all about the weaknesses of humans. That is why He never put his trust in people, but in God.

You and I must learn from Jesus. People disappoint us because they have shortcomings and faults. We must never put our trust in people. We should rather trust God with all our hearts. We must ask him to help us and support us. Ask him to give you people that you can trust and who will comfort you.

WWJD
Jesus would put his trust in God alone.

Do not put trust in princes, in mortal men who cannot save. (Ps. 146:3)

May 20

The small man

He wanted to see who Jesus was, but being a short man he could not, because of the crowd. (Lk. 19:3)

Some of us are tall and others are short. Short people have a problem seeing anything when they are surrounded by people in a crowd. Zacchaeus was a rich and important man in his town. Because he was short, he could not see Jesus passing by, because of the crowds. So he climbed into a fig tree, because he wanted to see this wonderful Man who performed all the miracles.

Then there was another miracle! When Jesus passed by, underneath the tree Zacchaeus was in, He looked up and said, *"Zacchaeus, come down immediately. I must stay at your house today"* (Lk. 19:5). When he got over the shock, he invited Jesus to his house. Some of the religious people were upset. They thought it was wrong of Jesus to stay at the house of a sinner. But Jesus had a plan with Zacchaeus' life.

That night Jesus told Zacchaeus all about his kingdom and that He wanted to forgive the sins of the world. Zacchaeus promised to stop his crooked ways immediately, and to start treating people fairly and with love from then on. This was another miracle!

You and I must also go to people's houses, visit them there and tell them about Jesus' love and his forgiveness. Maybe it will also work a miracle in their lives.

WWJD
In Jesus no one will be lost.

... call on him while he is near. (Is. 55:6)

May 21

Nearly, but not quite

"Do you think that in such a short time you can persuade me to be a Christian?" (Acts 26:28)

Paul was charged by the Jews because he followed Jesus. They brought him before King Agrippa of the Roman Empire. He had heard about this Jesus, and wanted to know more about him. So he asked Paul about Jesus and he also wanted to know why Paul followed him.

Paul thought it was wonderful that he was given an opportunity to speak to this important king about Jesus. He explained everything about Jesus' life on earth, and how He came to set up his kingdom on earth. Agrippa listened carefully. Paul tried to convince him that what Jesus said was the truth. Agrippa told Paul, "You are almost convincing me to become a Christian." Paul wanted Agrippa to accept Jesus as his Redeemer and become a Christian. He was on the point of becoming a Christian, but the Bible doesn't say if he became one in the end.

Many people are almost-Christians. They believe with half a heart in Jesus and the Bible. Still, they just don't get round to accepting him. You and I should, like Paul, go on telling them it is worthwhile to serve Jesus.

WWJD
Jesus would tell everybody about the kingdom.

Jesus went throughout Galilee ... teaching ... preaching the good news of the kingdom ... (Mt. 4:23)

May 22

The bad woman

... he ... married Jezebel ... and began to serve Baal and worship him. (1 Kings 16:31)

King Ahab was a king of Israel. Unfortunately he was not a very good king, because he did what was wrong in the eyes of the Lord. One of the big mistakes he made was to marry a woman who did not love the Lord. Her name was Jezebel. She was a heathen woman, and she worshipped a god named Baal.

Jezebel was a bad woman because she tried to kill the prophets of the Lord. She took care of a few hundred false prophets that served Baal. She wanted to lure the people of Israel away from the Lord and she also wanted to kill Elijah.

There are also people today who do not want to do the will of the Lord. Some of them are leaders. Like Jezebel, they are trying to sabotage the work of the Lord. We must be very careful of these people. The Lord says in his Word that those who serve him, must be praised. We must pray for bad people like Jezebel and show them that it is better to serve the Lord.

Perhaps you know someone who does not love and serve the Lord. Be careful of his or her advice, and pray for this person.

WWJD
Jesus would change the lives of sinners.

... if anyone is in Christ, he is a new creation ... (2 Cor. 5:17)

May 23

The Comforter

" ... He will give you another Counselor ... the Spirit of truth." (Jn. 14:16,17)

A counsellor is also a comforter. Has anyone ever comforted you? Of course! When we hurt ourselves, or something bad happens in our lives, it is wonderful to have someone that comforts us. A comforter is someone who says, "Never mind, things will get better."

The Lord knows that we, the people on earth, suffer. That is why He sent us a Counsellor or Comforter. The Comforter's name is the Holy Spirit. He came down to earth on the day of Pentecost. He lives in the heart of everyone who has accepted Jesus. The Holy Spirit is wonderful. He comforts us in difficult times. He encourages us. He inspires us and motivates us.

The fuller we are of The Holy Spirit, the easier it is for him to comfort us. Are you finding life hard to bear? Are you hurting because of someone or something? Ask the Holy Spirit to comfort you.

WWJD
Jesus would comfort you through the Spirit.

(The Holy Spirit) ... will teach you all things and will remind you of everything I have said to you. (Jn. 14:26)

May 24

Shoes

(A)nd with your feet fitted with the readiness that comes from the gospel of peace. (Eph. 6:15)

We know that soldiers who fight a battle must wear the right shoes. They cannot go to war barefoot. It is dangerous and they will not be able to fight properly. The Bible uses the image to say that we also need the right "shoes" when we do battle with the devil.

The image of the shoes that the Bible mentions, is the preparedness to talk about Jesus. As a soldier puts on the right shoes for the battle, you and I, as children of the Lord, must also wear the right shoes. We must be prepared to tell others about Jesus and we must be prepared to live for him. If we want to, we can sing about him, or teach people about him, as long as we are prepared to tell them He is the king of our lives. When we do this we are like a soldier suitably dressed for battle. Then the enemy is in trouble. It is when we witness for Jesus, that the devil stands to lose. That is why he tries to shame us, so that we don't want to tell, or show others that Jesus lives in us.

Are you prepared to tell others about Jesus? See that you start today. In this way, good soldiers win the war.

WWJD
Jesus would not be ashamed to talk and spread the gospel.

 I am not ashamed of the gospel ... (Rom. 1:16)

May 25

The dove

... heaven was opened and the Holy Spirit descended on him in bodily form like a dove ... (Lk. 21, 22)

The dove is a symbol of peace. Perhaps you have seen how doves are released at important gatherings. It is truly beautiful to see the doves fly in the blue sky. Maybe the dove is a symbol of peace because it is a tame bird. It is not really frightened of people. And the soft cooing of a dove brings peace to the soul. Doves are not birds of prey. Doves are not aggressive. Doves are friendly birds.

When Jesus was baptized, the Holy Spirit descended upon him in the form of a dove. It must have been beautiful to see. The Holy Spirit enabled Jesus to do his work. The peace of the Holy Spirit also descended on Jesus at the same time. Jesus is also called Prince of Peace. Yes, the Holy Spirit brings peace for you and me through the Prince of Peace, Jesus Christ. When the Holy Spirit lives in us, we also have peace in our hearts.

Ask the Lord to fill you with the peace of his Holy Spirit.

WWJD
Through his Holy Spirit Jesus will fill you with peace.

Peace I leave with you; my
peace I give you ... (Jn. 14:27)

May 26

You are a house

Do you not know that your body is a temple of the Holy Spirit, who is in you ... (1 Cor. 6:19)

In the Old Testament the people of Israel built the Lord a place where they could meet with him. They called it the house of God. Other words for it are temple, tabernacle, place of assembly and later, synagogue. But the Lord does not live in man-made buildings any more. When Jesus came, He decided to live in a new home: your and my bodies. It sounds almost too good to be true. How can the mighty God of heaven and earth live in our bodies? Yes, it is true! When we accept the Lord, He comes to live inside us. Because Jesus went back to heaven, He sent the Holy Spirit to come and live in us in his place. That is why the Bible calls our bodies, yours and mine, the temple of the Holy Spirit.

Because the mighty, wonderful Lord lives inside you and me, we must care for our bodies well, look after them, and we must make sure our thoughts are clean and holy. You are not allowed to harm your body, because it is the temple of God. Live in such a way today, that the Lord likes living in your body.

WWJD
Jesus will live in you, through the Holy Spirit.

... the Spirit of God lives in you ... (Rom. 8:9)

May 27

Let him guide you

"But when He, the Spirit of truth, comes, He will guide you into all truth ..." (Jn. 16:13)

Have you ever seen someone lead a blind person? A blind person cannot see where he goes at all. That is why someone takes his hand and leads him in the right direction. Some blind people make use of guide dogs to lead the way.

The Bible tells us in Romans 8:14 that the Spirit guides the children of God. This means that he shows us the right way. He shows us where to walk, what to do, how to act. He leads us in the truth. This is not just about Church on Sunday or Sunday school. It is all about our thoughts, how we practise sports, how we relax, how we do our school work. The Holy Spirit wants to teach us how to behave in every situation. He leads us in the truth of God's Word.

When we do not listen to the Holy Spirit, then all kinds of things go wrong in our lives. Then we make wrong decisions and take the wrong road. When the Holy Spirit is our Guide, we can be sure that we will always have the peace of the Lord in our hearts. Ask the Holy Spirit today to guide you in everything you do.

WWJD
Jesus will guide you through the Holy Spirit.

Since we live by the Spirit, let us keep in step with the Spirit. (Gal. 5:25)

May 28

A stammered prayer

"He ... beat his breast and said, 'God, have mercy on me, a sinner.'" (Lk. 18:13)

Jesus told the parable of two men who went to the temple to pray. In Jesus' time the temple was like the church is today. This is where we go to listen to the Word of God and to pray and sing. When these two men got to the temple, they acted differently. One was a Pharisee. This meant he had a very important position in the church. The other was a tax collector. Tax collectors were not good people. They were not to be trusted. They did not have a good name.

When the Pharisee prayed he thanked the Lord that he was good, and not bad, like the tax collctor. This Pharisee was haughty and his heart was filled with pride. The Lord does not like this. The tax collector, on the other hand, felt very bad. he knew he was nothing but a sinner. He felt quite ashamed to be in the presence of the Lord. That is why he begged for forgiveness and asked the Lord to have mercy on him.

Jesus said that the prayer of the tax collector was the best one. He was humble and knew he needed the Lord. He asked for forgiveness. That is why God answered his prayer and not that of the Pharisee. You and I must also be humble before the Lord.

WWJD
Jesus would be humble.

(Jesus) ... gentle and riding
on a donkey ... (Mt. 21:5)

May 29

Sow the seed

"A farmer went out to sow his seed." (Mt. 13:3)

Farmers plough a piece of land and then they sow seed in that land so that it can come up and bear fruit. In this way maize and wheat and all kinds of other plants that you and I eat are planted and sown. Some of the seed the farmer plants, does not come up. Maybe that seed landed in the wrong place. It could aslo be that weeds choked this seed so that it could not grow.

The Lord said that his gospel is like seed that falls on good or bad ground. Every Christian is a sower. You and I must try to sow God's seed in the lives of people. Wherever we go, we can tell people about God and explain his Word to them. This is seed that can come up in one's heart and bear lovely fruit that will make God happy. But sometimes this seed falls on hard soil. This is an image of people with hard hearts who don't want to accept God's Word. Sometimes there are weeds that choke the seed. This is the sin in a life, that keeps the Word of God from coming up. Sow good seeds today, wherever you go.

WWJD
Jesus would sow his message like seed.

" ...the seed is the Word of God." (Lk. 8:11)

May 30

"Storm be still!"

He got up and rebuked the wind and the raging waters ...
(Lk. 8:24)

One day Jesus and his disciples got into a boat and he told them to go over to the other side of the lake. While they were sailing, Jesus fell asleep. He must have been very tired. A very heavy storm broke over the lake and water came into the boat. Soon they were in great danger. They went to Jesus and woke him up. They asked him to help quickly; the boat was sinking.

Jesus got up and did an interesting thing: He spoke sternly to the wind; the waves died down and there was silence. It was a miracle. Just by talking, Jesus calmed the storm.

If you have problems, the Lord can also speak one word, and your life can change. Trust him with your problems. Ask him to help; the disciples did. He loves you very much and He takes care of you.

WWJD
Jesus would take care of you.

" ... will He not much more clothe
(take care of) you ... " (Mt. 6:30)

May 31

Not little, but lots

They all ate and were satisfied, and the disciples picked up twelve baskets full of broken pieces. (Lk. 9:17)

Once Jesus preached near the Sea of Galilee. The crowds were hanging on his every word. The day passed quickly and they could hardly believe their eyes when they realised that evening had already come. The crowds were hungry and there was not enough food for everybody.

A little boy brought Jesus two fish and five small loaves of bread. Jesus looked up to heaven, said grace and started passing the bread around. Thousands ate and still there was food left over!

The gospel of Jesus does not just make good reading, but it is also strength from God. It can work a miracle in one's life. It is unlikely that a loaf of bread will become more in your house, but God can perform other miracles. He can heal you from illness in a wonderful way. The Lord is still the Lord of miracles. The greatest miracle is that He forgives our sins so that we can live with God in his peace.

You and I must make sure that what we have, is available to the Lord, so that He can use it. The two little fish and five small loaves were good enough for the Lord to perform a miracle. Bring what you have to the Lord: your life, talents, time, money, and just see him work a miracle with it.

WWJD
Jesus will perform a miracle in your life.

" ...that I might display my power in you ... " (Rom. 9:17)

June 1

On this rock

" ... and on this rock I will build my church ... " (Mt. 16:18)

One day Jesus gave Simon, son of Jonah, a new name. Jesus wanted to change his name to Peter, because he had a special plan with his life. Peter means "rock".

There are many names that sound like Peter and they have the same meaning: Pete, Petrie, Petru, Pierre and many more. This shows us that Peter is an important name. Why did Jesus give this particular name to Peter?

Jesus gave Peter this name after asking what people were saying about him. People are forever talking behind one's back and they talked about Jesus too. But was it the truth? That is why Jesus asked this question. The reply was that people said He was a great prophet like Elijah. When Jesus asked his disciples who they thought He was, Peter answered that He is the Redeemer and the Anointed One, that He is the Son of God. This answer pleased Jesus and He said, *" ... on this rock I will build my church ... "* (Mt. 16:18). What Peter said is true and if we believe it, we are building the kingdom of Jesus.

When you confess that Jesus is Lord, the Redeemer and the Son of God, your words are also like a Peter-rock that the Lord can use to build his kingdom. Tell people that Jesus is alive!

WWJD
Jesus will build his kingdom with your testimony.

"Therefore go and make disciples of all nations ..." (Mt. 28:19)

June 2

Your life is precious

"What good will it be for a man if he gains the whole world, yet forfeits his soul?" (Mt. 16:26)

Jesus taught his disciples something very important. He also teaches you and me this. He says that our lives are very precious. That is why we protect ourselves. That is why we look after ourselves when we are ill. That is why we are afraid of criminals and murderers; they can destroy our lives.

Jesus teaches us that the best thing you can do to protect your life, is to give it to him. You can be selfish and keep your life to yourself. This means that you want to be in control of your life. You want your heart to yourself. You don't want to give your heart and your life to Jesus. Jesus warns that if you think you are going to keep or protect your life in this way, you are definitely going to lose it. If we open up our hearts and give our lives to the Lord, then we will save our lives. Then we will be safe. So we see that we save our lives by doing what the Lord tells us to. We must take up our cross, like Jesus took up his cross, and follow him.

One can have everything in the whole world. You can have lots of money, a motor car, have lots of toys, many friends and many other possessions, and yet, you can lose your life.

Decide today that you would rather follow Jesus, so that you don't lose your life. You can only win if you do that.

WWJD
Jesus will also protect your life.

Even though I walk through the valley of the shadow of death, I will fear no evil ... (Ps. 23:4)

June 3

Sin is sin

For whoever keeps the whole law and yet stumbles at just one point is guilty of breaking all of it. (Jas. 2:10)

There is no such thing as small and big sins. We think it is not such a big sin if we pinch something small; we will be forgiven easily. But murder is a big thing, and maybe we won't be forgiven for that. It does not work this way in God's eyes.

Sinning means that we fail. If we fail in a big or a small way, we fail. The Lord says stealing a pencil is just as bad as committing a murder. Sin is sin.

The Lord forgives both small and big sins. He is not like us. We will forgive something small quite readily, but whenever a big sin is committed towards us, it is very difficult to forgive. God forgives us if we confess our sins, whether it's a big or a small sin.

It is true that the effects or result of one sin can be much more serious than that of another. If you have pinched something small, it won't affect others all that much. On the other hand, if you shoot and kill eighteen people, all those families will be devastated. In God's eyes both sins must be confessed and forgiven.

Let's thank the Lord that He is willing to forgive all sins. But let's try not to sin.

WWJD
Jesus would forgive your sins.

" ...the Son of Man has authority
on earth to forgive sins ... " (Mt. 9:6)

June 4

Build the temple

"'Not by might nor by power, but by my Spirit,' say the Lord almighty." (Zech. 4:6)

When the people of Israel were taken away to Babylon, the temple in Jerusalem was destroyed. The Lord sent his people back to Jerusalem to rebuild the temple.

The people who had to rebuild the temple, were really not up to this task. They did not have the heart nor the money to start building. They couldn't get hold of building material. How were they to rebuild the temple? The Lord answered them in a vision. He showed Zechariah how they could build: not with might and power, but by the Spirit of the Lord. Zechariah told Zerubbabel, the man who had to build the temple, that all he had to do was get started, with the guidance of the Holy Spirit. He must use whatever he can lay his hands on, and soon he would see the work running smoothly. The Holy Spirit would give him the courage to do the work. He would also provide building material.

Zerubbabel got started and, lo and behold, everything happened the way Zechariah said it would. The temple was completed and everybody said, "Lovely, lovely!" Although Zerubbabel began in a small way, the temple was indeed completed. Maybe you also have a task that is getting you down. Ask the Holy Spirit to help you. If it is God's will, you will also be successful.

WWJD
Jesus will be with you and help you.

... be strong ... For I am with you ... (Hag. 2:4)

June 5

Deep in your heart

All a man's ways seem innocent to him, but motives are weighed by the Lord. (Prov. 16:2)

We see people on the outside. We see someone laugh, being merry, or friendly. It could be that this person is being friendly because he wants something from you. His motives are not quite honest, but you don't notice it at first. It can also happen that someone seems angry. For example, a teacher is very strict with you or with your class. Deep in the heart of that teacher she may have a sincere wish to help you, and that is the reason for her behaviour. Her motives are good.

The Lord does not look at the outside. He looks into a heart. He knows what our motives are. He knows why we do things. This is important to the Lord. He does not only see how we try to serve him on the outside. He sees many people going to church, or singing songs for him, or even praying to him. It could be that one does this for the wrong reasons. God looks into our hearts. Do we really want to serve him? Do we really want to be in his presence? Do we really want to love him? The Lord sees the answer deep in our hearts.

Why do you serve the Lord? I hope it is because you really love him. The Lord will know. Serve him for the right reasons.

WWJD
Jesus would look at the motives in your heart.

"Man looks at the outward appearance, but the Lord looks at the heart." (1 Sam. 16:7)

June 6

The right words

... how good is a timely word! (Prov. 15:23)

Words carry across a message. What we say has a meaning. If you say there is a snake in the house, you are carrying across a fact. Then everybody gets a fright. If you say a flower is pretty, you say it because you saw a pretty flower and you want others to know it.

Words can also be used in the wrong way. Sometimes we say one thing and mean another. We must learn to use language correctly.

It can also happen that one uses the right words but at the wrong time. Say you see someone who looks unhappy, and instead of saying something that cheers him up, you say something like, "Oh, come on, don't be silly." Then you have said the wrong thing. Yes, one can sometimes joke when one should be serious. Or one can be too serious when the time isn't right for it.

We need wisdom to say the right words at the right time. Let's ask the Lord to help us. I have learnt that the Holy Spirit helps me to say the right things. Still, I must also, same as you, always ask the Lord to help me so that I don't say the wrong thing.

WWJD
Jesus would know what answer to give.

Do not repay evil with evil ... but with blessing ...
so that you may inherit a blessing. (I Pet. 3:9)

June 7

Work hard

... diligent hands bring wealth. (Prov. 10:4)

Being diligent means being hard-working. It is the opposite of being lazy. Diligent people know that there is work to do. They are not too lazy to do it. They don't sleep too late. When they are working, they do not allow their thoughts to be busy with other things. They are disciplined. They have decided that hard work is good for one.

The Bible says one gets rich if one is diligent. Yes, if we work hard, the Lord blesses our work, so that things work out for us. Lazy people usually have a hard time. Many people just beg and don't want to work. They want to lie in the sun in some park all day long, and then ask others for money to buy bread.

I don't think this is right. Yes, it is true, many people are losing their jobs these days and they are suffering. But if they are diligent and ask the Lord to give them a new job – no matter how small, or what it is – I am sure the Lord will bless them. Someone who is not afraid to use his hands, is someone who always has bread on the table. I hope you are diligent. Do your homework diligently. Help Mom in the house. Don't be lazy. Then you will also be one of those people who always have enough in life.

WWJD
Jesus would be diligent.

Whoever sows sparingly will also reap sparingly, and whoever sows generously will also reap generously. (2 Cor. 9:6)

June 8

Refreshing others

... he who refreshes others will himself be refreshed. (Prov. 11:25)

There are so many needy people around us. There are hungry people. There are thirsty people. There are people who need clothes. There are people who need love. There are people who need friendship. Yes, and there are people with a "thirst" in their hearts.

We often think our own needs are so many that we cannot afford to help others. Sometimes we are stingy with what we have, and we don't want to share with others. The Bible teaches us an important lesson: you and I should rather give than receive. If you and I have learnt this great lesson, all will be well in our lives.

I don't know a single person who gives freely to others, and who doesn't receive much more. Someone once said you can never give others more than what God can give back to you. The Lord knows what we give others. If we give others water to drink to quench their thirst, the Lord tells us He will also give us water to quench our thirst. Don't be stingy. Give to others, and you will also receive.

WWJD
Jesus would quench your thirst.

Give everyone what you owe him ... (Rom. 13:7)

June 9

Words like silver

And the words of the Lord are flawless, like silver ... (Ps. 12:6)

We often say something that we don't really mean. Often we say we will do something, but then we don't feel like doing it. We just talked; our words did not become deeds.

If you said you would do something and you don't, your words were false. You lied. Your words meant nothing, they were just sounds. We must try to do what we promised. Sometimes something comes up and we can't keep our promises. But we must really try not to speak false words.

If we compliment someone on a pretty dress or a good voice, it must come from the heart. We must use words that we mean. We must not be false. Flattery is when you say something just to make someone feel good, without meaning what you say.

There is someone whose words are never false: the Lord. What He says is true. He cannot lie. He cannot bluff us with his words, because He is holy. His words are the truth. His words are like genuine silver. It's good to know that, in a world full of false words there are genuine, true words.

WWJD
Jesus would speak only the truth.

God is not a man, that he should lie ... (Num. 23:19)

June 10

The best!

... and he found none equal to Daniel, Hananiah, Mishael and Azariah; so they entered the king's service. (Dan. 1:19)

The Lord wants to be proud of his children. He wants to use them. They must be witnesses of his greatness. In everything, they must strive for the best. This does not mean that God's children are the cleverest in the world, or can do the best. They must give their best according to the talents that the Lord gave them.

In the time of King Nebuchadnezzar there were four men who knew the Lord and served him. The Bible says the Lord gave these men intelligence and also insight into everything they learnt. They were full of the Lord's wisdom. They were better than the heathen young men, because they loved the Lord. They lived the way the Lord prescribed. That is why they didn't eat the king's food and drink his wine. They ate only healthy food as they had been doing since childhood. That is why they looked healthy. They learnt hard, they stood out from their friends, and they glorified the Lord. The king appointed them to work in his palace.

When we serve the Lord, God also uses us, just like Daniel and his friends. What the Lord prescribes is always best.

WWJD
Jesus would live according to the Word.

The commands of the Lord are
radiant, giving light to the eyes. (Ps. 19:8)

June 11

Advice for the king

... be pleased to accept my advice: Renounce your sins by doing what is right ... then your prosperity will continue. (Dan. 4:27)

The young man Daniel served the Lord. God loved Daniel very much and wanted to use him, even in a heathen country. That is why He gave him the ability to interpret or explain dreams. One night King Nebuchadnezzar had a dream that upset him. His advisers could not interpret the dream. Then the Lord helped Daniel to interpret the king's dream.

Daniel explained the dream and also had to give the king a message. Daniel was only a servant, but he gave the Lord's message to the king, loud and clear. The king had to stop sinning and doing things that were wrong. The king had to do what was right, and help the needy. After Daniel had said all this, he must have held his breath. What if his message had annoyed the great king? He could have Daniel killed. Luckily he did not. But the king didn't listen to Daniel. He went on doing bad things. Later on he was not in his right mind any more, and ate grass like cattle. One must listen when God speaks.

You and I must give people the Lord's messages faithfully and respectfully.

WWJD
Jesus would give the Lord's messages faithfully.

For I gave them the words you gave me ... (Jn. 17:8)

June 12

Tame lions

... they brought Daniel and threw him into the lions' den. (Dan. 6:16)

I'm sure you know the story of Daniel who was thrown into the lions' den. The enemies of the Lord tried everything to find something they could use against Daniel, but they could find nothing. They made a sly plan. They knew that Daniel prayed to God three times a day. Then they went and asked the king to forbid the people to worship anybody but King Darius. Can you believe it? A person worshipping another person!

Because Daniel worshipped only God, they captured him and threw him into a lions' den so the lions could eat him. But God protected Daniel by sending his angel to shut the mouths of the lions, so that they could not harm Daniel. The king was very glad that the lions hadn't eaten Daniel, because He loved Daniel very much.

King Darius realised that the people had been scheming against Daniel, and he ordered that the guilty ones had to be thrown into the lions' den. They had not even landed properly in the lions' den before the lions tore them to pieces.

No matter who makes wicked plans against you, the Lord will help you out. Just trust him and be faithful like Daniel. Keep on praying to your God; He will be with you.

WWJD
Jesus would keep on praying in difficult times.

And being in anguish, He prayed more earnestly ... (Lk. 22:44)

June 13

Wait for strength

... those who hope in the Lord will renew their strength ... (Js. 40:31)

When you walk far, your legs get tired and weak, and it feels as if you have no more strength left. Then you must take a rest to renew your strength. Only when your legs have new strength, can you go on.

Your spirit can also get tired. We usually say a person who is tired in his or her spirit is depressed or despondent. There are many people around us who are so depressed they don't even want to live any more. They feel weak and have no strength. The Lord teaches us how we can get strength back into our spirit. It sounds almost too easy to work. But we must listen what the Lord says, because if we do what He suggests, we will really have new strength. He says if we are despondent or feel weak, we must first be still for a moment. We must wait for him. We must quiet down our hearts, and by reading his Bible and speaking to him, we will get new strength from him. In a wonderful way the Lord will give us new strength and courage. The secret is to wait for him and to trust him. You must tell the Lord that you trust him only. Be quiet before him, listen to his voice and find new strength.

WWJD
Jesus would become quiet.

...in quietness and trust is your strength ... (Is. 30:15)

June 14

I want it!

An inheritance quickly gained ... will not be blessed at the end. (Prov. 20:21)

There are things you want and don't always get. Yet you keep on thinking about them. You want them so badly that you nag your parents. You even ask the Lord to give you what you want.

It is not wrong to want certain things. Just make sure that things are not more important to you than people or God. If we want something badly, it is not wrong to ask the Lord. When I was a young boy there was something I wanted very badly. For quite a few months I wished I could have it; I even asked the Lord for it. When I gave up hope, the Lord gave it to me in a wonderful way, through an aunt and an uncle. The Lord sometimes gives us our heart's desire.

The Bible says we must not get something in a dishonest way. Some people want something so badly that they are prepared to be dishonest. They steal it. Even if you go on nagging your mother so much that she finally gives in and gets it for you, is also dishonest. Grown-ups sometimes get possessions in a dishonest way. They tell lies. The Lord hates it.

Tell the Lord your wishes, and leave the matter in his hands.

WWJD
Jesus would trust the Father with his needs.

... in everything ... present your requests to God. (Phil. 4:6)

June 15

Youth Day

How can a young man keep his way pure? By living according to your word. (Ps. 119:9)

Today we in South Africa think of all the young people who stay and live in our country. You are also young, and you must know that this is a special day also for you.

The youth is precious to the Lord. He wants to give them the best. His Word also speaks to young people. It is important to the Lord that young people keep their lives pure. If you are unclean in your youth, then you become a dirty grown-up. And you pass that dirt on to your children. When is one dirty in God's eyes? When sin has become a habit in your life. Many young people in our country are caught up in the web of sin. They are destroying their own lives. Many young people are addicted to dagga, and some even have sexual relationships at a very early age. It hurts them, breaks them, and makes them dirty.

The Lord says a young person can keep his life pure in one way only: when we live according to the Lord's Word. If we do what He wants, our lives will be pure. Let's pray that the Word of God will be preached in our country so loudly and clearly that the lives of many young people will be cleansed by it. See that you also hear the Word of God all the time and live according to it.

WWJD
Jesus would live according to God's Word.

Your Word is a lamp to my feet ... (Ps. 119:105)

June 16

What remains?

" ... the earth ... and the heavens ... will perish, but you remain ... " (Heb. 1:10,11)

What a pity that fun things don't last for ever. A holiday is fun, but it passes so quickly. That delicious chocolate is finished before you know it. You wish you had more, but it is all finished. It is the same with life. Here on earth nothing lasts for ever.

The Bible says God made heaven and earth. There are so many wonderful things on earth to enjoy. But these things pass. They will not be there for ever. It is such a shame that some people live as if the earth will stay the same for ever. They spend all their time and energy on their earthly possessions.

Yet, only God will be there for ever. That is why we should belong to him and He must be our Lord. We will never lose him. He is always there. He lives for ever, and if we love him, we will live with him for ever.

Make sure the Lord is important to you. Serve him and follow him. Love him. God and his kingdom, and that which He gives, will last for ever. It will never pass.

WWJD
Jesus would store up his treasures in heaven.

"But store up for yourselves treasures in heaven ..." (Mt. 6:20)

June 17

Bare trees

... They are ... autumn trees, without fruit and uprooted — twice dead. (Jude 1:12)

Some people plant fruit-trees in their gardens so that they can enjoy the delicious fruit that the trees bear. They don't just plant the tree, they water it and fertilize it so that the fruit can be good. They wait the whole season for the fruit to ripen, so that they can enjoy it.

It sometimes happens that the fruit of a tree is disappointing, in spite of the fact that it was looked after. Instead of nice ripe fruit, there is sometimes no fruit at all, or the fruit does not taste good. What a disappointment!

There are also people who don't bear good fruit. The Bible says it is already late in the season, and some people are still not bearing fruit. This means that they are already getting old and still have no fruit in their lives. One would expect people who have belonged to the church for a long time and know about the things of the Lord, to bear good fruit so that everyone can enjoy the fruit on their tree of life. But they are like dead trees that bear no fruit.

You must start bearing fruit when you are still young. This is how you praise the name of the Lord.

WWJD
Jesus would bear delicious fruit.

" ...For out of the overflow of his heart his mouth speaks." (Lk. 6:45)

June 18

Rich and poor are equal

Rich and poor have this in common: The Lord is the Maker of them all. (Prov. 22:2)

It is typical of people to look down on those who are not as well off as they are. The rich sometimes have too much pride in their hearts and think a tramp or someone who is very poor, is not important. They think they are more important, just because they have more money.

How fortunate we are that the Lord does not see us in that way. He doesn't mind if we are rich or poor. It does not matter to him how important we are in the eyes of people. It does not matter to him how much money we have in the bank. He doesn't even care if we are good-looking or ugly. He loves us just the way we are. He loves rich and poor – we're all equal in his eyes.

You and I must try to see people the way the Lord sees them. We must not treat some better just because they look better than others. You must not love that poor friend in your class less than the popular one who is rich. Ask the Lord that you will love all people equally, the same as He does.

WWJD
Jesus would love all people equally.

"For God so loved the world that He gave his one and only Son ..." (Jn. 3:16)

June 19

Sun-scorched and dry

The Lord will guide you always; He will satisfy your needs in a sun-scorched land ... (Js. 58:11)

Israel is a very dry country. There are parts that are very barren, just like a desert. In the time of the Bible there were no motor cars. People had to walk where they wanted to be. It was a slow process and they usually had some or other pack-animal with them. This also made the journey difficult. In such a dry and barren place there is very little water. It is also usually very hot in a desert.

Our lives also sometimes go through dry and barren patches. This means that things don't always go well for us. Sometimes you go through bad times, and you seem to be walking through a barren, sun-scorched desert. It could be that your mom and dad are busy getting divorced. You could be ill. Or you could be in some or other trouble at school. This makes you very unhappy.

The Lord promises that He will help you and me, and that He will guide us, his children, through the dry patches in our lives. He will take care of us. We need not be afraid. Even if you feel a bit down today, know that the Lord will take care of you and lead the way. Just trust him.

WWJD
Jesus would ask for guidance in difficult times.

"Father, if you are willing ... not my will, but yours be done." (Lk. 22:42)

June 20

I give back

" ... Whose ox have I taken? ... Whom have I cheated? ... I will make it right." (1 Sam. 12:3)

Sometimes it's just not good enough to say you're sorry. You must also give back. If you have borrowed someone's pen and it broke, you must be willing to give that person a new one. If you have taken something from someone by accident, you must give it back. If you pick up something that someone has lost, you must try and find the owner so that you can give it back.

When Samuel came to the end of his life, he wanted to make sure that he did not have anything with him that belonged to another person. That is why he asked if he owed anyone anything. He wanted to set matters straight and give back. He wanted nobody to blame him for something he had not returned.

Maybe you have something that belongs to another person. You took it, or are still borrowing it. Give it back to its owner as soon as possible. Write a note or a card and say thank you for having it. Maybe you haven't thanked someone for something they did for you. Do it now. Don't be stingy with your thank yous.

WWJD
Jesus would never take what does not belong to him.

 "You shall not steal." (Ex. 20:15)

June 21

First ask

(H)e inquired of the Lord ... Once again David inquired of the Lord. (1 Sam. 22:2, 4)

David was king of Israel and he had to fight the Philistines. The Philistines wanted to kill the Isrealites. The Bible says that David inquired of the Lord. When you inquire about something, you ask about it. This means we must become quiet before the Lord. We must go to one side and speak to the Lord. We must pray and yes, we must also listen. We believe that He will give us wisdom. That is why we ask him. David asked.

Often something comes up in our thoughts, and we decide this is exactly what we want to do. We don't really ask anyone. Nor do we tell someone that we plan to do it. We just decide to do it. The safest way is to do what David did: first ask the Lord. Does the Lord want us to do it? Is it his will? First ask! Then we will not make so many mistakes.

Is there something important you have decided to do? Be quiet before the Lord, and first ask him to help you. Ask him to open, or close, the door according to his will.

WWJD
Jesus would ask the Lord before He does anything.

"Father, if you are willing ... not my will, but yours be done." (Lk. 22:42)

June 22

Like a flea

" ... The king of Israel has come out to look for a flea – as one hunts a partridge in the mountains." (1 Sam. 26:20)

Saul was the first king of Israel. He sinned against God and the Lord renounced him. An evil, jealous spirit came into Saul's heart. One of the bad things he did was to try and kill David.

Saul and a few of his men went after David. David fled into the mountains and hid in caves. He knew Saul would kill him if he should get hold of him.

Yet, David was not bitter towards Saul. He trusted in the Lord. He still respected the king because the Lord had made him king of Israel. There were times when David could have killed Saul, but he didn't. One day he was very close to Saul, and this is when he said he was like a flea, a tiny partridge that lives in the mountains. David's humbleness was so sincere that Saul felt sick at heart, *"I have sinned ... I will not try to harm you again ... "* (v. 21). Saul did not keep his promise, but the Lord kept David safe.

We must not think more highly of ourselves than we should. Be humble. The Lord will uplift you.

WWJD
Jesus would be humble.

Do not think of yourself more
highly than you ought ... (Rom. 12:3)

June 23

The Lord lives!

The Lord lives! Praise be to my Rock! (Ps. 18:47)

Jesus died on the cross for our sins. When He breathed his last, his spirit passed into the hands of his Father. Then they took Jesus down from the cross. He was dead. They washed him and wrapped his broken body in a clean linen cloth. Then they went and put him down in a grave. Graves in those days were different to ours. They were like small rooms cut out of a rock. There they placed Jesus.

Jesus was in the grave for two days. On the third day there a miracle took place: Jesus woke up! The power of life in God overcame death in the body of Jesus. His heart began beating again. He was raised from the dead. The Lord was alive again. And He still lives!

If Jesus did not live today, we would not have been able to talk to him. He would also not have been in heaven to pray for us and to prepare a place for us. That Jesus lives, is very important. Because He lives, He can talk to us through his Word and his Spirit. Because He lives, He is with us every moment of the day. You must allow him to live in your heart. Then you will also live with him for ever.

Be still for a while. Tell the Lord you are very thankful that He is not dead. Praise him because He lives.

WWJD
Jesus will always be with you.

"And surely I am with you always,
to the very end of the age." (Mt. 28:20)

June 24

The strange donkey

Then the Lord opened the donkey's mouth, and she said to Balaam ... (Num. 22:28)

Balaam was a messenger of the Lord. When the king of Moab wanted to use him to put a curse on the Israelites, God told Balaam that he must not do it. No one is allowed to put a curse on the people of the Lord. The king of Moab offered him a lot of money. But Balaam knew he should not go against God's will.

God said Balaam could go with the king's men, but Balaam was to say just what He wanted him to say. The Lord was a little angry with Balaam. Balaam had a donkey that was on the road with him. When the donkey refused to walk any farther, Balaam hit the donkey. Suddenly the donkey spoke to Balaam. Can you imagine what a fright Balaam must have got? Surely donkeys cannot talk! After a while Balaam realised it was an angel talking to him. The angel told Balaam that his path was a dangerous one. Balaam then realised he just had to do what the Lord said.

Because the Lord loves us and wants to use us, He gives us good advice. He can talk to us in many ways, and when we least expect it. Keep your ears open, so that you can hear what the Lord wants to tell you. He even talked to Balaam through a donkey!

WWJD
Jesus will talk to you in many ways.

One day ... he had a vision ... He distinctly saw an angel of God ... (Acts 10:3)

June 25

The prize

Run in such a way as to get the prize. (1 Cor. 9:24)

Athletes who run a race, run to win a prize. The best athlete of the day gets the Victor Ludorum prize. This prize is usually a cup or a trophy or a medal. Also cricket teams, netball teams or hockey teams can win a prize. In some sports, like tennis, winners can win a big money prize.

We humans will also be rewarded or be given a prize at the end of our lives. There are both winners and losers in life, just like in a race or a match. The Bible says if you don't believe in Jesus, and don't want to walk the road of life with him, you will be a loser one day. You won't get a prize. Only eternal damnation will be waiting for you. On the other hand, everyone who asks Jesus' forgiveness, and who has been led onto the right road by him, will get the prize of everlasting life.

Let's serve the Lord with all our hearts and with our whole lives. Then we too will, one day at the end of our lives, get the prize from Jesus' hands.

WWJD
Jesus will give you the best prize: everlasting life.

He who has the Son has life ... (1 Jn. 5:12)

June 26

The right ointment

... the anointing you received from him remains in you ... (1 Jn. 2:27)

In the time of the Bible, kings, priests or prophets were anointed with special oil. This oil had a lovely smell, almost like the nicest perfume today. This oil was usually poured onto someone's head as a sign that that person would be able to do his work. The ointment or oil was the sign of the Holy Spirit who would help that person.

When the Holy Spirit came down on Jesus, He was also anointed for the work He had to do. The Bible says you and I have also been anointed. Yes, when we give our lives to Jesus, the Holy Spirit is also like an ointment or oil that gives us what is necessary to do the work of the Lord, just like in the Old Testament. The only difference is that every child of God is an anointed one, and not only special people. The Lord uses you and me, and He gives us the Holy Spirit so that we can be his instruments.

Thank the Lord that you have also received his Holy Spirit so that you can be used as his anointed one.

WWJD
Jesus will anoint you with the Holy Spirit.

Then the Spirit of the Lord
came upon Gideon ... (Judg. 6:34)

June 27

Greet one another!

Greet one another with a kiss of love ... (1 Pet. 5:14)

In some countries even men greet one another with a kiss. In other countries it is not really done. There are cultures where people don't kiss one another on the mouth, but they rub noses. So we see that every country has its own customs, also with kissing.

In the time of the Bible all people – not only those who were in love – kissed one another. When they greeted one another, they kissed. It was a sign that they loved and cared for one another. In our country people who are close, like family or friends, also kiss when they greet each other.

We don't have to kiss everyone we see, but we must give one another a hearty greeting. A friendly person doesn't just walk past others, he or she greets them. It is always nice to be greeted with a smile by a friendly person. The Bible also says that Christians should always greet one another. They must do it heartily. They must show other Christians that they love them. They must not look the other way when they walk past someone.

Greet everybody you meet today, especially your Christian friends; and be friendly.

WWJD
Jesus would greet everybody in a friendly way.

Grace and peace to you from God our Father and from the Lord Jesus Christ. (Rom. 1:7)

June 28

Come back

" ... return to Me with all your heart ... He is gracious and compassionate, slow to anger and abounding in love ... " (Joel 2:12, 13)

Sometimes people run away from God. Adam and Eve did. They lived close to God, but then decided to be disobedient. They ran away from God. It got so bad that they were chased out of the Garden of Eden. You and I can also run away from God. The Lord calls us to be close to him, but sometimes we go our own way.

Do you remember the story of the prodigal son? He decided to leave home; to go away from his father. He wanted to do his own thing and not what his father said. So he left home and thought he would have the time of his life in a country far away. But he made a mess of his life. He wasted all his money and started going hungry. He realised that he had made a mistake. So he picked himself up and went back to his dad. There he was happy again. His father gave him only the best. It was good to be back home.

The safest and best place to be is close to God. The Lord is full of love and very patient. If you are far away from him today, come back straight away. Tell him you are sorry that you strayed from him. He is waiting for you.

WWJD
Jesus would not leave his Father's home.

"But while he was still a long way off, his father saw him ... he ran to his son, threw his arms around him ... " (Lk. 15:20)

June 29

Sow and reap

Do not be deceived; God cannot be mocked. A man reaps what he sows. (Gal. 6:7)

Everything you and I do has consequences. If we put our hand on the hot stove, we burn. If we drive into a wall, we will get hurt. If we keep on watching ugly things on TV we will become ugly in our hearts.

There are also positive consequences of what we do. If you have learnt hard you will probably get good marks. If you sleep enough, you will be well rested. If you treat others well, they will do the same to you. When you serve the Lord, your love for him grows.

The Bible says what you sow, you will reap. A farmer sows wheat grain and expects to get wheat. If you plant mealies, peach-trees won't come up there. The fruit in our lives depends on the good or poor seed we sowed. If you think bad things, you will do bad things: *The one who sows to please his sinful nature, from that nature will reap destruction; the one who sows to please the Spirit, from the Spirit will reap eternal life* (v. 8).

See that you do what is good and right according to God's will.

WWJD
Jesus would sow good seeds.

Whoever sows sparingly, will reap sparingly, and whoever sows generously will also reap generously. (2 Cor. 9:6)

June 30

Who are you inviting?

Philip found Nathanael and told him ... "Come and see ... "
(Jn. 20:25)

There once was a man called Philip. He had a friend named Nathanael. One day Philip met up with Nathanael. They stood talking and then Philip told Nathanael about an exciting thing that had happened to him. It was something very important.

Philip came across Jesus one day. He saw him and heard what He had to say. Philip was very surprised. While he was listening to Jesus, he was sure that Jesus was the Redeemer that God had sent. The more he listened to Jesus, the more he realised the truth of this. When he saw Nathanael, he was very excited and told him about Jesus and that He was the one Moses wrote about in the Law, and the one about whom the prophets had spoken. Nathanael was not impressed. His first reaction was to ask if anything good could possibly come from Nazareth. He could not believe that this Jesus could be so important. But Philip invited Nathanael to come and see for himself. A miracle took place. Jesus talked to Nathanael and Nathanael realised that Jesus was the Son of God.

Nathanael believed in Jesus because his friend Philip told him about Jesus. Do you tell people about Jesus?

WWJD
Jesus would tell everybody He is the Redeemer.

So the other disciples told him (Thomas),
"We have seen the Lord!" (Jn. 20:25)

July 1

Two roads

" ... wide is the gate and broad is the road that leads to destruction ... But small is the gate and narrow the road that leads to life ... " (Mt. 7:13, 14)

The Bible tells us there are only two roads to take. One road is a broad road. It looks like a good road. There are many people on this road. Unfortunately this road leads to a very nasty place. The Bible calls it the place of destruction. It is just another name for the place where the devil rules. We also call it hell. Fortunately, there is also another road. According to the Bible this is a narrow road. Not so many people take this road. Few people manage to find this road. This is the road that leads to life. Although few people walk on this road, they know they are on the right road if they do. They are very lucky, because the Lord walks this road with them. This is the road to life, or heaven.

One must choose which road you want to take. Some people have been on the broad road since birth, and never decide to change to the narrow road. The Lord calls us to choose the narrow road. It is the Lord's road. On this road we ask what the Lord's will is and then we live according to it. On this road we follow Jesus. Which road are you on?

WWJD
Jesus would take the narrow road.

"Make every effort to enter through the narrow door ... " (Lk. 13:24)

July 2

On the road with Jesus

"Were not our hearts burning within us while He talked with us on the road and opened the Scriptures to us?" (Lk. 24:32)

After Jesus' resurrection two of his disciples were on the road to Emmaus. As they talked, Jesus came up to them and started interpreting the Scriptures to them. This means He taught them about the things written in the Word of God. While they were on the way, they learnt what the Lord's will was, especially about his own death and resurrection.

Later on He ate something with them and then they realised it was Jesus. Then He suddenly disappeared. They were amazed and started talking to each other. They were excited about what had happened, and they told each other what a wonderful warm feeling came into their hearts when He talked to them about the things of his Father.

Something you cannot explain happens to you when the Lord speaks to your heart. You get a feeling of peace and joy. It is a warm feeling. Not hot like a boiling kettle, but nice and warm deep down inside you. You and I must make time regularly to listen to the Lord, so that He can nourish our spirit and fill us with the warmth of his love.

Go on the road with Jesus today. Also talk to him while you are on your way. Allow him to explain his Word to you.

WWJD
Jesus would teach you from his Word.

The unfolding of your Word gives... understanding to the simple. (Ps. 119:130)

July 3

Under his feet

"Sit at my right hand until I put your enemies under your feet." (Mk. 12:36)

The enemy of the kingdom is evil. The devil fights against the Lord. The devil is the prince of darkness and the Lord is the Prince of light. Jesus overcame the devil when He died on the cross and was raised from the dead. In this way He upset the work of the devil. Now people can believe in Jesus, and break loose from the devil.

Unfortunately the devil has not been defeated completely. He has not been finally destroyed. He hurts many people. He still leads many people astray to follow him. Even if Jesus defeated him on the cross, he has not been finally bound.

A day will come when the Lord will have the devil under his control completely, and destroy him once and for all. He will have no more influence on the people on earth. The final judgement will take place. Each will receive according to his or her works. Whoever did good things and followed Jesus, will be rewarded. The others will go with the devil. Jesus will reign and rule for ever and ever. The devil will be under his feet and have no more influence.

Until Jesus finally rules over the devil, we must just faithfully follow in his footsteps. He keeps us from evil.

WWJD
Jesus would keep us from evil.

... take up this shield of faith, with which you can extinguish all the flaming arrows of the evil one. (Eph. 6:16)

July 4

Who are your friends?

Blessed is the man who does not walk in the counsel of the wicked or stand in the way of sinners or sit in the seat of mockers. (Ps. 1:1)

Although we are children of this world, we do not live like people who don't know the Lord, and don't want to obey his Word. We chose to follow Jesus, and that is why we try to do what the Lord tells us to.

The Word tells us that we will be blessed if we do certain things, and others not. Our scripture says we will be blessed if we choose our friends well. A Christian is friendly to all people, whether they know the Lord or not. But a Christian cannot become close friends with just anybody. Our best friends must be friends who also know the Lord and love him.

If we are best friends with people who don't have the Lord in their hearts (the wicked), or do not think the way they should (mockers), or have not yet given their sins to Jesus to be washed clean (sinners), we might find it all the more difficult to serve the Lord. Bad friends can influence us in a bad way. It would be better to choose your friends from those who follow the counsel of the Lord and want to think like him, and who have been washed clean of their sins. Who are your best friends?

WWJD
Jesus would choose friends who follow him.

... so I stand aloof from the counsel of the wicked. (Job 21:16)

July 5

Unrest

Why do the nations conspire and the peoples plot ... ? (Ps. 2:1)

All over the world there is unrest and strife. Every day we see on TV or read in the papers about warring countries. People kill one another, we hear of uprisings and dissatisfaction. Many children go hungry or get hurt and die, because they are caught up in a war where they live. Why is there so much unrest and strife?

Psalm 2 tells us that the real reason for all the warring and strife is that the kings on earth are rising up against the Lord and against Jesus. They are saying, *"Let us break their chains ... and throw off their fetters ... "* (v. 3). It is because kings and presidents and the leaders of countries do not want to bow to God and Jesus, and accept his rule, that there is unrest in their countries.

Jesus came to build a kingdom of peace. He promised if we follow him, we will live in peace. If countries and parliaments and leaders will accept the kingship of Jesus, there will be peace.

Let us pray for our country and our leaders. Ask that they will follow Jesus and do things according to his Word.

WWJD
Jesus would pray for South Africa and the whole world.

... we have one who speaks to the Father in our defense – Jesus Christ ... (1 Jn. 2:1)

July 6

Lift up my head

... you bestow glory on me and lift up my head. (Ps. 3:4)

What God thinks of you and me is most important. It is, however, also important what others think of us. Every one of us has an opinion of another human being. Opinions differ and are often wrong, but yet it is important what people think of you.

Sometimes we do something that makes people change their opinion of us. If we do something good, someone might think we are not as bad as he thought we were. If we do something wrong, someone's opinion of us can also change. Someone may have thought you are good inside, but now he's not sure any more.

It is important that the Lord's opinion of us must be correct. We all make mistakes and all of us sometimes do things that are not right. If we tell the Lord that we are sorry, He forgives us. His opinion doesn't change. He knows we are sinful, but He sees we are feeling bad about it, and that is enough for him. He can give us back our esteem and lift up our heads. If we, from today, live our forgiveness as we should, the Lord will see to it that people's bad opinions of us will be righted. You just serve the Lord faithfully. He will lift up your head.

WWJD
Jesus would change people's opinions of him.

"Repent and believe the good news!" (Mk. 1:15)

July 7

My heart is overflowing

You have filled my heart with greater joy than when ... grain and new wine abound. (Ps. 4:7)

We all make the mistake of thinking if we have possessions we will be happy. Some think if they get a bigger house they will be happy. Others think if they can drive a better car they will be happy. Perhaps you think if you can get a new bicycle you will be happy. Or a nice watch, or a lovely dress, or that special something you so badly want.

David was a king and he had many possessions. Still he wrote these words to tell you and me that he has learnt that many possessions do not really make one happy. It is not what you have that makes you happy, but what you have in you. You are not made happy by things that come from outside. It depends on what is in your heart. There are many happy people who have very few earthly possessions. There are also many unhappy people with lots of possessions.

The Lord gives us much more happiness in our lives than anything else can. This is what David says. His heart was overflowing with the joy of the Lord.

WWJD
Jesus would choose life above earthly possessions.

"What good will it be for a man if he gains the whole world, yet forfeits his soul?" (Mt. 16:26)

July 8

Scared of the night

I will lie down and sleep in peace, for you alone, O Lord, make me dwell in safety. (Ps. 4:8)

We live in a very unsafe world. Every day we hear about people who are attacked and shot even in their own homes. This is enough to scare one. Bad people often use the dark of the night to commit their crimes. Maybe it is this that makes you scared of the dark.

David, as a king, had many worries. One day his son, Absalom, also did something very bad. He rebelled against his dad. It was so bad that David had to flee for his life. Yet we hear him say that he will lie down and sleep in peace. This tells us that David had complete trust in the Lord. He believed that God alone could protect him. He slept peacefully.

You and I must tell the Lord every day and every night that He alone can protect us. Then we will be able to sleep peacefully. He is with us. He never slumbers or sleeps.

WWJD
Jesus would not be afraid.

Even though I walk through the valley of the shadow of death, I will fear no evil, for you are with me ... (Ps. 23:4)

July 9

The new morning

In the morning, O Lord, you hear my voice; in the morning I lay my requests before you and wait in expectation. (Ps. 5:3)

In the morning when we get up, there is usually lots to do. Some of us must make our beds. We must rub the sleep from our eyes and quickly wash. We must eat breakfast and get ready for the day. We must brush our teeth and make sure that our hair is combed neatly.

An important thing we must not forget is that we must, as soon as possible after we have woken up, speak to the Lord. As soon as you are awake, say, "Good morning, Lord." Ask him to be with you all day long. If you have a moment later on, read a few lines, see what He says and pray for specific things. The Lord listens to your voice in the morning.

If we pray, we will receive. Talk to the Lord now.

WWJD
Jesus would get up early and speak to his Father.

He wakens me morning by morning, wakens my ear to listen like one being taught. (Is. 50:4)

July 10

Heal me

O Lord, heal me, for my bones are in agony. (Ps. 6:2)

There are many millions of people in the world who are sick today. Maybe you are also sick. It's not nice to be ill, because then you cannot play like other children.

There are many children of God who are in hospital today or in a wheelchair. With the fall of man, everything the Lord made broke into pieces. Our sick bodies are part of the brokenness, the consequence of the sin of Adam and Eve, and often not because you and I have sinned.

Fortunately we as Christians can ask the Lord to help us when we are ill. David did. He asked the Lord to please make him well. The Lord helps us in all our troubles. He helps us when we are ill. He helps us in his way. Many people don't get well, but they can feel that the Lord is helping them. The way in which they can still joyfully praise the Lord, is a wonderful testimony.

Ask the Lord in faith to heal you also. If you are not ill, think of someone you know who is ill. Pray for him now, or write a card and say you will pray for him and are thinking of him. Thank the Lord for your health.

WWJD
Jesus would care for sick people.

... (p)eople brought to him all who were ill ... and He healed them. (Mt. 4:24)

July 11

It's not fair!

WWJD

God is a righteous judge ... (Ps. 7:12)

It often happens that one is treated unfairly. It means that we get what we did not deserve. Someone else did something wrong and now you get blamed. You were not supposed to be punished, but you got the hiding. Someone else was naughty and now you are scolded! Surely that's not fair.

Sometimes you and I can say we didn't do it, we were not guilty. There are times we cannot even do that. We just hear that someone blamed us behind our backs for something we didn't do. It is impossible for us to defend ourselves. Then it is sometimes just better to let it go and to accept that there is nothing you can do. There will always be unfairness in life. It can happen that someone's electricity gets cut off because other residents in the neighbourhood didn't pay their bill. That sounds most unfair!

Luckily there is a fair judge: the Lord. He knows what goes on in your heart. He can be trusted. Every one of us will stand before his throne one day. God will pass judgement. Every time you and I were treated unfairly, or were accused of something we didn't do, will come out into the open. The Lord will clear us. He will also punish as He sees fit. If you are treated unfairly today, give the matter to God. Just make sure you live the way you should and do what He tells you.

WWJD
Jesus would leave everything to the Father.

You are always righteous, O Lord, when
I bring a case before you ... (Jer. 12:1)

July 12

Sing a new song

Sing to the Lord a new song; sing to the Lord all the earth.
(Ps. 96:1)

The Bible says in a few places that we must sing a new song to the Lord. Does this mean that we must look for songs that we have never heard? That we must sing only fresh, new songs?

When something is old, it is the opposite of something that is new. Thus the Bible says that old songs are songs sung in the hearts and thoughts of people still living with sin. Sin always makes things feel old. Sin always looks fresh and new, but very soon you find out that this is not true. Sin hurts. Sin gets mouldy. Sin is dull. Sin brings unhappiness. Jesus, on the other hand, gives us new life. Together with new life, new songs come.

A broken guitar or a broken violin cannot play beautiful music. A broken instrument makes music that is off key, "old" music. Only when you fix the guitar or violin can you play fresh, new music. In the same way the Lord fixes us when we have sinned, and we can sing new songs to please him. Everything in our lives and in our hearts that praise the Lord – that is what the Bible calls a new song.

Let us praise the Lord with our new lives, and let's sing him a new song!

WWJD
Jesus would sing a new song.

I will sing of your love and justice ... (Ps. 101:1)

July 13

Time is important

... make the most of every opportunity. (Col. 4:5)

Time is like a stream: the water flows past and when that drop of water which is in the stream, has flowed past, it will never come that way again. It is the same with our time. We have an opportunity to do things today. If we don't do it, we might never be able to do it again. Today's time we cannot have over tomorrow.

It is important to the Lord that we will use every opportunity to live for him. Every second is precious. Every minute is important. Every hour that we can live for him. We must know that every day could be our last. Every month gives us the opportunity to tell others about him and to live for him. Every year is a precious opportunity to learn more about the Lord.

We don't know how old we will get. We don't know if we will still be alive next year. That is why it is important to make the best of the time we have. Of course we must work, eat, play, rest, chat and lots more. But while we are doing it, we must make sure we do it to the best of our ability and to the glory of God.

Thank the Lord now for this day. Make the best of it!

WWJD
Jesus would make the best use of every moment.

(M)aking the most of every opportunity... (Eph. 5:16)

July 14

Embrace him!

Exalt the Lord our God ... (Ps. 99:5)

To praise the Lord is wonderful. When we praise him, we sing merry, joyful songs that say the Lord is great and wonderful. Songs of praise are full of joy. We make sounds to say that we are excited because the Lord is wonderful.

Christians don't sing only songs of praise, but also songs to worship. Worshipping the Lord is a little different than praising him. The Bible uses a word for worship, which means something like "to come closer, to embrace, or to kiss". It is the Greek word "proskuneo". What this word wants to say is that we must sometimes be quiet before the Lord, and have the need in our hearts to embrace and to kiss him. When you love someone like your mom or dad, you enjoy holding them, giving them a hug, or kissing them.

We cannot embrace the Lord or kiss him like a human. He is not in a body here with us. But we can love the Lord with our hearts and in our thoughts and we can show him this love. We can tell him and feel it deep in our hearts. We can also sing him songs of worship. Come, let's worship him right now.

WWJD
Jesus would worship the Father.

... worship him who lives for ever and ever... (Rev. 4:10)

July 15

Like grass

As for man, his days are like grass ... the wind blows over it and it is gone. (Ps. 103:15, 16)

Some people reach the age of ninety. Others forty. Then there are those who die very young. Our lives are transient. This means that nothing lasts for ever, it comes to an end. I'm sure you have flowers in your garden. Today you see a beautiful flower, but tomorrow or the next day the flower has wilted and has died. You will never see that flower again. It is the same with the grass in the fields. One day the grass is green and luxuriant, but soon it wilts and dies. You will never see that grass again. Yes, it is the same with a human life. We don't live on earth for ever. Also people who may be fit and strong today, could be dead tomorrow.

Only people who accept the new life Jesus gives, will live for ever. The Bible says only the Word of God will live for ever. If we keep his Word in our hearts, this Word inside us makes that you and I will not perish, but live for ever. Yes, of course we will die, but we live for ever in Jesus. God's Word is in you and me. Are you also pleased that you will live for ever?

WWJD
Jesus will let you live for ever.

"He who believes in Me will live, even though he dies." (Jn. 11:25)

July 16

The stone

The stone the builders rejected has become the capstone. (Ps. 118:22)

One day some people wanted to erect a building. They built with stone. Among all the other stones was a very special stone. The builders were very fussy and they didn't want to use just any stone. This stone looked quite ordinary to them. They wanted to use only the nicest and precious stones to build with. They took this stone and threw it to one side. God picked up the stone and saw that it was a special stone. He used it as the most important stone in his building. He made it the corner-stone or foundation of the building.

This is just a story, but this is what happened to Jesus. When He came to earth the Pharisees and scribes thought that He was just an ordinary person. Jesus was very special even if they didn't think so. They renounced him and had him killed. But God used Jesus' life to become the most important stone in his kingdom. God used Jesus as a corner-stone to build the new Jerusalem, where all the children of God will live together happily.

Praise the Lord that He used Jesus as corner-stone.

WWJD
Jesus would choose God's plan.

... come to him, the living stone ... (1 Pet. 2:4)

July 17

Call out Lord!

I call on the Lord in my distress, and he answers me. (Ps. 120:1)

Have you ever been in big trouble? Sometimes things happen to us that make us so anxious that we feel quite sick. It could be that you lost something very valuable. At that moment when you realised it, you heart missed a beat. Or you could have been somewhere on a rock and your foot slipped. You could have been hurt very badly. You really got a fright. It can also happen that you are walking down the road and see some-one following you, and you suspect that he is trouble. It is as if a cold hand is gripping your heart.

The Bible says a child of the Lord calls out to his God in a moment of crisis. It is the right thing to do. You can even start praying out loud when you realise you are in trouble. Don't be ashamed to do it. Call out to God, He is there with you. It will also be good for everyone to hear that you put your trust in the Lord. Also the devil and his henchmen, because the name of the Lord that you are calling upon, is like a strong tower to hide in.

Remember that you can always call upon the Lord in your distress.

WWJD
Jesus would call upon the Father.

" ... call upon me ... I will deliver you ... " (Ps. 50:15)

July 18

The tears were flowing

By the rivers of Babylon we sat and wept when we remembered Zion. (Ps. 137:1)

Israel did what was wrong in the eyes of the Lord. Then God allowed that they were exiled to Babylon. The Babylonians were a heathen nation. They did not believe in God. The Israelites found it very difficult to live in a foreign heathen country.

Someone then wrote a song that tells how they sat at the rivers of Babylon and cried, because they missed Zion, the hill on which the beautiful big city, Jerusalem, stood. Actually they didn't even want to sing any more: *How can we sing the songs of the Lord while in a foreign land?* (v. 4). Although the Israelites did sing, their songs sounded like songs of mourning, because they were sad and their tears were flowing.

If you are not prepared to do the will of the Lord, you cannot really be happy. If you drag your sins along with you, you always reach a point where the happiness and joy in your heart disappear. Sin always brings unhappiness. You and I cannot sing in our hearts and be joyful if we sin. Then the tears flow in our hearts, and the joy of the Lord disappears.

Won't you make sure that you don't land up at the rivers of Babylon. It is a place of sin. There is no joy. There are no songs. There are only tears.

WWJD
Jesus would wipe the tears from your eyes.

He will wipe every tear from their eyes... (Rev. 21:4)

July 19

A parent's advice

Listen, my sons, to a father's instruction; pay attention and gain understanding. (Prov. 4:1)

Moms and dads must teach their children and advise them. When fathers and mothers don't really love their children, then it's not important to them what their children do. Parents who care about them, teach their children well. It is good when parents teach their children right from wrong.

Children, on the other hand, don't always take the advice of their parents to heart. This means they don't take notice of it. Or they can be irritated by it. They don't want their parents' advice. The Bible says this is wrong. It is a foolish child who does not want to accept advice from his or her parents. One does not always like getting advice from older people, because we often think what we want to do is better. Accept that grown-ups have more experience in life, and that is why their advice is good. Remember, they were children too, they know how a child feels.

My father and mother are not alive any more, but I am very glad about the advice they gave me. It helped me to take the right decisions. Be thankful if you still have a father and a mother who can help you, can talk to you, give you advice, and show you the right way. Thank the Lord for your parents right now.

WWJD
Jesus would accept his Father's advice.

Children, obey your parents... (Eph. 6:1)

July 20

Like the rising sun

" ... may they who love you be like the sun when it rises in its strength." (Judg. 5:31)

Especially in winter, it is lovely when the sun shines brightly. Sun brings warmth. When you open the curtains in a cold house, the room quickly becomes nice and warm. When we sit in the winter sun, our bodies warm up. Do you also think sunrise is better than the cold, dark night?

The Bible says whoever loves the Lord can shine brightly like the rising sun. Their lives, the way they act, their friendliness and love, can be like bright sunshine on a cold winter's day. You and I can, as children of the Lord, bring light and warmth wherever we go. Jesus said we must be the light of the world. Jesus himself is called the light of the world. If He, the brightest light, lives in us, our lives are also lit up and we will shine like bright sunbeams in the dark.

There is much darkness in life: darkness of sin. There is pain, distress and heartache. Many people have no hope in their hearts. To them life is dark. You and I can make a difference in their lives. Let us shine with and for Jesus.

Bring sunshine today wherever you go.

WWJD
Jesus would let his light shine in the darkness.

 The light shines in the darkness... (Jn. 1:5)

July 21

Enough

"Even if she gathers among the sheaves, don't embarrass her." (Ruth 2:15)

Ruth was Naomi's daughter-in-law. Naomi lived in a far country and she wanted to go back to Bethlehem where she came from. Ruth decided to go with her mother-in-law, to be with her to support and help her. Ruth was a good woman.

In Bethlehem they had to find food to eat. Ruth went to the fields where they were harvesting the wheat. As the men were gathering the sheaves, some leftover grain remained in the fields. In those times poor people were allowed to gather behind the harvesters. This cornfield belonged to Boaz. Boaz was a good man. He saw how hard Ruth was working and he told his men to leave more grain behind, so that she could gather more. It was the Lord working in Boaz' heart, so that he took pity on Ruth. Later on Ruth and Boaz fell in love with each other, and Boaz took Ruth as his wife.

The Lord looks after his children. Ruth didn't know where she would find food, but the Lord saw to it that she was noticed. Ruth worked hard and the Lord blessed her. The Lord wants to take care of you too. He has a plan with your life and He knows what you should have. He will see to it that you are noticed if it is his will. Just trust him, like Ruth, and the Lord will also bless your future.

WWJD
Jesus would trust the Father.

"... am coming to you now ... " (Jn. 17:13)

July 22

Leaders

In those days Israel had no king; everyone did as he saw fit. (Judg. 21:25)

In Judges 21 we read how the young men from Benjamin (the Benjamites) hid in the vineyards, and when the young girls from the town Shiloh came out to dance in the field, they rushed out from the vineyards, and each one grabbed himself a wife. What a way to get a wife! I don't know if the Lord was very happy with this way, because that chapter closes saying that at the time there was no king, and everyone did as they pleased. If all of us to what we please, life will be very confusing. Just think: if everyone drives a car as fast as he likes, there will be even more accidents on the roads. If all of us could steal or take what we like, none of our things would ever be safe again.

That is why it is so important to have leaders. Leaders are people who are chosen or appointed to see that rules are obeyed. Rules or laws are necessary for order. Your school has rules. You can't do just as you please; you must keep to the rules. There are prefects or leaders who see to this. Obey them, pray for them, support them. It is your duty to keep to the rules and obey leaders.

WWJD
Jesus would respect leaders.

The authorities... have been established by God. (Rom. 13:1)

July 23

She pleaded

She named him Samuel, saying, "Because I asked the Lord for him." (1 Sam. 1:20)

Long ago there was a woman called Hannah. Her husband's name was Elkanah. He loved Hannah very much. Although Hannah lived a good life, she was deeply troubled. She could not have a baby. She wanted a baby so badly, but although they had been married a long time, she and her husband had no children. Then Hannah went to the temple.

Hannah wanted a child so badly that she pleaded with God and begged that He would work a miracle. She also made the Lord a promise. She said if she had a child, she would give this child to the Lord. She would bring this child to the temple, and he could work there for the Lord and serve him. The Lord answered Hannah's prayer. A miracle happened! Suddenly she was expecting a baby. Later on the baby was born. His name was Samuel. When Samuel was big enough, she took him to the temple and there he worked for the Lord. Samuel became an important man in Israel. He was a prophet of the Lord. He told people about the Lord.

Hannah kept her promise. She asked the Lord for something and she did what she promised. Perhaps there is something you want very badly. Ask the Lord for it. And remember, if you make a promise to the Lord, you must keep it.

WWJD
Jesus would keep his promises.

"Simply let your 'Yes' be 'Yes'
and your 'No' 'No' ... " (Mt. 5:37)

July 24

The right friends

... accompanied by valiant men whose hearts God had touched. (1 Sam. 10:26)

The people of Israel wanted a king. Actually the Lord was their king, but because they did not have enough faith, they wanted an earthly king like all the other nations. So the Lord gave them a king, but He warned them that kings can make life difficult. The first king was Saul. Saul was just an ordinary young man and the son of a farmer. Suddenly he was a king. He must have felt a bit lonely and also unsure of how he should behave.

Then God made a plan. The Lord "touched" the hearts of a number of brave men. This means that the Lord put it into their hearts that they should support Saul. Deep in their hearts they got the feeling that they had to go with Saul and help him. We can also say the Lord called them to support the new king.

The Lord knows that you and I can sometimes not do what we have to do, alone. Then He touches the hearts of friends so that they can love and support us. It is wonderful when the Lord gives us people to be with us and to help us. Of course, the devil also sends bad people to us, because he wants to take us away from God. Pray that the Lord will send you the right friends.

WWJD
Jesus would choose the right friends.

... "Is this the love you show your friend? Why didn't you go with your friend?" (2 Sam. 16:17)

July 25

God's answers

... But God did not answer him that day. (1 Sam. 14:37)

We know that we can't hear the voice of the Lord the way we can another person's. God's voice has no sound. God talks in different ways. He speaks to us through the Holy Spirit and through his Word. Sometimes He speaks through people, but what they say will never go against God's Word.

The Lord answers us. If you have prayed about a thing and you ask the Lord to give you wisdom, He will sometimes give you an answer deep inside your heart. You just know what his will is. Then there are times when you ask and ask and get no reply. It is as if the Lord is keeping quiet. Often it is because you are asking things that go against his will. Sometimes you ask the Lord to give you things and you don't get them. You wonder why. The reason is most probably that it would not be good for you to have those things. Then the Lord keeps quiet. He does not give an answer to your prayer. You must just trust that the Lord knows best. If what you have asked for is really meant for you, He will give it to you, at the right time.

Go on trusting Jesus, even if you sometimes wonder why He doesn't answer the way you want him to.

WWJD
Jesus would be patient when God keeps quiet.

O my God, I cry out by day,
but you do not answer. (Ps. 22:3)

July 26

God sees inside

" ... The Lord does not look at the things man looks at. Man looks at the outward appearance, but the Lord looks at the heart." (1 Sam. 16:7)

King Saul disappointed the Lord, and so the Lord decided to choose a new king. In the olden days the prophets anointed a new king. They poured oil onto his head, and that was the sign that he was the new king. Here, Samuel was the prophet who had to anoint the new king. He didn't know who he had to anoint. All that he knew, was that it would be one of the sons of a man named Jesse.

Jesse had eight sons. They were good-looking, big and strong. Samuel thought the biggest and strongest and most attractive son would most probably become the king of Israel. But God wanted someone who was attractive in his heart. The Lord did not choose any of the elder brothers, and soon only one was left. He was the youngest, and not the strongest or the best-looking. When Samuel saw David, because that was his name, the Lord spoke in Samuel's heart and told him that this was the new king, and that he had to anoint him.

The Lord does not always choose the strongest or the most attractive people. He chooses every one of us who is willing to do his will.

WWJD
Jesus would look at your heart.

... motives are weighed by the Lord. (Prov. 16:2)

July 27

Peace in music

Whenever the spirit ... came upon Saul, David would take his harp and play. Then relief would come to Saul, and the evil spirit would leave him. (1 Sam. 16:23)

Because Saul sinned, the Lord allowed an evil spirit to go into him to trouble him and make him unhappy. If we don't have the Holy Spirit in our hearts, evil spirits can come into our lives and make us very unhappy.

David played the harp beautifully. It is a stringed instrument, nearly like a guitar. David learnt to play the harp when he looked after his father's sheep in the fields. That is where he sang many of the psalms that we can still read in the Bible today. Saul often asked David to play him some music. This happened especially when Saul's heart was troubled and full of evil, because of the evil spirit in him. Afterwards the evil spirit would leave him, and he had peace in his heart again.

Songs or music sung or played by Christians, help to bring Christ's light and peace into the world.

WWJD
Jesus would be there, in your songs of praise.

... you are enthroned as the Holy One;
you are the praise of Israel. (Ps. 22:3)

July 28

Someone else

He is the one who will build a house for my name … (2 Sam. 7:13)

King David loved the Lord. He was a successful king and very famous. The Israelites prospered when he was king. David was happy and blessed.

Still, there was something David wanted to do very badly: he wanted to build a house for the Lord. In the Old Testament the Lord did not live inside people like today. They had to go to a building or tent which was there specially for talking to the Lord or worshipping him. David saw that there were no really beautiful buildings where people could worship the Lord. That is why he wanted to build a big and beautiful temple. He dreamt about it and he plannd to build this place for the Lord.

But the Lord had his own plan. The Lord wanted David's son to build this temple. The prophet Nathan came to tell David this.

Maybe David was very disappointed. But he accepted God's decision. Sometimes you and I also want to do something badly, but the Lord wants to use someone else. We may be disappointed, but the Lord knows best.

WWJD
Jesus would always obey the Lord's orders.

 … Then you will be prosperous and successful. (Josh. 1:8)

July 29

An evil plan

... he got up and went down to take possession of Naboth's vineyard. (1 Kgs. 21:16)

King Ahab was a bad man who did not do what the Lord wanted. He even married a heathen woman, Jezebel.

Ahab had enough money and possessions. But he was not satisfied. He saw a very nice vineyard. It belonged to Naboth. He told Naboth that he wanted to buy the vineyard. Naboth did not want to do that because he had inherited the ground. It was special to him. Then king Ahab started sulking and lay down on his bed with his face to the wall, and he didn't want to eat. His bad wife told him what to do; it was an evil plan.

Ahab arranged for two bad men to make false accusations against Naboth. This means they said Naboth had done a terrible thing, while it was not true at all. The bad men then came to the king and told him that Naboth had cursed both God and the king. Ahab ordered that Naboth had to be stoned to death. After Naboth's death the king took Naboth's vineyard for himself.

People will sometimes do terrible things for very wrong reasons. Rather ask the Lord to give you what you want. Don't ever hurt someone just because you want something that belongs to him.

WWJD
Jesus would be satisfied with what God gives him.

"You shall not covet ... anything that belongs to your neighbor." (Ex. 20:17)

July 30

You will be comforted

As a mother comforts her child, so will I comfort you ... (Is. 66:13)

If you pick up a baby unexpectedly or put him in the arms of a stranger, he will usually start crying. This happens because the baby does not feel safe. You and I also have things that make us feel insecure and afraid.

The Lord does not want us to feel insecure. The devil likes it when we are scared at night and lie awake because we see all kinds of scary pictures in our heads of people killing or hurting one another. One of the weapons the devil uses is fear. The more he can scare us, the happier he is, for then he knows we can't give our best.

When a child feels insecure, he or she usually runs to Mommy, where there is safety. A mother or father protects their children, and takes them in their arms so that they can feel there is no danger. If there is any danger, Dad or Mom will make sure that I am not hurt, the child thinks. As a mother comforts her child, the Lord will also comfort you and me. We must just trust him, run to him and shelter with him. We can tell him all our fears. He will put his arms around us and we will feel safe.

Are you afraid of something? Allow the peace of the Lord into your heart. Put your trust in him. He will comfort you.

WWJD
Jesus would put his trust in the Father.

So do not fear, for I am with you ... (Is. 41:10)

July 31

Three important things

"This is the one I esteem: he who is humble and contrite in spirit, and trembles at my word." (Is. 66:2)

When the Lord looks at a person, there are some things that are important to him. If He finds them in a person, He is like a father who looks at his child with satisfaction and love. The first thing of importance is that we must not be proud. We must realise our need and ask help. If we do, we can be helped. A proud person will not admit that he needs help. That is why the Lord cannot help a proud person.

The second thing is to repent our sins. Someone who doesn't say he or she is sorry about their sins, cannot be forgiven. People who don't want to admit to their sins pretend they do not need God. The Lord likes people who are sorry about their sins. If you confess your sins, God will forgive you.

The third important thing the Lord likes very much, is when his words are important to us. He likes people who respect his words. In the Bible it says, "people who tremble at his word". This means that we must have respect for what the Lord says, and we must know that it is important not only to hear what He says, but also to do it.

I hope that if the Lord looks at you today, He will feel satisfied because you tell him that you need him, are sorry about your sins, and listen to his words and then do what He says.

WWJD
Jesus would do what the Word says.

With my lips I recount all the laws that come from your mouth. (Ps. 119:13)

August 1

Broken cisterns

... broken cisterns that cannot hold water. (Jer. 2:13)

In the time of the Bible, people didn't have taps in their homes that they could just turn on to get water. They had to go to a fountain, or a source of water, and there they had to draw water and carry it home in something like a stone jug or a pail.

A jug or a pail can hold water only if it does not have holes in it. Otherwise it will leak. Can you think how stupid it would be if you keep on drawing water and the more you draw, the less you have in your jug. This will not work.

One day the Lord told Jeremiah that his followers are just like people trying to draw water with a jug that has a hole in it. The more water they draw, the less water they have, because they keep on losing the water. The Lord uses this image to show that people do not put their trust in him, but in ordinary people with shortcomings. They cannot provide like the Lord. During that time, Israel had come to an agreement with Egypt, that Egypt would help them. But God said they must not put their trust in Egypt, but in him. He would help them.

You and I also put our trust in other things, or people to help us. No, says the Bible, we must trust God. We must ask his help. He will never disappoint us like a broken jug.

WWJD
Jesus would trust the Father.

Do not put your trust in princes, in mortal men, who cannot save. (Ps. 146:3)

August 2

God's sad heart

... my heart is faint within me. Listen to the cry of my people from a land far away. (Jer. 8:18, 19)

Have you ever wondered if the Lord can also be sad? After all, He is the great God of heaven and earth. Can He also feel like you and I do? Yes, the Bible talks about the Lord as if he can.

We read in the Bible that the Lord was very sad when He looked at the people of Israel. He wanted only the best for them, but they sinned. Then He looked at them and saw how they were suffering. A person who lives with sin always suffers. What the Lord saw made him sad and it upset him. He saw how troubled they were in their distress. Then He said, Since my people are crushed, I am crushed; I mourn, and horror grips me (v. 21).

The Lord so badly wants to comfort his people and heal them, to be like an ointment that will heal the wounds of their hurt. He wishes they will accept him and come back to him. He knows that will be the only solution. Only He can help them.

Sometimes the Lord is also worried about you and me. He is also sad because we do the wrong things. He knows it won't make us happy. He wants so badly for us to come closer to him, so that He can heal us. Come to the Lord today so that his heart can be filled with joy.

WWJD
Jesus would make the Father happy.

...so that my joy may be in you and that your joy may be complete. (Jn. 15:11)

August 3

Be careful of boasting

(B)ut let him who boasts boast about this ... that he knows Me. (Jer. 9:24)

When we can do something well, it is easy to boast. When we boast, we tell others how good we are at certain things. Of course we are sometimes good at something. Some people sing beautifully, others run fast, or are clever with their hands. Often our fathers and mothers or grandmothers or grandfathers boast about us. It is always better if someone else boasts about you. One must never boast about oneself.

The Lord said a wise man must not boast about his wisdom. The soldier must not boast about his great strength. A rich man must not boast about his great wealth. If we have to boast, there is only one thing to boast about, and that is the Lord himself. Someone who is clever never boasts about himself, but says the Lord is good and wonderful. This person shows that he or she knows the Lord, and understands who He is. God is so great and wonderful and without sin, that we can really boast about him. He is without faults. The Lord is fantastic. If we really want to boast, we must look away from ourselves and praise his name. He is the one who gives us our talents. He must take credit for it.

WWJD
Jesus would never boast about himself.

I will boast about a man like that, but I will not boast about myself ... (2 Cor. 12:5)

August 4

When all is well ...

Give glory to the Lord your God before ... your feet stumble on the darkening hills ... (Jer. 13:16)

Most people call out to God only when things go wrong. Every day they just go on living their lives, and when something goes wrong, then they call upon the Lord. He must help quickly. The Lord wants us to put our trust in him, and He wants to help people in need. But He does not like it if we ask his help just when we are in trouble. Christians follow and serve the Lord, not only when they are in trouble, but also when all is well in their lives.

The Lord says his people must glorify him before it gets dark in their lives. In the dark we can't see where we are going, and the Lord uses this image to say, "They will be like people who bump into the mountain in the dark." Once you have stumbled over a stone, it is too late to call upon God. You should have spoken to him long before you got to the hills. We must not wait until the moment of need. Speak to the Lord now, and glorify and praise him for everything He is and does. If trouble comes then, the Lord is with you already. Actually He will warn you even before you get to the hills.

God wants to share our lives with us, not only our troubles.

WWJD
Jesus would talk to the Lord about everything.

You will fill me with joy in your presence. (Acts 2:28)

August 5

He is everywhere

"Do I not fill heaven and earth?" declares the Lord. (Jer. 23:24)

There are really people who think they can hide from the Lord. The Lord says no one can *"hide in secret places so that I cannot see him"* (v. 24). God sees everything, because He is everywhere we are. His eyes can see right through a wall or right through a person's body. He can see deep into our hearts. Yes, God knows everything and He sees everything. The Lord hears everything. It scares some people to think that God knows everything about them and can see everything. If you are the Lord's child, it doesn't scare you, it makes you happy. It means that the Lord understands you. He knows what you are struggling with. He knows what your problems are. He also knows what your dreams are and what you want. He sees you when you are alone, and when you cry, and when you are afraid. Because God knows everything, He can help us the way we have to be helped, at the right time.

The Lord knows about all our sins. Because He sent Jesus to pay for our sins, this is not a problem. We can be honest with God about our sins, we don't have to hide from him. If we are honest about our sins, the Lord promises to forgive us.

Thank the Lord that He knows all about you, and sees everything you do, and that He still loves you very much.

WWJD
Jesus will be with you wherever you are.

"And surely I am with you always, to the very end of the age." (Mt. 28:20)

August 6

The fire and the hammer

"Is not my word like fire," declares the Lord, "and like a hammer that breaks a rock in pieces?" (Mt. 28:19)

The Bible is very, very powerful. Many people have read the Bible just because they were inquisitive, and then their whole lives changed. There are many people who have slept over in a hotel room where a Bible was placed next to the bed, and when they started reading it, it was as if their attention was fixed on it, and they could not put it down. Suddenly they realised that God was talking to them, and they made their peace with God.

Small wonder that the Bible says God's Word is like fire. Fire can burn down a whole town. Fire can also destroy a person's life. The Bible is like fire because it has the power to change a person's life.

The Bible is also like a hammer sometimes. You do not only use it to drive nails in, but you can also use it to break down walls. With a big hammer one can even break a large stone, or rock. Many people have hearts like stone, and when the Word of the Lord speaks to them, it is as if their hard hearts are broken. They become soft and open to the Lord.

The Word can change your life. We must share this Word with others, so that the power of God can change their lives.

WWJD
Jesus would share the Word with others.

" ... go and make disciples of all nations ... " (Mt. 28:19)

August 7

The past is past

... do not dwell on the past. See I am doing a new thing!
(Is. 43:18, 19)

We can all remember something that happened in the past. Perhaps it was something good, or perhaps something bad. What happened in the past, can have an influence on our lives even now. If something terrible happened in your family, you don't forget it easily. We also remember the good things. Sometimes we take out our photo albums and think back to all the wonderful things that happened in the past.

One must not allow the ugly things of the past to spoil today's joy. The Lord prefers that we live each day to the full; one day at a time. We know that the Lord is the one who wants to make the good things in our lives even better. He wants to give us new experiences, new dreams. That is why He says we must not think too much about past things, because He is going to do something new, and it is about to happen. The Lord also makes another promise. Even if tomorrow is a desert, He will give us enough water.

The Lord tells you and me today that we must not look back too much, and not dwell too much on the past. Grab the opportunity the Lord offers today, and allow him to do something new for you. Leave all the hurt of the past in his hands, and trust him to give you a new, bright future.

WWJD
Jesus would not look back.

"No one who looks back ... is fit for ... the kingdom of God." (Lk. 9:62)

August 8

Women's Day

... a woman who fears the Lord is to be praised. (Prov. 31:30)

In the beginning God made a man and a woman. The Lord made the woman beautiful. She loved the Lord and followed him and served him. Then sin came into the world. There are still many pretty women, but the hearts of some are full of sin, until Jesus forgives them.

The Bible says, *Charm is deceptive, and beauty is fleeting, but a woman who fears the Lord is to be praised*(v. 30). It is important that we must tell all women that they can become new in Jesus Christ, and then they will not have only an attractive outward appearance, but that their whole being will be beautiful. Women are very precious, and because they behave in a very specific way, we cannot do without them in our society. When we celebrate Women's Day today, we also praise what women have done, not only in our country, but all over the world. Our prayer is that all women will accept Jesus Christ as Redeemer. Then they will become like the woman of Proverbs 31.

WWJD
Jesus would share his message with everybody.

"If you knew the gift of God ... you would have asked him ... " (Jn. 4:10)

August 9

Musicians

... four thousand are to praise the Lord with the musical instruments I have provided for that purpose. (1 Chr. 23:5)

Today there are many musicians and singers who are used by the Lord to glorify and praise him. Many congregations have members who sing beautifully, and they lead the congregation in praising the Lord. We often hear singers on the radio or television, who make CDs that one can listen to. The message that they sing, is the message of the wonderful gospel of Jesus.

This is nothing new. Although they did not have CDs or radios in the time of the Old Testament, singers and musicians were appointed, and it was their full-time job to help people praise and glorify the Lord. King David was a musician himself. In his time he appointed thousands of singers and paid them all a salary to praise the Lord. It was their job. They served in the house of the Lord.

Thank the Lord for singers and musicians who help us praise the Lord better, and to love him better. Also pray that the Lord will bless them, so that they can build his kingdom.

WWJD
Jesus would thank the Father for musicians and singers.

As they began to sing and praise,
the Lord set ambushes ... (2 Chr. 20:22)

August 10

Joshua's filthy clothes

... Joshua the high priest ... was dressed in filthy clothes ...
(Zech. 3:1, 3)

Zechariah was one of the Lord's prophets. One day he saw a vision. A vision is when you see something happen, but it is not really there. It is like a dream. You dream of something happening, and you can see it clearly, you can remember everything afterwards, but it didn't really happen. The Lord often talked to his prophets in dreams. In these dreams the Lord tried to tell them something He wanted them to know.

Zechariah's dream was about the priest called Joshua who did very important work. He was the high priest. Next to Joshua stood the devil. He was busy accusing Joshua. But the Lord scolded Satan because He still had a plan with Joshua. Joshua's clothes were filthy with sin. The Lord told an angel to take off his dirty clothes. Then the Lord said to Joshua, *"See, I have taken away your sin, and I will put rich garments [clean clothes] on you"* (v. 4).

Even a minister, or someone who is in the service of the Lord, sins. That is why we must pray often for our ministers and everybody in leadership positions. He forgave Joshua's sins, and dressed him in clean, white clothes. Pray for your minister, that he can be clean when he stands before the Lord.

WWJD
Jesus would pray for ministers and leaders.

Pray also for me, that ... words
may be given me ... (Eph. 6:19)

August 11

Good company

WWJD

"Bad company corrupts good character." (1 Cor. 15:33)

It is always interesting to see how people react when they are in the company of different people. Company is conversation you have when you are with other people. When the minister or the pastor comes to visit, there are people who get such a serious tone of voice. The same people talk differently when they are with friends they like visiting, or at a party. When they are in the company of noisy people who swear and argue, you will hear them, soon enough, behaving in the same way. Our behaviour is influenced by the company we keep. You can talk softly, but the minute someone starts shouting at you, it is not long before you shout right back at him. When someone is ticking you off and you speak softly, it is interesting that the noisy person quickly starts talking softly.

This is the way we influence one another. The company you keep is important. If you are always in the company of people who say and do ugly things, you eventually become just like them. That is why the Bible tells us we must be careful of the company we keep. If your friends are good, and they are good company, it is easier for you to live a good life.

Make sure you keep the right company today, so that your behaviour will be to the glory of God.

WWJD
Being in Jesus' company will influence people's lives.

Large crowds ... followed him. (Mt. 4:25)

August 12

Good gifts

There are different kinds of gifts, but the same Spirit. (1 Cor. 12:4)

It is always exciting to receive gifts. If you are a child of the Lord, you also receive gifts. The gifts the Lord gives you, are handed out by the Holy Spirit who lives in a Christian. The Bible calls these gifts "gifts of grace". "Grace" means that these gifts are free; you and I just get them, not because we deserve them. "Gift" means just that – it is a present. So gifts of grace are gifts we haven't earned, we get them free from the hand of God.

The gifts handed out by the Holy Spirit are not given to you and me to make only us happy, but to make, especially people around us, happy. These are gifts to share with others. Every Christian has received a gift from God. This gift is something like wisdom, knowledge, special faith, or even to heal others. The Holy Spirit hands out these gifts to the children of God the way He decides to. You and I must just ask that the Lord will show us which gift He gave us.

As you grow closer to the Lord, He will show you which gifts He gave you, so that you can use them to make others happy. Thank him for all the gifts He has given you.

WWJD
Jesus would use his gifts to benefit others.

Now to each one the manifestation of the Spirit is given for the common good. (I Cor. 12:7)

August 13

Pray for South Africa

Righteousness exalts a nation, but sin is a disgrace to any people. (1 Tim. 2:1, 2)

We live in a beautiful country. It is a country of sunshine, lovely places where beautiful game is found, and friendly people. Many people come from far and wide to visit our country. We call them tourists. Tourists like coming to South Africa because it is such a beautiful country.

Unfortunately there are also things in our country that are not at all beautiful. Terrible things happen and the people who do these evil things do not know the Lord, and do not love him. They are people who sin. Sin always brings shame on a country and its people. We are ashamed when we think of so many people being killed in our country, or whose cars are stolen, or who are being sexually abused. We are ashamed of people who steal money as they please, even if they are leaders. That is why we need to pray a lot for our country.

The Lord says when we pray, He will answer our prayers and help us. Why don't you and I ask the Lord's forgiveness for all our sins, on behalf of our country. We must say, "Lord, we are sorry that not all of us want to serve You. Forgive us, and help us, and heal our country. Grant that we can live here in safety, and in peace." Pray now for our country and its leaders.

WWJD
Jesus would pray for our country and its leaders.

... that ... prayers ... and thanksgiving be made ... for kings and all those in authority ... (1Tim. 2:1, 2)

August 14

Not nice any more

Better a meal of vegetables where there is love than a
fattened calf with hatred. (Prov. 15:17)

You can have the most delicious food at table: lovely fried
potatoes and leg of lamb, with pudding afterwards, or just all
kinds of goodies. But, if the atmosphere at table is not pleasant, then the food does not taste as good as it should.

Perhaps it has also happened to you that you were enjoying
a good meal, when all of a sudden some argument started.
When we argue we get cross with one another and start saying ugly things to each other. I bet the food was suddenly not
as nice any more. You didn't even feel like finishing it. You just
wanted the fighting to stop.

A clever man said he would rather eat plain vegetables served with love, than a delicious exotic meal, served with hatred.
It is so important that we create the right atmosphere when
we are having a meal. You also does not digest your food well
if you are in a bad mood. Peace, love and friendly talk create the
best atmosphere at a table. Every day you say grace before a
meal, pray that the love and peace of the Lord be there with you
all. Don't start an argument at table.

WWJD
Jesus would create a nice atmosphere at table.

... do it all in the name of the Lord Jesus ... (Col. 3:17)

August 15

Brothers and sisters

... He said, "Here are my mother and my brothers. For whoever does the will of my Father in heaven is my brother and sister and mother." (Mt. 12:49, 50)

Some people have very big families. My father had twelve brothers and sisters. To have family is wonderful. The members of a family can help, protect and love one another. Normally, family are supposed to give warmth and love to one another. Nearly like a harbour where boats can dock safely.

Christian families are not only brothers and sisters living in the same house. Jesus surprised people when He said He did not have only one mother and father and a few brothers. He said everyone who does the will of his Father is a brother or a sister to him. We too, have more family than our blood brothers or sisters; we have millions of brothers and sisters all over the world. There are many people in many countries who decide to follow Jesus. We don't even know their names. If it was possible to meet them, wouldn't we have a lot to talk about! There is so much to say about our Father in heaven.

Christians must love one another like brothers and sisters. We must care for one another, support one another and encourage one another to serve the Lord. Who are your brothers and sisters who believe in Jesus? Love them.

WWJD
Jesus would accept you as a brother or a sister.

... Jesus is not ashamed to call them brothers. (Heb. 2:11)

August 16

Do it now

Do not say ... *"Come back later; I'll give it tomorrow"* ... (Prov. 3:28)

It always feels good to help others. But when you are asked to help out, it isn't always easy to turn your attention to them-immediately. Also, it might not be so easy or pleasant while you are busy helping them. But when you have helped them, you have a good feeling inside. It is good when people help one another.

Sometimes we are so busy that we do not think it will be possible to help this person asking for it now. Then we say, "I'll help you later." Perhaps it's your mother asking you to do something for her, and you reply, "I'll do it just now, Mommy." The Bible says we shouldn't do that. When someone asks us, we must do it immediately. If you tell them you will help to-morrow, it can happen that you are not even alive tomorrow.

Or something can come up, so that you just don't get round to helping him or her. No, if we are asked to help, do it now.

WWJD
Jesus would help people immediately.

Do not merely listen to the Word ... Do what it says. (Jas. 1:22)

August 17

Punishment is ouch

He who spares the rod hates his son, but he who loves him is careful to discipline him. (Prov. 13:24)

When we are naughty, we usually get a hiding. I'm sure you can remember a hiding you got when you were little. Perhaps your backside was stinging from the punishment your parents gave you because you were naughty.

Parents punish their children because they want to teach them right from wrong. The government punishes people who break the law. The Lord punishes people who break his laws. Punishment is part of our lives.

Sometimes we think our parents don't love us when they discipline us. No parent or teacher or anyone else may punish someone without a good reason. Unnecessary punishment is unfair. If however, we deserve to be punished, it will make us think twice the next time we want to do something wrong.

Because your parents love you, they punish you by either smacking you, or taking something away from you, or making you stay in your room. If you have been punished, think why you were punished. Apologize, and try not to do the same thing again.

WWJD
Jesus would be obedient.

"But be sure to fear (obey) the Lord and serve him faithfully." (1 Sam. 12:24)

August 18

The precious pearl

"When he found one of great value [a pearl], he went away and sold everything he had and bought it." (Mt. 13:46)

Jesus told stories to teach people important things. He told the story of a man who worked with jewels. He was a jeweller who knew a lot about pearls. He was always on the look-out for good pearls to string and sell, and he made a lot of money like this.

This jeweller came across a very wonderful pearl one day. It was the best pearl he had ever seen. He knew immediately that it was very valuable. He knew that he could sell this pearl again at a profit, so he immediately went and sold all his things, so that he could buy this most important, most valuable pearl. He knew that nothing he had ever had, was as important to him as this pearl.

Jesus told this story to tell us that his kingdom is just as important as the most valuable pearl. There is nothing more important than to know the Lord, to serve him as your king, and be his follower in this kingdom. That is why people will do anything and give everything, yes even their own lives and their hearts, to know Jesus and to follow him. Nothing is more important than this.

WWJD
Jesus would give everything up for the kingdom.

You were bought at a price ... (1 Cor. 7:23)

August 19

Seed becomes tree

"Though it is the smallest of your seeds, yet when it grows, it is the largest of garden plants and becomes a tree ..." (Mt. 13:32)

The seed of the mustard plant is so small that you can hardly see it. But this little seed can become a big tree.

One can hardly believe that some big trees grow from a small seed. A small mustard seed also grows into a tall tree, and many birds build their nests in the branches of that tree. This is the image the Lord used to say that his kingdom will be like that. Just think of this: Jesus began, as one Person on earth, to tell people about his kingdom, and today millions of people are part of this kingdom. From one person to millions! Yes, the seed of the kingdom falls into a person's heart and then it comes up just like a real seed, and very soon a tree is growing. This tree bears fruit and from it we get more seeds to plant, so that there can be more trees. This is how Christians build the kingdom. We carry the seed of the Word and it grows in our hearts; we give some to others so that the seed can also come up in their hearts. Before we know it, the kingdom is like a big garden with many trees. All of this started with only one seed.

Pray and ask the Lord that the seed of his kingdom will keep on coming up, so that many people will believe in him.

WWJD
Jesus would preach the Word.

Jesus went throughout Galilee ... teaching ... preaching the good news of the kingdom. (Mt. 4:23)

August 20

On the water

But when he [Peter] saw the wind, he was afraid and, beginning to sink, cried out, "Lord, save me!" (Mt. 14:30)

Jesus did the most wonderful things to show how mighty his Father was, so that people could believe in him and follow him.

One day the disciples were all in a boat a few kilometres from the shore. Jesus had stayed behind on the mountain to pray. Suddenly the wind started blowing and it whipped up great waves on the Sea of Galilee. The disciples were on this stormy sea all night. At daybreak Jesus came walking towards them on the sea. The disciples got a fright, because they thought it was a ghost. Jesus said to them, "Don't be afraid, it is I." Peter could not believe it was Jesus. He said, "Jesus, if this is really you, tell me to walk on the water to you." Jesus told him to do that.

Peter began walking on the water, but when he saw how big the waves were, he was afraid and started sinking. Only when he called out to Jesus to help him, could he get back into the boat again.

We must trust in the Lord completely. If He tells us something, we can be sure He won't make a mistake. The minute we start thinking about the position we are in or the waves, we sink. Keep your eyes on Jesus.

WWJD
Jesus would trust in God alone.

... let us throw off everything that hinders ...
Let us fix our eyes on Jesus ... (Heb. 12:1, 2)

August 21

The lone sheep

" ... will he not leave the ninety-nine ... and go to look for the one that wandered off?" (Mt. 18:12)

Jesus told the parable of a man who had one hundred sheep. Every day he left them to graze in the fields, so that they could eat enough and get fat.

One sheep was after the green grass and went after it. This sheep strayed from the others. All of a sudden he was alone and couldn't see the other sheep anywhere. What if a beast of prey should come along and eat him, or if it got dark and he was all alone?

Because the shepherd knows all his sheep, he soon noticed that one sheep was missing. He left the ninety-nine others together and went looking for the lost sheep. When he found him, he was so happy that he held him close. At that moment he was happier about that one sheep, than about the ninety-nine waiting for him where he had left them.

People are like sheep. The Lord is the Shepherd. He knows which sheep have strayed. He loves each and every one so much that He wants to go and find any lost sheep. They are people who are very far away from the Lord. He will take trouble to find them. And if He does, He is very pleased.

You and I must also be like this. We must go and find all the lost people for Jesus. They are very important to him.

WWJD
Jesus will lay down his life for his sheep.

 "The good shepherd lays down his life for the sheep." (Jn. 10:11)

August 22

Commandments

"Love the Lord your God with all your heart … Love your neighbor as yourself." (Mt. 22:37, 39)

If we should ask what the Lord really expects from you and me, we would be able to give two answers. The Bible says there are two things the Lord wants from us.

The first important thing is that we must love the Lord our God with all our heart and all our soul and all our mind. This means only that we must love the Lord with all our life. We must choose God. We must tell him that we love him. We must also tell him that we are thankful that He forgives our sins and makes us new. We must want to live for him. This is the first and greatest commandment.

The second thing the Lords wants from us, is that we must love, not only him, but also all people around us. We must love our neighbour. Our neighbour is every person near us. Not only family and friends, but all people we come into con-tact with every day. We must show them the love of the Lord. We must care for them. We must help them. We must show them the way to heaven.

Love for the Lord and love for people – this is what the Lord wants to see. Love God today and also everyone you meet.

WWJD
Jesus would love his Father and also people.

Whoever loves God must also love his brother. (1 Jn. 4:21)

August 23

Preparing the way

"A voice ... calling in the desert, 'Prepare the way for the Lord, make straight paths for him ... And all mankind will see God's salvation.'" (Lk. 3:4, 6)

Already in Isaiah it was prophesied that someone will do the work to prepare the way for the Lord. Was it a real road that they built that Jesus could walk on? No, this was the work of a man called John the Baptist.

Before Jesus started telling people about his kingdom, John the Baptist (who was a relative of his), was already preaching in the desert near the river Jordan. He told people to repent. He also told them that someone was coming who would bring salvation. In this way he prepared the way for Jesus. This is to say, he told people that Jesus would come with a plan for salvation.

John the Baptist realised he was just an instrument that had to explain God's salvation plan to people. He only prepared people for the great and wonderful work that Jesus would do himself.

You and I must also try to make it easier for Jesus to reach people with the gospel of salvation. You and I must, like John, "make straight paths for him", so that people can be prepared for him.

WWJD
Jesus would help you to witness.

"But you will receive power when the Holy Spirit comes on you; and you will be my witnesses." (Acts 1:8)

August 24

Useless lamps

"Give us some of your oil ... " (Mt. 25:8)

Jesus told the parable of ten girls who took their lamps to meet the bridegroom. In Jesus' time wedding celebrations lasted much longer than they do today. They celebrated for a week. Because it was getting dark they needed lamps. Five of the girls didn't take extra oil with them. The bridegroom was late and their lamps started going out. They asked the other girls for oil, but there was not enough for everyone and they had to go and buy oil. While they were gone, the bridegroom arrived, and everyone went with him. When the girls whose lamps had gone out came back, the bridegroom and his guests had already left. The other five sensible girls who had taken enough oil with them, were ready to go with the bridegroom.

This parable means that you and I must always be ready, so that when Jesus comes, we must be ready to go with him. We must not be like the foolish girls, but like the sensible ones. We must not be caught napping. We must not think the Second Coming is still far off. Jesus can come back tonight or tomorrow. We must be ready.

WWJD
Jesus would be prepared.

But the day of the Lord will
come like a thief. (2 Pet. 3:10)

August 25

Perfume for Jesus

(A) woman came to him with an alabaster jar of very expensive perfume, which she poured on his head ... (Mt. 26:7)

In the days when Jesus was on earth, people also liked sweet-smelling stuff. They used perfumed oil. This oil was made of all kinds of scented things and was very expensive. It was usually kept in an alabaster jar.

One day when Jesus was in Bethany, in the home of Simon, a woman came to him where He was sitting at the table, and poured a very expensive jar of oil on his head. It was a wonderful thing to do. These days we don't put perfume on our hair, but in those days it was an honour if someone put such expensive oil on your head. Jesus was very thankful and pleased with what the woman had done. One of Jesus' disciples was cross because so much money was wasted on Jesus' hair, but Jesus knew that this woman was glorifying him. That is why He was thankful.

You and I cannot honour Jesus with scented oil, but we honour him when we praise him, give our lives to him and follow him, and just tell him that we love him. This is just as precious to him as scented oil.

WWJD
Jesus would be thankful for love.

The poor you will always have with you,
but you will not always have Me. (Mt. 26:11)

August 26

Are you hospitable?

Practice hospitality. (Rom. 12:13)

It is always nice to visit hospitable people. Hospitable people have open hearts for visitors. Anyone who walks through that door, instantly feels welcome. There is an atmosphere of warmth and friendliness. It almost feels as if you are at home.

Hospitality is a very good characteristic. If you open up your heart and home to others, they enjoy being with you. The Lord likes us to be hospitable. He likes it when we show others that we love them. We show our love when we make others feel at home. We make them a nice cup of tea or coffee, we offer them food if they are hungry. If they want to sleep over, we like to give them a warm bed.

Think of ways you can be hospitable today. Although we must be careful to let just anybody into our homes, we can offer hospitality and love to those we know.

WWJD
Jesus would be hospitable.

Offer hospitality to one another without grumbling. (1 Pet. 4:9)

August 27

Your good favour

The king had granted him everything he asked, for the hand of the Lord his God was on him. (Ezra 7:6)

The people of Israel were exiled to Persia because they did not do the will of the Lord. Ezra was one of the Israelites who lived in Babylon, in Persia. God had a plan with Ezra.

The Lord decided that his people had lived in a foreign country long enough. It was time for them to go back to Israel. He wanted the temple to be rebuilt. Ezra was one of the important people He wanted to use for this purpose. The Lord kept his hand on Ezra in a special way, and he found favour with the king of Persia, Artaxerxes. When you find favour in somebody's eyes, it means that that person will go out of his way to help you. Not only did the king order that Ezra go back to Jerusalem, but he also gave him silver and gold to rebuild the temple. And just listen what the king said, *"And anything else needed for the temple of your God ... you may provide from the royal treasury"* (v. 20). Small wonder that we read in Ezra 7 how happy Ezra was, *"Praise be to the Lord ... who has put it into the king's heart to bring honor to the house of the Lord ... and who has extended his good favor to me ..."* (v. 27, 28).

If you serve the Lord, He will even use non-Christians to favour you, so that you can finish your work.

WWJD
Jesus will keep his hand over you.

The Lord ... blesses his people with peace. (Ps. 29:11)

August 28

Three things

... Ezra had devoted himself to the study ... of the Law of the Lord, and to teaching its decrees and laws in Israel. (Ezra 7:10)

Often people ask us what we are going to do during the holidays. Or what we want to do when we have finished school. We all have a dream or an ideal. What is your ideal? Ezra had a specific task. The Bible says he devoted himself to do certain things. "Devoted" means we do something with enthusiasm and faith. If you want to see or do something very badly, you will go to a lot of trouble to make it happen.

Ezra'a first dream was to know the law of the Lord. (The law of the Lord is the Word of God.) He decided that he would study the law of the Lord. You and I must also learn the Lord's Word with devotion.

The second thing he wanted to do was to learn the Word of God so that he could live it. It is one thing to learn it and another to do it. You and I should also live the Word of God.

It was not enough for Ezra that he knew and lived the Word; he wanted all his friends to know and do the same. You also have friends that need to know and live the Word of the Lord.

Follow Ezra's example.

WWJD
Jesus would learn the Word of God.

Let me understand the teaching
of your precepts (law) ... (Ps. 119:27)

August 29

The Lord always wins

They hired counselors to work against them and frustrate their plans ... (Ezra 4:5)

When Ezra came from Persia to rebuild the temple, the devil tried everything to put a stop to it. He knew if the temple was rebuilt, the Israelites would praise and serve the Lord. That is why he tried to prevent the building of the temple.

The people who were not satisfied with the building of the temple first told Ezra that they would help build. But Ezra knew that they were actually enemies, and he did not want to allow them to help with the work. They would not do good work. Then the enemies tried to frighten the builders and discourage them to go on with the building operations (cf. v. 4). They told the king he would lose money if they finished this project.

Fortunately the Lord saw to it that the devil's plan to stop building operations altogether, did not work. Unfortunately though, the work was stopped for fifteen years.

If you serve the Lord you will notice that people will try to discourage you. They will also try to frighten you. You will be blamed for all sorts of things and people will tell stories about you. Don't worry. The Lord always wins.

WWJD
Jesus would carry on, no matter what.

" ...he who stands firm to the end will be saved." (Mt. 10:22)

August 30

Be strong, be brave

"Be strong and courageous. Do not be afraid ... there is a greater power with us than with him." (2 Chr. 32:7)

Hezekiah was a king of Israel. He reigned in Jerusalem almost thirty years. He was a good king and really wanted to serve the Lord. One of the wonderful things he did was to clean up the house of the Lord. He had everything unclean taken out of the temple so that it could be holy again.

Then a king of another foreign country came on the scene. He invaded Israel and he wanted to put and end to Hezekiah's rule. Hezekiah had faith in God and so he spoke to his army, *"Be strong and courageous. Do not be afraid or discouraged because of the king of Assyria and the vast army with him, for there is a greater power with us than with him. With him is only the arm of flesh, but with us is the Lord our God to help us and to fight our battles"* (v. 7, 8). These are beautiful words. They tell us that Hezekiah had faith in the Lord. No wonder the Lord worked a miracle. He sent an angel and every soldier and leader and official in the enemy camp was killed. This is how the Lord saved Hezekiah and the people of Jerusalem from a bad king.

If you have God on your side, you are always a winner. Put your trust in him today.

WWJD
Jesus would put his trust in God.

Do not be terrified ... for ... God will be with you wherever you go. (Josh. 1:9)

August 31

The test

God left him to test him and to know everything that was in his heart. (2 Chr. 32:31)

All of us have to do tests so that we can see if we know things. King Hezekiah of Judah was also tested.

Hezekiah was a rich and respected man. He had treasuries built for his valuables. He also built cities and had many possessions. He was prosperous in everything he did. It was because God blessed him. However, Hezekiah became seriously ill and he prayed to God. The Lord made a miracle happen. Hezekiah got well again. But the Bible says Hezekiah was not thankful that the Lord had mercy on him. He started feeling self-satisfied. He started boasting. Luckily he repented and said he was sorry. One day the Lord decided to test Hezekiah. The Bible says God left Hezekiah or withdrew from him. When God withdraws from you and me, things get very bad for us. God did this so that Hezekiah could know his own heart.

Not his real heart, but his attitude and his feelings towards the Lord. This is what the Lord tests. And Hezekiah's heart was not altogether what it should be. God tested him so that he could know his own heart.

Test your heart today. Is your attitude towards the Lord what it should be? Is there also pride in your heart? Or sin? Confess it!

WWJD
Jesus would have the right attitude.

 "Blessed are the pure in heart ... " (Mt. 5:8)

September 1

Officials and judges

... officials and judges over Israel. (1 Chr. 26:29)

If there is no law and order and justice in a country, there is confusion. We need order and justice. Order means everything is arranged and run properly.

In every country there are people who maintain or keep order. It is usually done by the police and traffic officers. All people who have to maintain order are important. We must never look down on them. It is God's will that there must be order in a country, or in a town, or in a school. That is why we have to obey the police and traffic officers, and pray for them. It is not easy to maintain order in our country. Even in the time of the Bible Kenaniah and his sons were instructed to maintain order in Israel.

When two people have a disagreement, a judge must decide who is in the wrong and who is right. This is decided in a court of law. This is where people are tried. We must pray often for people who must pass judgement. We must pray that they will be fair and decide according to God's will.

Thank the Lord now for those who help with law and order and justice in our country.

WWJD
Jesus would obey authority.

... thanksgiving (must) be made for everyone ...
for kings and those in authority ... (1 Tim. 2:1, 2)

September 2

We want to be like them

"Then we will be like all the other nations ... " (1 Sam. 8:20)

We often see things others have, and then wish we could have the same. Perhaps your friends have certain toys that you wish you could also have. You feel out of place, because you don't have what they do.

The Israelites were not happy. Yes, the Lord was their king and he did bring them out of Egypt. He also gave them the ten commandments and showed them how to live. Furthermore, He sent them priests and prophets to speak to them and show them the right way. But they were not happy. They wanted more. What did they want?

They saw that all the heathen nations around them, and all the other nations on earth had a king. They felt out of things. It was quite unnecessary, because they had the best king, the Lord himself. He ruled over them and He wanted to keep it that way, but no, they did not want to. They wanted a king like other nations.

Samuel warned them that it would not be the best thing for them. Later on the kings of Israel made things very difficult for the people. Because of the disobedience of the kings, the people of Israel often suffered.

Don't want something just because someone else has it. Ask the Lord what his will is, and trust that He knows best.

WWJD
Jesus would do the will of the Father.

 "Father, if you are willing ... not my will, but yours be done." (Lk. 22:42)

September 3

The ark

"Have them make a chest of acacia wood ... " (Ex. 25:10)

The Lord instructed the Israelites to make an interesting thing. It is called the ark of the Covenant. It was one and a quarter metre long, three quarters of a metre wide and the same height. It was covered with pure gold and made of acacia wood.

This almost square wooden chest had an important function. It was carried all over when the Israelites were busy moving. It was as if the Lord wanted to tell them He was with them, as the ark was with them. It was as if He wanted to tell them He was in the ark, and that they could talk to him there. He would also meet them there. The ark was usually placed in a tent, the tabernacle, and there the spiritual leaders, and also the people, worshipped the Lord. When the people moved on, the tent was taken down and they picked up the ark and carried it along with them. In this way they knew God went with them.

You and I don't need an ark anymore to carry around with us. Neither do we need to pitch a tent or go to a building to meet God. We serve him right inside of us if we open the doors of our lives for him. He goes wherever we go. Serve the Lord today with your life.

WWJD
Jesus will always be with us.

"So you will be my people, and I will be your God." (Jer. 30:22)

September 4

Is He going with you?

(B)ut if the cloud did not lift, they did not set out – until the day it lifted. (Ex. 40:37)

When the Israelites moved out of Egypt, the Lord was with them on the road, during the whole journey. No one should be on the road without him. We need the Lord to bless us and to be with us. This the Israelites knew very well.

Whenever they reached a place where they would stop over, they pitched camp. They also put up the tabernacle (the Tent of Meeting), and put the ark inside. Something wonderful happened: a cloud covered the tabernacle, and the mighty presence of the Lord filled the tent. The cloud stayed there until the Lord wanted them to go on. When the cloud lifted from the tabernacle, the people knew they had to move on. If the cloud did not lift, they stayed on until it did. If they were to move without the cloud, the Lord would not be with them. Then they would be in trouble.

Learn today, that you shouldn't just do things without first making sure the Lord will go with you.

WWJD
Jesus would walk with God.

"If your Presence does not go with us,
do not send us up from here." (Ex. 33:15)

September 5

Offerings

"When any of you brings an offering to the Lord ... " (Lev. 1:2)

In the time of the Bible, and especially the Old Testament, many offerings were brought to the Lord. We read of many different kinds of offerings: burnt offerings, grain offerings, animal offerings, fragrant offerings, guilt offerings, and a few others. An offering was brought because people felt they had to give God something. Because we are human we are all sinful, and we also need to answer to God for our sins. The offerings of the Old Testament did this. Offerings were also brought to God because it was a way of thanking him.

The Old Testament offering is not in use any more. Does this mean that we no longer want to give the Lord something? Does it mean that we no longer have sins that need to be taken away?

Jesus brought an offering in our place. His offering pays for our sins. We must just accept it. The thanks-offering that you and I can bring now, is the offering of our hearts and our lives.

WWJD
Jesus would give thanks to the Father.

Enter his gates with thanksgiving
and ... give thanks to him ... (Ps. 100:4)

September 6

"Christians"

The disciples were called Christians first at Antioch. (Heb. 11:26)

Many people in our country call themselves Christians. People talk about Christian nations and even say we live in a "Christian country". Where does the word "Christian" come from?

The name "Christian" comes from "Christ". Christ means "the anointed one", and that is one of Jesus' names. Remember He was anointed by the Holy Spirit so that He could do his work. Christians are people who follow Christ, and because we are his followers we also take his name. It was in Antioch that people were called Christians for the first time, because they told and showed everybody that they belonged to Christ.

Actually it is wrong to call someone a Christian if that person does not know and follow Christ. Many people are only Christians in name. If we want to call ourselves Christians, we must follow Christ.

If Christ means " the anointed one" then Christians are also "anointed ones". That is why the Holy Spirit anointed us. Like the fragrant anointing oil of the olden days, you and I must also spread the aroma and fragrance of the gospel to everybody around us. Live like a true Christian today.

WWJD
In Jesus you will be a Christian.

... through us spreads everywhere the fragrance of the knowledge of him. (2 Cor. 2:10)

September 7

God's thoughts

"For my thoughts are not your thoughts ... " (Is. 55:8)

We think with our brain, and what a wonderful instrument it is. It gives us all kinds of thoughts. Each one of us has many thoughts. Our thoughts make that we behave in a certain way. God also has thoughts. He thinks in the same way that you and I do, but his thoughts are not like our human thoughts.

You and I often think wrong thoughts. Sometimes we think we are right, but then we have made a mistake. Because we don't know everything, we often think just as far as we know. Because we don't have more facts, our thoughts are limited. The Lord is not limited. He knows everything and He sees everything and what He thinks is perfect.

Often we ask the Lord certain things, and we expect him to give them to us. If He doesn't, we wonder why. It is then that we must trust him. His thoughts are not like our thoughts. He looks differently at what we want. He sees the whole picture. He knows if it will be good for us to have. He knows if it will be good for our lives to have it. And if He decides we are not to have it, it is because He knows best. He says, *"As the heavens are higher than the earth, so are my ways higher than your ways and my thoughts than your thoughts"* (v. 9).

WWJD
Jesus would trust the Father in everything.

Commit to the Lord whatever you do,
and your plans will succeed. (Prov. 16:3)

September 8

Chickens or eagles?

They will soar on wings like eagles ... (Js. 40:31)

Chickens are quite different to eagles. Chickens stay on the ground. They make their nests on the ground. Chickens cannot really fly. A chicken will try to fly only when it gets a fright. That doesn't really mean a thing though, because it doesn't fly high at all. Before it is properly airborne, it's on its way down again.

An eagle is a majestic bird and by this I mean it is kingly. An eagle is not like a chicken! An eagle does not build its nest on the ground, but high up in the mountains. He can also fly magnificently, and ride the wind for hours on end. An eagle is very strong and fast. Oh yes, there is a big difference between a chicken and an eagle.

I can't think the Lord wants us to be like chickens. He wants us to be like eagles. He wants us to be as strong and as majestic as an eagle. That is why He says in his Word that if we put our trust in him, or wait upon him, we will be given new strength, and we will take off like eagles. He wants us to reach heights because He gives us the strength to do so. He does not want us to move awkwardly, like chickens. God's strength helps you and me to be winners.

Listen to the voice of the Lord today, allow his Spirit to fill you and soar with the eagle wings of faith.

WWJD
Jesus would live like a winner.

He is the God who ... puts the nations under me. (2 Sam. 22:48)

September 9

Never understanding

... [these people are] ever hearing, but never under-standing ... (Is. 6:10)

We are not all clever. Some of us take longer to understand things than others. We could say some are quick on the up-take, while others are slow. There are people who will go as far as saying that someone who is slow to understand is stupid. I don't think that's a nice thing to say. One should never make fun of people who do not understand as quickly as you do.

The Lord looked at his people, Israel, and He thought they were a bit on the slow side. He says they heard, but did not understand. This was because he told and taught them certain things, and although they heard what He said and seemed to understand, they didn't do what He said. This is being stupid: when you hear things and even understand, but still you don't want to do whatever it is you are told to do. Especially if it will be good for you. It is almost like someone who doesn't eat and goes hungry, while there is plenty to eat. Israel was like this. They were "never understanding". They did not want to do the right things.

You and I must ask the Lord to help us so that we must not be "never understanding" when it comes to his things. Ask him to make you diligent and willing and also clever, so that you can know his will, and also do it.

WWJD
Jesus would ask his Father for wisdom.

If any of you lacks wisdom, he should
ask God, who gives generously ... (Jas. 1:5)

September 10

Fearless

The wolf will live with the lamb ... The infant will play near the hole of the cobra ... (Is. 11:6, 8)

I'm sure you've seen on television how careful buck are when they drink water, or walk in the veld. They are afraid of lions and leopards that can catch and eat them. Then again, leopards hunt buck to stay alive.

Snakes are poisonous reptiles. Not all snakes are poisonous, but if a poisonous adder should bite you, you have to get to a doctor very quickly, or you will die. That is why we avoid snakes or we kill them if we should find them in our homes. If a baby should put his hand out as if to touch a snake, you will hold your breath and try to get the child away from the snake. People are afraid of snakes.

Isaiah prophesies that a time will come when peope wil not fear snakes any more. Babies will be allowed to play near the hole of a cobra. Buck will no longer be afraid of leopards, they will live together. Of course he is talking about heaven. Oh, you and I can look forward to living together with everything we were afraid of, because there will not be any fear in heaven.

Thank the Lord that He makes it possible for us to look forward to a place where there will be no more evil or fear.

WWJD
Jesus will take all fear away one day.

... perfect love drives out fear ... (1 Jn. 4:18)

September 11

To love

Love the Lord your God and keep his requirements ...
(Deut. 11:1)

When we love someone, we want to do what makes that person happy. True love is taking someone else into consideration and we don't do just what we want to do. If you love your mommy and you know she expects you to behave in a certain manner, you show your love for her by being obedient and doing what she would like you to. The Bible says if we love the Lord, we will also do what He asks us to. John writes, *This is love for God: to obey his commands* (1 Jn. 5:3).

How can one love God? We can't see him. We can't touch him. He doesn't talk to us in a way that we can hear him. Is it really possible to love God? Yes, of course! The best reason for loving God, is because He sent us his Son Jesus, and Jesus was prepared to give his whole life for us. He was tortured and hurt, but He died on the cross for you and me. God loves us so much, that He gave us his Son. Because He loved us first, we love him back.

Show your love by doing today what He wants you to.

WWJD
Jesus would obey the Lord's commands.

This is love for God: to obey his commands. (1 Jn. 5:3)

September 12

She gave everything

" ... this poor widow has put more into the treasury than all the others ... " (Mk. 12:43)

One day Jesus sat at the temple opposite the place where the offerings were brought. He saw people putting their money into the temple treasury. Rich people came past and put a lot of money into the box. Then Jesus saw a poor widow. She opened her purse and put two small coins in the box. They were not worth much. But Jesus knew that she was very poor. Calling his disciples to him, Jesus said, *"I tell you the truth, this poor widow has put more into the treasury than all the others"* (v. 43).

Jesus said this because He knew the rich people had so much money that they would hardly miss what they put into the box. The poor widow, on the other hand, was so poor that she couldn't even really afford to put those two coins in the box; she needed the money for food. But because she loved God, she gave just about everything she had.

God likes us to give because we love him. Not because we have a lot, but because we want to give, even if it is all we have. Give God your everything today. Remember also, whenever you get a little money; give, every now and then, a little something for the Lord's work.

WWJD
Jesus would give us his everything.

... offer your bodies as living sacrifices, holy and pleasing to God ... (Rom. 12:1)

September 13

Judas' weakness

With the reward he got for his wickedness, Judas bought a field ... (Acts 1:18)

Jesus chose Judas to follow him, and he taught Judas about the things of the kingdom. Judas loved Jesus. He had the very important job to look after the money matters of the disciples. But Judas had a weakness.

Every one of us has a weak spot. Some people get angry very quickly and this makes trouble for them. Others always want things and because they long for them so badly, they will even do something wrong to get hold of what they want. Some people are too proud. They think they are better than others. Judas liked money, and he was greedy. He always wanted more and more. He was never satisfied with the money he had.

The devil knew about Judas' weakness, and that is why he saw to it that the Pharisees bribed Judas with money, to hand Jesus over to them. He pointed Jesus out to the Pharisees so that they could capture him. Later on Judas felt very bad about this. He bought himself ground, but there he hanged himself.

Ask the Lord what your weakness is. Ask him to make you strong, so that your weakness will not tempt you to do the wrong thing.

WWJD
Jesus would resist temptation.

... "Away from me, Satan ..." (Mt. 4:10)

September 14

Stop doubting

"Stop doubting and believe." (Jn. 20:27)

Thomas was one of the disciples Jesus chose to follow him. After the death of Jesus and the resurrection, He appeared to his disciples. On the day Jesus rose from the dead, He went to his disciples and said to them, *"Peace be with you!"*(v. 19). The disciples were very happy to see Jesus. Thomas was not with the disciples at the time. The first thing the disciples told him when they saw him again, was that they had seen Jesus. He did not believe them.

Thomas could not believe that Jesus had risen from the dead. He said if he didn't see the nail marks in Jesus' hands, he would never believe it. Eight days later Jesus appeared to his disciples again and this time Thomas was with them. Jesus said to Thomas, *"Put your finger here; see my hands ... Stop doubting and believe ... "*(v. 27). Just there Thomas went down on his knees and worshipped Jesus.

You and I must not doubt, like Thomas. Jesus said He would rise from the grave, but Thomas did not believe it. We can believe everything that Jesus says in his Word.

WWJD
Jesus would motivate us to believe with all our hearts.

"God is not a man, that he should lie ... " (Num. 23:19)

September 15

All that important?

"How hard it is for the rich to enter the kingdom of God!" (Lk. 18:24)

One day there was a rich young man. He had a lot of money and many possessions. His money and possessions were more important to him than anything else. Yet, deep inside his heart he had a need, because he came to Jesus and asked him how he could get everlasting life. Jesus knew that this young man had a problem: he was not prepared to let go of his obsession with money. When you are obsessed with something, it is all you think about and it becomes your master. Money was this young man's master. That is why Jesus said a strange thing. Jesus told him to sell all his belongings and follow him. This was a bitter pill for the young man to swallow, because he was not prepared to do that. Money was too important to him.

You and I also need money. We need certain things to stay alive. Money is important, and possessions are also important. But, they may never be the most important things in our lives. Money is not as important as knowing the Lord, following him, and being rich, inside. We are rich if we do the Lord's will and experience what He gives so plentifully. Make sure that money doesn't become the most important thing in your life.

WWJD
Jesus would store up riches in heaven.

"For where your treasure is, there your heart will be also." (Mt. 6:21)

September 16

I'm stressing

"Who of you by worrying can add a single hour to his life?" (Mt. 6:27)

Some people are worried about things all their lives. They stress about anything and everything. They complain and see problems, and more problems. They are afraid of all sorts of things. They lie awake nights about the things they fear. They are worried people.

We all have our worries at times. Yes, we do worry about things that can go wrong. Yet the Bible tells us that we should not get into the bad habit of worrying about everything. To tell the truth, Jesus did not allow his disciples to worry about their lives. He said, " ... *do not worry about your life ... "* (v. 25). He also gave them a question, asking if it was possible that a person's worries could make him live even one hour longer. As a matter of fact, all the clever people tell us that worries make your life shorter. This is true, because worrying is bad for us. It makes us stress and that makes us unhappy. Yes, and it also makes our bodies ill.

Rather learn to put your trust in the Lord and thank him for everything. Don't stress!

WWJD
Jesus would talk to the Father about his worries.

Do not be anxious about anything ... (Phil. 4:6)

September 17

They forgot

But they did not understand what He was saying to them.
(Lk. 2:50)

Before Jesus was born, the angel told Mary and Joseph that they would be his father and mother on earth. They also knew that He was the Son of God, and that it made him different to other children. He is the great Redeemer who would pay for the sins of the world, even if He had a human form.

One day Mary and Joseph journeyed to Jerusalem for the Feast of the Passover. Jesus was twelve years old at the time. Mary and Joseph started the journey back to Nazareth in a group with many grown-ups and children. After a day on the road, they noticed that Jesus was not with them. They turned back to Jerusalem to go and look for him. Three days later they found him at the temple where He was listening to the learned people and asking them questions. His parents asked him why he had made them worry about him like that. Jesus answered, *"Didn't you know I had to be in my Father's house?"* (v. 49). Mary and Joseph did not quite understand what He meant by this. For a moment they forgot that He was the Son of God, and that his life was not like that of other children.

Don't forget that the Lord does not think like us. He is not a human being like you and me. Even if there are things you don't understand, just trust him. He knows best.

WWJD
Jesus would do the will of his Father.

"For my thoughts are not your thoughts, neither are your ways my ways ... " (Is. 55:8)

September 18

Ashamed?

I am not ashamed of the gospel ... it is the power of God for the salvation of everyone who believes ... (Rom. 1:16)

"**A**shamed" can mean one doesn't want to be seen or heard. When Saul was anointed as king, he hid because he didn't want people to see him. That is more like being embarrassed, which is a little different, but nearly the same as being ashamed. You and I are also sometimes embarrassed, say if we have spilt something on our clothes in front of strangers.

One can also be ashamed to identify with Jesus. "Identify" means we openly agree with what Jesus is, and what He teaches; we want to be like him. Christians identify with Christ. They have accepted him as their Savior and Lord. When you are still a young Christian, then you are sometimes embarrassed to show others and to tell them that you belong to Jesus. Perhaps it is because you don't know how they will react.

As one gets stronger and you grow in Jesus, it becomes easier to admit openly that you are his follower. You know, as Paul did, that it is nothing to be ashamed of. We should rather be very happy and talk about it, because then it can also help others confess their sins. Jesus' message is a happy message. It is a gospel. Share it with others without being ashamed, so that they can find out for themselves how wonderful it is to know him.

WWJD
Jesus would preach the gospel unashamedly.

Jesus went throughout Galilee, teaching (and) ... preaching the good news of the kingdom ... (Mt. 4:23)

September 19

They laughed

But they laughed at him. (Mk. 5:40)

One of the ugliest things we can do is to tease others or to make fun of them. When you make fun of others, you make them feel small; you humiliate them. It's OK to laugh because we are happy – no one can feel bad about that.

One day Jesus was busy healing people, and a ruler of the synagogue saw everything Jesus did. While he was watching Jesus' miracle healings, someone came from his house and told him that his little girl had died. Jesus heard this sad message and He told the synagogue ruler, *"Don't be afraid; just believe ... "* (v. 36).

Jesus went to the house of the ruler and saw the people there weeping bitterly. Jesus told them the little girl had not died, she was just sleeping. They laughed at him, mocked him and scorned him. They had seen for themselves the child was dead. Then Jesus took the child, Talitha, by the hand. When He told her to get up, she did just that. Everybody was speechless with surprise.

Today there are still many people who scorn the message of Jesus. They laugh and say the Bible is just stories. But we know the truth. Pray that people will not laugh at the Lord, but will praise him.

WWJD
Jesus would keep on believing, no matter what.

"Do not let your hearts be troubled. Trust in God; trust also in me." (Jn. 14:1)

September 20

Go for it

"Well done ... You have been faithful with a few things; I will put you in charge of many things." (Mt. 25:21)

Jesus told the story of a man who wanted to go on a journey. He asked the people who worked for him to look after his property while he was away. He gave one worker five gold coins, another one two, and the third received one coin. The master told them to use what he had entrusted to them, in the best way.

The worker who received five coins, put his money to work and made a profit of five coins. The worker who received two coins, doubled the money to four. But the worker who got one, was worried that he would lose it and so he buried the coin.

When the master came back from his journey, he praised the first two workers, but he was fed up with the last worker who had not put his money to good use. With this story, Jesus wants to give us a message: We must work with what He gives us, in such a way that we build his kingdom. We must develop the talents He has given us, as well as all our spiritual gifts, and use them well. Go for it! As we use what He has given us to his glory, He will give us even more, so that his name is glorified.

Thank the Lord for everything He has given you. Decide to be diligent. Don't bury your talents.

WWJD
Jesus would use his talents.

Now to each one the manifestation of the Spirit is given for the common good. (I Cor. 12:7)

September 21

No favourites

" ... you pay no attention to who they are." (Mt. 22:16)

Sometimes we treat people as if some are more important than others. Yes, I know that there are people who are important because of their rank or position. Think of the state president. He is an important person because he has an important position. This, however, does not mean that as a person, he is worth more to God than you or me. God has no favourites. All people are equal before God. The state president will not be treated better than you and me one day before the throne of God. To God we are all equal.

The Pharisees saw that Jesus did not favour certain people, and ignore others. *"(W)e know you are a man of integrity and that you teach ... in accordance with the truth. You aren't swayed by men, because you pay no attention to who they are ... "*(v. 16). Jesus did not curry favour with people. Something else He didn't like, was when people tried to win his favour, just for show. He was always honest.

Remember that you are just as important to the Lord as any other person. If Jesus likes you it is not because you are pretty or good. He loves you and cares for you. You don't need to impress him. Just be yourself. Decide to serve him with all your heart. He will always be honest with you.

WWJD
Jesus would be honest.

" ... we know you are a man of integrity ... " (Mk. 12:14)

September 22

King on a donkey

"See, your king comes to you, gentle and riding on a donkey, on a colt, the foal of a donkey." (Mt. 21:5)

Donkeys are very humble animals. In the olden days donkeys were used more often than today. Nowadays we only see a donkey-cart on out-of-the-way farm roads.

It the time of Jesus, a donkey was a very common pack-animal. People put their goods on a donkey's back, and usually walked alongside the donkey, or maybe rode on another donkey. In this way they transported their goods and travelled from one place to another.

Jesus decided to ride into Jerusalem on a donkey. Many years ago a man called Zechariah prophesied that Jesus would enter Jerusalem in this way (cf. Zech. 9:9). Zechariah said that Jesus was the king, but not a proud king who would look down on people. No, He is a king who shows us how humble He is, because He rode into Jerusalem on the back of a donkey. The king of our lives, Jesus Christ, is not haughty or boastful. He is humble. Doesn't the fact that He came down from heaven to live on earth, prove that He is humble? He, the Son of God, was prepared to become human, a human like you and me.

As the children of a humble king like Jesus, we must also behave humbly. We must not think too much of ourselves.

WWJD
Jesus would be humble.

" ... for I am gentle and humble in heart ... " (Mt. 11:29)

September 23

Heritage Day

... surely I have a delightful inheritance. (Ps. 16:6)

Every day new babies are born. Their lives start new. As they grow older, they will start noticing the world around them, and they will start living life. Everything will be new and fresh to them. And yet the earth has existed millions of years. As Ecclesiastes says, there is actually nothing new under the sun.

There are many things around us that you and I can enjoy. Just think of the beauty of nature. Every day we can still discover something new – that is, new to us – we are given these things. The Lord made everything for us to enjoy.

Today is Heritage Day. We think about things that have been, that we have inherited, that have been passed down to us. There are people in this country whose families have lived here for ages. Your grandfather and grandmother and their grandfathers and grandmothers before them, most probably lived here, and they also passed certain things down to us. Like our language, our religion, and all kinds of everyday things.

Our national sport is rugby, and these days soccer is also popular. Other countries have other favourite sports that are more important to them than to us. All this is inheritance.

You and I can thank the Lord today for all the good things we have received. Everything comes from the hand of the Lord, but there are also people who worked hard to keep what the Lord gave them in a good condition for you and me.

WWJD
Jesus would be thankful in everything.

And be thankful. (Col. 3:15)

September 24

Tomorrow

Do not boast about tomorrow ... (Prov. 27:1)

You can live tomorrow and the day after in your thoughts, so much so, that you let today pass you by. It is good to have plans for the future, but we must not be so excited about tomorrow, that we don't live today.

The Bible says one must not boast about what you expect tomorrow. Whoever boasts about tomorrow, pretends that he or she has already received what must still come tomorrow. That is dangerous. How can we know what is waiting for us tomorrow? We don't even know what is going to happen to us in the next hour. That is why Christians say, "God willing ... " meaning, it all depends on the Lord if we will have a tomorrow. Perhaps you have heard of "DV". This is short for the Latin "Deo Volente", which means "if God is willing".

Are you looking forward to something? Then say to yourself, if God is willing, then it will happen.

WWJD
Jesus would not worry about tomorrow.

"Why, you do not even know what will happen tomorrow." (Jas. 4:14)

September 25

Good for evil

If your enemy is hungry, give him food to eat ... (Prov. 25:21)

The Lord's way of doing things is so much different to our way. If someone doesn't like us it is very easy not to like that person. If someone is cross with us, it is just as easy to be cross with that person. The Lord's way is different. He says we must love our enemies, we must not hate them. If someone who hates us is hungry, we must give him something to eat, and if he is thirsty, we must give him something to drink.

Only God can help us to love people like this. It is also a very good way to show that we love Jesus and belong to him. We must not return evil for evil. Ask the Lord to help you show love to that person. Perhaps the love you show him or her will make that person stop hating you, and it will please the Lord if the heart of such a person is changed.

Is there someone who goes out of his way to hurt you and hate you? Be nice to that person. Give him or her something. Give it with love. In this way you are the Lord's instrument of love.

WWJD
Jesus would be nice to his enemies.

"Love your enemies ... " (Mt. 5:44)

September 26

At peace

A heart at peace gives life to the body ... (Prov. 14:30)

Your heart is the place deep down where you feel. Sometimes we feel good, sometimes not so good. Sometimes we feel excited, sometimes we are calm and relaxed. When we are scared our hearts are filled with fear. If we are glad, our hearts are full of joy. If we are anxious, our hearts are stormy, almost like the waves of the sea that can't stop breaking.

Doctors and the Bible tell us that it is not good for us if we are anxious all the time. Restlessness, worry or fear are all things that upset us, and that is not good for our bodies. It is much better to be calm and restful.

The Lord helps you to have peace in your heart. Give him all your worries, pray to him and trust him. He will fill you with his peace. This will also help make your body healthier.

WWJD
Jesus will give you peace.

"Peace I leave with you; my peace I give you." (Jn. 14:27)

September 27

Stand up for them

... Moses ... stood in the breach before him ... (Ps. 106:23)

We read in Psalm 106 how the people of Israel forgot God, their Savior. He did great things in Egypt and brought them out of this country. Still they did not go on believing in him, but kept on doing bad things. The Lord was very angry with them and decided to destroy them. He wanted them all to die. The Lord will not decide lightly to do such a thing, unless a person has sinned very, very badly. (If you are a child of the Lord, you don't have to worry that He will destroy you, because Jesus paid the price of your guilt and took your sins upon him.)

Fortunately Moses was prepared to speak to God on behalf of these people. The Bible says he "stood in the breach" for Israel. This means that he asked God very nicely to forgive them, and the Lord decided to spare their lives. Just because one man prayed, the lives of thousands and thousands of people were spared.

Moses stood in the breach for others. You and I can also do it. There are many people who live under the judgement of God because they renounced Jesus, but you and I can pray for them and plead for them, and ask the Lord to change their hearts and spare their lives. If you see someone who is careless about living for the Lord, you must plead with the Lord for him or her.

WWJD
Jesus would stand in the breach before the Father for us.

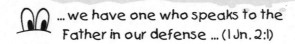 ... we have one who speaks to the
Father in our defense ... (1 Jn. 2:1)

September 28

Satisfied

But if we have food and clothing, we will be content with that. (1 Tim. 6:8)

It is so easy to complain about the things we don't have. So many things are advertised and everything looks so attractive that we think we cannot go without it. One can want something so badly, that you become dissatisfied with what you have.

To be satisfied with what you have is a wonderful characteristic. Some people have so much, and yet they are never satisfied. Others have very little, yet they are happy and satisfied. The Bible says if we have food and clothes, we have nothing to complain about. Then we must be satisfied. Food keeps us alive, and clothes keep us warm and protected. It is as if the Bible is saying if we have the basic things in life, we must be happy. Of course there are other things just as important as food and clothes. Like having peace in your heart, and being happy in your relationship with your friends and with your parents. We are satisfied because we are thankful for what we have received. The Lord promised that He would give us food and clothing if we put our trust in him. Children of the Lord should never be dissatisfied.

Don't you want to thank the Lord for everything you have? If there is something you want very badly, tell the Lord, but don't be dissatisfied with your life.

WWJD
Jesus would be satisfied with what He has.

... let us be thankful ... (Heb. 12:28)

September 29

The nurse

"Let us look for a young [girl] ... to attend the king and take care of him." (1 Kgs. 1:2)

When king David was old, he suffered a lot. Like many old people even today, he was sickly and needed care. His servants suggested that they must look for a nurse who could be with him every minute of the day and night, to serve him and take care of him. From all the girls, they chose Abishag. The Bible says she was very young and also very pretty. One can just think how much she meant to David. She saw to all his needs and looked after him well.

Today nurses still care for sick people. It is a wonderful job because nurses care for those in need. They work in hospitals and also in private homes. They make sure that the sick are well taken care of. They also help the doctors who treat their patients.

Thank the Lord for nurses. Many of them are also Christians, and they care not only for the bodies of the sick, but also talk to them, encourage them, and tell them about Jesus. Pray for nurses today.

WWJD
Jesus would pray for nurses.

"Come, you who are blessed by my Father ... you looked after me ..." (Mt. 25:34, 36)

September 30

Road signs

"Set up road signs; put up guideposts." (Jer. 31:21)

We find road signs on all major roads. Signboards are placed along the roads to give information as to where we should go. There are road signs that tell us speeding is dangerous, or to warn us of a sharp curve ahead. Other road signs give us information of a rest-stop along the road, or a petrol station where we can fill up. Then there are signposts that indicate direction. They point out in which direction a specific town lies. The Lord told his people to erect road signs and guideposts. This is the Lord's way of telling them that they must keep to the road which has been indicated and make sure they reach the right destination. You and I also need road signs and signposts which show us the way. What road signs are these?

Examples of road signs or guideposts for you and me are ministers, pastors, teachers, good advice from friends, advice and couselling from our parents, and of course, the Word of God and the Holy Spirit. Take note of all these road signs and obey them. Erect your signboards today, keep your eyes on the main Road and don't wander off in your own direction.

WWJD
Jesus would show you the way to the Father.

"I am the way and the truth and the life." (Jn. 14:6)

October 1

Who does He think He is?

... And they took offence at him. (Mk. 6:3)

Jesus did many wonderful things. In his own home town, Nazareth, he started teaching in the synagogue. Many people came to listen to him, and they were amazed and touched by his message. Yet, they asked one another, *"Isn't this the carpenter? Isn't this Mary's son and the brother of James? Aren't his sisters here with us?"* (v. 3). And they didn't want to have anything more to do with him.

It was because they had known Jesus since childhood that they didn't take him seriously. They thought of him as an ordinary person because He grew up before their eyes. That is why Jesus said a prophet is respected everywhere, except where he grew up. Jesus even said his own family would not accept him as others did. Jesus did not perform even one miracle in his home town, because his own people were so unbelieving.

Often we find it more difficult to live for Jesus and to be a witness for him in our own surroundings. People don't readily accept that you can give them a message from the Lord, because they know you so well. Perhaps you are finding it difficult to follow Jesus in your own home, but just keep at it, even if your own family are negative and discourage you. The same thing happened to Jesus. You just go on praying for your family and friends.

WWJD
Jesus would preach the gospel everywhere.

... He was teaching the people in the temple ... (Lk. 20:1)

October 2

Cheered up

For they refreshed my spirit ... (1 Cor. 16:18)

Paul did wonderful work for the Lord. He worked very hard. Paul was a tent-maker, but in between he preached and helped people find the Lord, and grow in faith and in knowledge of the Lord. Sometimes he worked so hard that he became very, very tired, body and soul.

Paul writes in a letter to his friends in Corinth, how pleased he was when three men visited him. They had very interesting names: Stephanas, Fortunatus and Achaicus. Then Paul tells them why he was so glad to see these men. They refreshed his spirit, in other words, they cheered him up. I'm sure they talked and laughed a lot, and praised the Lord and prayed together. After this visit Paul was filled with new courage and strength for all the work he had to do for the Lord.

You and I also need friends who can be with us when we need encouragement and cheering up. Good friends are like a nice glass of water when you are thirsty. They refresh you and make you feel much better. Thank the Lord for your friends who are there for you and cheer you up when you need it. Be a friend like this to others.

WWJD
Jesus would cheer others up.

(The Lord) has sent me to bind up the brokenhearted ... (Is. 61:1)

October 3

The thorn

... there was given me a thorn in my flesh ... (2 Cor. 12:7)

Have you ever had a thorn in your foot? It makes your foot very sensitive, and after a while you can't really walk on it any more. One of the reasons why we wear shoes is so that we don't get thorns in our feet.

Paul also talks about a thorn in his foot. This was not a real thorn, and it was also not really in his foot. He had some or other hurt in his life. We don't really know what it was. Some say it was a weakness he had. Others think it was some kind of illness, or that his eyes were very weak. So we don't really know what was wrong. Three times he asked the Lord very earnestly to take this away. The Lord's answer was short and sweet: *"My grace is sufficient for you ... "* (v. 9). Later on Paul writes that he knows he has this problem to keep him humble. It made him realise that he needed God.

Is there something that makes your life difficult? Perhaps you also want the Lord to take it away. Perhaps this weakness is there for the same reason as Paul's. One thing we know: the Lord's grace is enough for us. Yes, He carries us through and supports us.

WWJD
Jesus will be with us even in our hurt.

There you saw how the Lord your God carried you, as a father carries his son. (Deut. 1:31)

October 4

Where is Demas?

… Demas, because he loved this world, has deserted me …
(2 Tim. 4:10)

Demas was a Christian and at first he served the Lord with all his heart. We don't know much about his life, but what the Bible tells us of Demas is not very positive. It is rather a shame if the Bible mentions your name, but everything it says about you counts against you.

Paul writes that Demas was with him at first. Most probably he worked with Paul and helped him, prayed with him and the two of them told people about Jesus. Then something went wrong, because Paul writes that Demas decided to leave him. Paul says the reason was that Demas loved the world.

When the Bible talks about "the world", it is everything that is not the will of the Lord. Everything that does not belong to the kingdom of Jesus, is "the world". There are many good and wonderful things in life, and also many wonderful people. But if they do not accept Jesus as king and Lord, they are part of "the world". Often it is exactly all the glitz and glamour of a world without Christ that seems so inviting to us. To Demas it was so attractive that he decided not to serve the Lord any more. He loved things better than the Lord and his kingdom. What a shame!

WWJD
Jesus would focus on the things of heaven.

Set your minds on things above,
not earthly things. (Col. 3:2)

October 5

Just you

... no one came to my support, but everyone deserted me. (2 Tim. 4:16)

Has anybody ever let you down? Have you ever landed up alone with something, because everybody made themselves scarce when the work had to be done? It happened to Paul.

Paul served the Lord with his whole being. He was not ashamed to be a witness for him, and to tell people that Jesus Christ is the only Savior. The devil did not like this at all. So he got some people together to go after Paul and make his life very difficult. This got so bad that Paul was even taken prisoner at a later stage for preaching the gospel. Many of his friends left him. Perhaps they were afraid, or some may have been embarrassed. Paul says when he had to appear in court the first time no one was there to support him. Can you think how unhappy that must have made him?

Yet, just listen what Paul adds, *But the Lord stood at my side and gave me stength ... I was delivered from the lion's mouth* (v. 17). Remember, even if people let you down and disappoint you, the Lord stays at your side. He will support you.

WWJD
Jesus would support you in everything.

... the Lord stood at my side and
gave me strength ... (2 Tim. 4:17)

October 6

Do love?

"A new command I give you: Love one another." (Jn. 13:34)

Many people think love is a feeling. If you feel good about someone, or you feel that you love someone very much, it is true love, you say. It is so that we have a special feeling for someone we love. But this does not mean we must first feel, before we can love.

The Bible sees true love as a command from the Lord. Because the Lord tells us to love one another, we must love one another, it's as simple as that. Don Francisco sings a song with the words: "Love is not a feeling, it is an act of your will." This means that you and I must say: We will love, because God tells us to. Then we love.

Love is one of God's commandments, and it means I must do deeds of love for all people, whether I like them or not. The question is not how we feel about people, but if we are pepared to love them like Jesus loves them. Even if we don't like them, we are friendly, and we help them, and we also support them, and we want what's best for them.

Decide that you will love all people that you meet today, even if you don't like them.

WWJD
Jesus would love his enemies.

" ...Love your enemies ... " (Mt. 5:44)

October 7

Ham makes a mistake

" ... The lowest of slaves will he be to his brothers." (Gen. 9:25)

Noah had faith in God. God told him to build an ark, and it did not put him off at all that everybody was making fun of him. Noah just went on doing what the Lord had told him to do.

Noah had three sons: Shem, Ham and Japheth. After the flood, Noah planted a vineyard. Noah made wine with the fruit of the vine and one day he drank too much wine and got drunk. He did not even realise that he had taken off all his clothes. Just then Ham came into his father's tent. It seems that Ham laughed at his father scornfully when he found him naked and drunk. He went and told his two brothers about this. His brothers were ashamed and took some clothing and covered their father. They did not scorn their father. Instead they wanted to give him back his dignity.

When Noah woke up, he realised that he was naked, and when he heard what Ham had done to him, he cursed Ham. Noah said Ham would be a good-for-nothing slave in his brothers' service. This prophecy came true.

The lesson is that we must respect our parents and honor them even if we don't like what they do. Even if they get drunk and do things that embarrass us, we must still love them and respect them, because love always protects (cf. 1 Cor. 13:7).

WWJD
Jesus would respect his parents.

 "Honor your father and your mother ... " (Ex. 20:12)

October 8

Abraham's big test

... The Lord Will Provide ... (Gen. 22:14)

Abraham was already very old when the Lord gave him a son. Abraham loved Isaac very much. When Isaac was a young boy, the Lord told Abraham to sacrifice his son.

In the Old Testament animals were sacrificed. They were placed on an altar and killed. How could God tell Abraham to do this to his son? The reason was that God wanted to test Abraham's love. God knew how much Abraham loved Isaac and God and he had a very specific plan with Abraham's life.

Abraham did what God had told him to do. He saddled his donkey and chopped wood for the burnt offering. Then he set off for the place the Lord had shown him. On the third day they saw the place in the distance. Isaac asked his father what animal they were going to sacrifice. Abraham answered that the Lord would provide. When they reached the place of sacrifice, he tied up his son and placed him on the altar. Just as Abraham took the knife to slaughter his son, an angel of the Lord called down from heaven and told him to stop. Then the Lord said, *"Now I know that you fear God, because you have not withheld from Me your son, your only son"* (v. 12). How much do you love the Lord?

WWJD
Jesus would obey his Father.

... He ... became obedient to death –
even death on a cross! (Phil. 2:8)

October 9

The grace of Jesus

May the grace of the Lord Jesus Christ ... be with you all.
(Gal. 13:14)

I'm sure you've heard a minister use these words as a blessing at the end of a church service. This blessing is the same prayer that Paul wrote in his letters to Christians living in different cities. He always ended his letters with these words: May the grace of the Lord Jesus Christ, and the love of God, and the fellowship of the Holy Spirit be with you all.

What does this mean? The word "grace" comes from the Greek word "charis" and in its simplest form it means simply "gifts". When the minister, or Paul, says that the grace of Jesus will be with us, they mean all the gifts that Jesus wants to hand out to us with his death and ressurection, become real. Which gifts?

Jesus saw to it that you and I are saved through his life and everything He came to do for us; that we are forgiven, and become new, and that we receive the fruit of the Holy Spirit and much more. All these are spiritual gifts or "mercy" that the Lord gives us.

My prayer is that you will receive the grace-gift of Jesus in your life.

WWJD
Jesus will bless you with gifts from heaven.

... Jesus Christ ... has blessed us in the heavenly realms with every spiritual blessing in Christ. (Eph. 1:3)

October 10

The gift of love

... the love of God ... be with you all. (2 Cor. 13:13)

Yesterday we saw that Paul's blessing was something he wished his Christian friends. He did not pray that they would receive Jesus' grace-gift only, but also the love of God.

Without God's love you and I cannot live meaningful lives. We need God's love. His love makes us strong. His love changes our lives. God proved his love for us when He gave us his Son. He loved us too much to allow that we perish, and that is why He sent Jesus. Yes, He proves his love through Jesus on the cross. It is this love that He wants to give also to you and me today.

He wants you to know now that He loves you very much, that He cares about you and that He will be with you in everything you do.

All of us need love. We cannot live without love. We need the love of people. But above all, we need the love of God. Jesus forgave us our sins so that we could have a loving relationship with him, our Father. The love of God will be with you.

WWJD
Jesus would always love others.

Love never fails. (1 Cor. 13:8)

October 11

What is fellowship?

... the fellowship of the Holy Spirit be with you all. (2 Cor. 13:13)

The last part of the blessing that Paul ended his letters with, mentions the fellowship of the Holy Spirit. He prays that people will experience that they have the fellowship of the Holy Spirit. What does this mean?

The word "fellowship" means two or more different people sharing a common interest or aim, and this unites them. When people have something in common it means they are the same in one or more ways. They may have the same colour eyes, or speak the same language, or have the same father.

When someone is a child of God, and has accepted Jesus Christ as Savior, that person has the Holy Spirit. All Christians have this in common: they have the Holy Spirit in their hearts and lives. This unites them, leads them in truth, fulfills them, and gives them the fruit and gifts they need. The Holy Spirit is like an invisible person in our hearts, and this makes that we look at things in the same way. This is how Christians can live together in harmony, because it is the same Spirit that encourages them to love one another.

I pray that you will share the fellowship of the Holy Spirit with other Christians today.

WWJD
Jesus will send the Holy Spirit to you as well.

... I will pour out my Spirit on all people ... (Joel 2:28)

October 12

Jesus and the whip

So He made a whip out of chords, and drove all from the temple ... (Jn. 2:15)

One can hardly think that Jesus was ever cross. But He was. The question is, if Jesus never sinned, why did He get angry?

Getting angry is not necessarily a sin. It is a sin to do something out of selfishness and go against the will of God. But God himself was also disappointed and angry about all the wicked things the people of Israel did.

Jesus was angry because the temple, where people were supposed to worship, was beginning to look like a supermarket. The main reason why people were coming to the temple was not to pray any more, but to make a lot of money. Jesus was angry and disappointed. He made a whip, and chased all those buying and selling out of the temple, together with their sheep and cattle. I think the merchants must have been very cross with Jesus. Newspapers would write about Jesus whipping people. Jesus did not care what the people thought of him. He wanted what was right.

We must also take a firm stand on things that are not right. It doesn't mean we have to whip people, but we need to be very firm out of respect for God.

WWJD
Jesus would be firm when necessary.

Jesus turned and said to Peter ... You are a stumbling block to me ... (Mt. 16:23)

October 13

What's done is done

But one thing I do: Forgetting what is behind and straining toward what is ahead. (Phil. 3:13)

Life is wonderful. Every day we have opportunities to do things. Tomorrow today's opportunities will be over and done with. Yesterday was unique. Yesterday is behind us.

When I think of certain things that happened in the past, I'm very glad it's over. We all know about things that happened in our past, that we don't like thinking about. The good news is that it's over.

Paul was very sorry about his past. He had people killed because he thought it was wrong to follow Jesus. That was a big mistake, but he could not make it go away. He was a murderer. Then the Lord changed his heart and he became a Christian. He asked the Lord to forgive him, and when he had been forgiven, he decided, "I am forgetting what is behind and looking toward what is ahead."

Do the same. Don't keep thinking about past failures and sins. Free yourself from things that happened yesterday. If you have confessed your sins, you are forgiven. Look ahead. Like an athlete, you must focus on what lies ahead.

WWJD
Jesus would look ahead.

... let us throw off everything that hinders ...
Let us fix our eyes on Jesus ... (Heb. 12:1, 2)

October 14

Before you were born

(Y)our eyes saw my unformed body ... (Ps. 139:16)

Medical technology is so wonderful nowadays that we can see a baby on a sonar even before it is born. In the time of the Bible none of these discoveries had been made yet. Yet the Lord saw us before we were born.

It is wonderful to know that the Lord has a plan with your and my lives, long before we are born. Even before your birth the Lord had already decided what your name would be, what you would look like, which talents He would give you, and what his plan with your life is. King David realised that he was not simply one man among many, but that the Lord knew him personally, long before his birth.

Who you are, and what you look like is all part of God's plan for your life. Thank him for all your talents and for what you are, even if you are not all that happy with yourself. Praise and thank the Lord that He knows all about you, yes even since before you were born. Decide today to live for him and his kingdom.

WWJD
Jesus would accept God's plan for his life.

For I know the plans I have for you ... plans to prosper you and not to harm you ... (Jn. 14:3)

October 15

We're getting married

... the wedding of the Lamb has come, and his bride has made herself ready. (Rev. 19:7)

Have you ever been to a wedding? A wedding is an exciting and festive occasion. The bride spends a lot of time on herself, doing her hair and face and then she puts on that stunning wedding dress. The bridegroom himself looks smart, because one's wedding day is a very important day. Usually many friends and family come to the wedding to share the happiness and excitement of the bridal couple.

In Revelation 19 we read about a very special wedding. It is called the "wedding of the Lamb". The Lamb is Jesus Christ. The Bible says Jesus is like a bridegroom. And who is the bride? You and I! Every one of us who belongs to Jesus, is Jesus' bride. One day He will come and fetch us and we will "get married" to him in heaven. Yes, and we will be with him for ever and ever. There we will celebrate and be joyful. Are you ready for the heavenly wedding?

WWJD
Jesus will come again to fetch us.

... I will come back and take you to be with me that you also may be where I am. (Jn. 14:3)

October 16

The open door

See, I have placed before you an open door that no one can shut. (Rev. 3:8)

Nowadays there are so many robbers and criminals that one has to keep the doors locked. Luckily one can buy strong locks. When you turn the key in the lock, the door is locked so securely that it is practically impossible to open it again without the right key. This is a wonderful message for every Christian. It is as if the Lord is telling us that He alone can open or shut a door for us. Often we want to open a "door" ourselves. Say you want to play the lead in the school play and you try just about everything to get that role. Or you so badly want to play in the first team for your school, so you try everything to make that team. You try opening the "door" to that team.

Rather ask God to open and lock doors for you. If He opens a door for you, no one on earth will ever close it again.

WWJD
Jesus would accept his Father's will.

"Father, if you are willing ... not my will, but yours be done." (Lk. 22:42)

October 17

Ready for harvesting

"The harvest is plentiful, but the workers are few." (Lk. 10:2)

One of the best things to see is a field ready for harvesting. Farmers work very hard to prepare a land before the seeds he sows or the tree he plants, can produce fruit, so that he can make a profit. Jesus also talks about a harvest field, a corn-field. A corn-field is green at first while the corn grows, and later the grain growing on the ears becomes yellow. Then it is ready for harvesting.

The Lord sees billions of people on earth, and He sees their needs. They are like uncountable ears of corn. There are millions of people in countries like India, China, Russia, America, Europe and Africa. The Lord says, "See, they are ripe on the fields." We must tell them about the kingdom of Christ. We must tell them they can be saved. That they can go to heaven. That they can be given a new life.

We must not only pray for the billions of people who have not even heard about Jesus; we must be prepared to tell them about Jesus. We must be like workers, willing to harvest.

WWJD
Jesus would preach the gospel all over the world.

Jesus went throughout Galilee, teaching ... preaching the good news of the kingdom ... (Mt. 4:23)

October 18

Workers

" ... to send out workers into his harvest field." (Mt. 9:38)

Farmers who have big farms and many corn-fields need a lot of workers to help with the harvest. Although we have large and wonderful machinery to harvest the crops, the help of people is still necessary. In the time of the Bible many workers were needed because then, of course, they did not have the modern machinery we have now.

Every worker on a farm has his or her own very specific task. Some drive tractors. Others must bag up the wheat. Others fasten the bags, or load and off-load the bags. If one decides not to do his bit, the whole harvest is slowed down. Every one must do his or her bit.

You and I are workers in his service, and we also have a task. Some are ministers or pastors, others have a specific duty to perform in the church, some are singers. Yet others take part in prayer meetings or talk to people about Jesus. Then there are those whose calling is to be witnesses for the Lord as doctors, nurses or businessmen. We all have a task to carry out. In this way God's bumper crop is harvested, because each of us is a worker in God's huge field. You must also pull your weight. You are a worker and you have to harvest the Lord's crop.

WWJD
Jesus would be a fellow worker in God's field.

For we are God's fellow workers ... (1 Cor. 3:9)

October 19

Just a cup of cold water

"And if anyone gives even a cup of cold water to one of these little ones because he is my disciple ... he will certainly not lose his reward." (Mt. 10:42)

Jesus said our hearts and our homes and our hands should be open to receive those who preach the message of his kingdom. He said, *"He who receives you receives Me, and he who receives Me receives the one who sent Me. Anyone who receives a prophet because he is a prophet will receive a prophet's reward, and anyone who receives a righteous man because he is a righteous man will receive a righteous man's reward"* (v. 40, 41).

We must help people who work full-time for the Lord and try to make their task easier. We must give them our support, give them money when necessary, and see that they get what they need to do the Lord's work. Even if we give them a cup of cold water when they are thirsty, the Lord sees it, and He will reward us. He promised.

Think of ways to help those who work for the Lord. Perhaps you can pray for them. Perhaps you can give them a hand and encourage them. Or you can contribute money. You can invite them to join you for a meal at your house. If we support people in this way, it is as if we are doing it for Jesus himself.

WWJD
Jesus would help others and support them.

So He went to her, took her hand and helped her up. (Mk. 1:31)

October 20

Worthless?

A bruised reed he will not break, and a smoldering wick he will not snuff out ... (Mt. 12:20)

Sometimes we think we are not good enough for the Lord. We feel that we have failed and because of that we have been disqualified. God does not think so. He can use anything. Even the greatest failure.

Reeds were used in the olden days by people who walked on stony roads. When they had to go through a river, the reed showed them how deep the water was. But a bent or bruised reed was no good. It could not be used any more. The Bible says even if you and I are sometimes like bruised reeds we can still be of use to the Lord.

There was no electricity in the time of the Bible. They used lamps that were filled with oil. Inside the lamp was a wick, and it was the wick that burnt and made the light. Sometimes the wick started smoldering and it would smoke. Then it was better to put it out, otherwise the whole house would be full of unpleasant smoke. A smoldering wick was useless. Even if you and I sometimes feel as worthless as a smoldering wick, our smoke getting into the eyes of the Lord, He will not put us out. He will still be able to use us.

Thank the Lord that He uses you in spite of all your short-coming.

WWJD
Jesus would regard you as an important person.

" ... you are worth more than many sparrows." (Mt. 10:31)

October 21

Don't pull them up!

"The servants asked him, 'Do you want us to go and pull them up?'" (Mt. 13:28)

Jesus told the parable of seed and weeds. A farmer sows seed to produce a good crop. Unfortunately farmers must have their lands weeded regularly, otherwise weeds will kill the seed. A weed is a worthless plant that can do much harm to the crops.

Jesus tells the story of a man who sowed good seed. One night when everyone was asleep, his enemy came and sowed weeds among the wheat. The weeds started becoming a danger to the seed. The farmer's servants asked him if they should pull up the weeds. He answered, *"No, ... because while you are pulling the weeds, you may root up the wheat with them. Let both grow together until the harvest. At that time I will tell the harvesters: First collect the weeds and tie them in bundles to be burned; then gather the wheat and bring it into my barn"* (v. 29, 30). What did Jesus mean?

Jesus is saying you and I must not judge people. If it seems as if someone doesn't love and serve the Lord, we must not shun or reject him. Don't pull him up like a weed. The Lord will decide for himself when the time comes, who is a seed and who is a weed.

WWJD
Jesus would be the good seed.

" ... the good seed stands for the sons of the kingdom ... " (Mt. 13:38)

October 22

No more questions

"In that day you will no longer ask Me anything." (1 Cor. 13:12)

Because we wonder about so many things, we ask a lot of questions. There are also many spiritual things we do not understand. Sometimes we ask our minister to explain something that we don't understand.

We ask questions especially when things happen that hurt us so very much and we don't understand why they happen. The poet Totius was a minister, but when two of his daughters died very young, he also asked many questions. Job also questioned God, because he could not understand why everything was suddenly going so horribly wrong for him. Some questions have clear and definite answers. Other questions however, are more difficult to answer. Even learned people sometimes disagree about answers to certain questions. Likewise, ministers differ about the answers to certain spiritual questions. Only God knows all the answers.

Luckily Jesus says a day will come that you and I need ask no more questions. That day we will know all the answers. Everything that we couldn't understand, will be crystal clear to us. This is the day that we will be in heaven with the Lord. We will know everything and understand everything. Until then we must just believe, and trust the Lord.

WWJD
Jesus will answer all your questions one day.

Now I know in part; then I shall know fully ... (1 Cor. 13:12)

October 23

I have to!

... I am compelled to preach. Woe to me if I do not preach the gospel! (1 Cor. 9:16)

Gospel means "good news". Paul says he can't help preaching the good news of Jesus Christ. He tells it and explains it to all who want to listen, if they understand it or not. He cannot help himself, he simply has to do it.

Paul tried to put a stop to the gospel of Jesus Christ at first. Those who preached the gospel were persecuted by him. Then the Lord touched his life and he repented and his whole life changed. Suddenly he had a longing in his heart to preach the gospel. Do you remember that the Lord called him to do it? God gave him the specific task to preach the gospel to the heathen nations in particular. The Holy Spirit encouraged him.

Every one of the Lord's children should, like Paul, have a longing to preach the gospel. Jesus wants the whole world to know about him. We must preach the gospel. Woe to us if we do not do it! We may never disobey the Lord. Tell him today that you too will preach the gospel.

WWJD
Jesus would preach the gospel.

"I must preach the good news of the kingdom of God ..." (Lk. 4:43)

October 24

Wild people

Where there is no revelation, the people cast off restraint ...
(Prov. 29:18)

Today's scripture means when the will of God is not made known to people they are uncontrolled and become wild. Wild horses are dangerous. If you should try to ride one, it is very likely that he will throw you, because he bucks and goes wild. Your life can even be in danger. It is the same with a wild bull. Many farmers and farmhands have been trampled by wild bulls. Wild people are just as bad. I'm sure you've heard people talk about a wild party. When people go wild (often because they have had too much to drink), they do all kinds of very stupid things. They hit one another, or break furniture and do a lot of irresponsible things.

Civilized, people are not wild, but "tame". They have peace in their hearts and are well-mannered. Wouldn't it be wonderful if all the people of our country could behave like this?

The Bible tells us if the will and the Word of God are not brought to the people, they become wild (they have no restraint). It is the Word of God that changes our hearts and his will, so that we become better people. Then we are not wild, but the way God wills it: everything with love.

Pray that God's Word and his will be preached loud and clear in our country.

WWJD
Jesus would preach God's Word to all people.

Now the tax collectors and "sinners" were all gathering around to hear him. (Lk. 15:1)

October 25

Don't you know me?

... "Don't you know Me, Philip, even after I have been among you such a long time?" (Jn. 14:9)

I think we often surprise the Lord, like Philip, one of his disciples did. Philip lived with the Lord and shared everything with him. Philip heard him talk about his kingdom. And then Philip asked a strange question, "Lord, show us the Father ... "

This was when Jesus said that it seemed as if he didn't know Jesus, although he had been with him such a long time.

The Lord speaks to us in many ways and in many places. Often we hear, but we don't really hear. Will the Lord not perhaps say to you or me, "You've known Me so long, how can you ask such stupid questions?" I don't think the Lord minds that we ask him questions, it's just that he sometimes expects us to know more answers, seeing that we have his Word and we are his children.

Make an effort to get to know the Lord even better.

WWJD
Jesus would teach you about the Lord.

" ...He will proclaim justice to the nations." (Mt. 12:18)

October 26

Go the extra mile

"If someone forces you to go one mile, go with him two miles." (Mt. 5:41)

This really does not seem fair. Why must I carry someone's things a longer distance, especially if he is forcing me in the first place? Most of us will refuse. The issue here is the attitude in our hearts. If God does not work in our hearts, it is impossible to do what Jesus says in this scripture. But, if He has changed our hearts, then we can do things we would never have done before.

It is precisely when we must do things that we don't enjoy, that we reveal Jesus' love and attitude. It is when we love our enemies that we glow with a wonderful testimony for all to see. It is when we serve others that people will ask why we are so different. Then we can tell them it is Jesus who taught us to be like him. He served. He gave people his best. He came to save us and give us life, although we did not deserve it. This is what our attitude should be.

We must amaze others with our loving ways. Especially those who least expect it, will be so surprised at a deed of love from the heart of the Lord himself. Come, let's walk that extra mile without being asked. Then we will please the Lord, and be a bright light in the dark world.

WWJD
Jesus would serve others without asking questions.

" ... I, your Lord and Teacher, have washed your feet ... " (Jn. 13:14)

October 27

Come a little closer

Come near to God and he will come near to you. (Jas. 4:8)

I'm sure you have tried to get closer to someone. Perhaps you were the odd one out in a group of friends. Often when we try to draw near to someone they won't allow us to. It is as if they keep us at arm's length. One can feel very lonely if people won't allow you to come close.

Fortunately the Lord is not like that at all. He wants us near him. He came nearer to us. That is why Jesus' other name is "Immanuel": God with you. Because God saw that we were far away from him, He decided to send us his Son. In this way He came near us. James tells you and me that we must draw nearer to God; draw near to him and He will draw near to you. This is a promise from God's Word. I do not know of a single person who tried to draw near to the Lord, and was pushed away by him. The arms of the Lord are always ready to receive us. He wants us to be very near to him. When He is near to us, our hearts are full of peace, and love and true happiness.

Decide that you want to draw even closer to the Lord today. Tell him this, and tell yourself. Don't allow anything to keep you away from the Lord. He is waiting for you with out-stretched arms if you want to come near to him.

WWJD
Jesus would not turn you away if you draw near to him.

Let us then approach the throne of grace with confidence ... (Heb. 4:16)

October 28

For the sake of

I have become all things to all men so that by all possible means I might save some. (1 Cor. 9:22)

Paul had such a burning desire to share the gospel that he was prepared to make allowances. This means you act differently because you want something to work.

For the sake of the gospel Paul was prepared to become a Jew to a Jew and a Greek to a Greek. He knew if he wanted to preach the gospel, he couldn't expect people to become like him. He had to become like them. This doesn't mean that he was prepared to sin, but that he could see to it that he was on the same level with them. He talked to the Jews in their language, and to the Greeks in theirs. With children, he talked on a child's level. With clever people he used suitable language for them. It's no good to try and tell people things if they don't understand you.

Jesus was also prepared to mingle with bad people so that he could speak to them. He even had friends who did not have a good reputation. Because Jesus loved people and didn't mind being on their level, He could preach the gospel to them.

You and I must also be like this. We must be able to speak to anybody about his or her interests, and when we get the opportunity, we must tell them about Jesus.

Let's make allowances to bring people to Jesus.

WWJD
Jesus would tell everybody the good news.

... the tax collectors and "sinners" were all gathering around to hear him. (Lk. 15:1)

October 29

Afraid, but obedient

Samuel ... was afraid to tell Eli the vision. (1 Sam. 3:15)

Do you remember how Samuel's mother prayed for a child? When Samuel was born she dedicated him to the Lord. Ever since he was a small boy he was in the temple where he was raised to serve the Lord.

One night as Samuel was sleeping, the Lord called him. When Samuel woke up, he thought at first that Eli had called him. Eli was the priest who worked in the temple. Later on Eli realised it was the Lord who had called Samuel, and he told Samuel to say, "Speak, Lord, for your servant is listening."

Then the Lord spoke to Samuel and gave him a message for Eli. Unfortunately it was not good news.

It couldn't have been easy for Samuel to give Eli this message. But he had to be obedient. Often we find it very difficult to tell someone the truth. Even if the truth hurts, we must tell it. But we must do it in love and obedience to the Lord. If Samuel had not obeyed the Lord, Eli would not have been prepared for what was going to happen. Then Samuel would not have had peace with God. When the Lord asks us to do something, we must do it.

WWJD
Jesus would tell the truth.

"Then you will know the truth, and the truth will set you free." (Jn. 8:32)

October 30

You must move

... Abraham ... obeyed and went, even though he did not know where he was going. (Heb. 11:8)

The Lord called Abraham from a far land, Ur. Because the Lord had a plan with his life, and the people of Israel would later descend from him, the Lord told him to move away from Ur. There was just one problem. Abraham had no idea where to.

The Lord calls many people to follow him, even today. You too. He also wants you to "move away" in the direction that He thinks is best for you. It's difficult if you don't really know where you're going. The Lord doesn't tell us exactly where we're headed either. What He does tell us, is that He will be with us. What He is asking is that we trust him. That is faith. Abraham believed that the Lord knew what He was doing, and so he moved away from Ur. Because he believed, the Lord did wonderful things through him.

Every day must be a step along the road with Jesus. We don't know what will happen this day, but let's trust him to show us the way. What an adventure! Following Jesus with your whole life, is not being sure about what tomorrow will bring, but knowing that if you are moving with God, you will be contented and happy.

WWJD
Jesus will be with you wherever you go.

"And surely I am with you always, to the very end of the age." (Mt. 28:20)

October 31

Look to the heavens

Lift your eyes and look to the heavens: Who created all these? (Is. 40:26)

In the time when Isaiah lived, the people of God could not see the Lord any more. They were too sinful and it made them spiritually dull, so that the Lord seemed vague and far away to them. They put their trust in heathen gods and not in God. Then Isaiah made them look at the heavens. He told them to see the stars again.

When one sees the wonders of the galaxy, you cannot help but realise that a great and mighty Creator made it all. We see so much of God's greatness in nature. We see him in the mountains, and the flowers, and even in modern technology. If we allow our minds to open our eyes, we will see God in everything around us. When Israel really looked at the stars again, they realised God lives. They started worshipping him once more.

At school you learn about wonderful things. You take in new knowledge. If you read books and encyclopaedias, you will get to know about the most wonderful things, and if you are a child of the Lord, you cannot help but see the hand of God in everything. You must thank and praise the Lord for all the wonderful things. He is the Creator and Lord of your life.

WWJD
Jesus would be happy with creation.

You have set your glory above the heavens. (Ps. 8:2)

November 1

All day long

(P)ray continually ... (1 Thes. 5:17)

One of the best habits one can get into, is to speak to the Lord all the time. The Lord wants us to speak to him; He is always with his children. In his Holy Spirit He lives inside us. That is why He is never away from us, and we can be in contact with him every moment of the day.

Paul writes a letter to a Christian church and tells them to pray continually. Continually means without stopping. So what he is actually saying is: Pray without stopping. How do we do it? You pray continually when you talk to the Lord in your thoughts all the time. You share everything with him: what you see, what you hear, and what you experience.

As the day goes on, we can talk to the Lord all the time, about everything that is happening to us. We can talk about our feelings. We can talk about things we want to see, or have. We can say thank you for things we enjoy. We can pray for the need of someone else. We can speak to the Lord if we feel we are in danger. Yes, we can really speak to the Lord about everything.

Let's make it a way of life to talk to the Lord continually. Share everything you do today with him, by talking to him in your thoughts or even out loud.

WWJD
Jesus would talk to the Lord all the time.

But Jesus often withdrew to lonely places and prayed. (Lk. 5:16)

November 2

Jealousy and quarreling

... For since there is jealousy and quarreling among you, are you not worldly? (1 Cor. 3:3)

Paul wrote this letter to the Corinthians. They accepted the Lord Jesus and followed him. Yet they sometimes still acted like non-Christians. This is a problem with all Christians. We still sometimes do things that are not proper and that God does not expect us to do.

Paul writes that they are sometimes jealous and quarrel with others. When one is jealous you don't want anyone else to have anything good, if you can't have it too. You don't want someone else to be successful. One is jealous of a friend if one wants him or her for oneself only. You don't want your friend to have any others friends but you.

To quarrel is to be angry and to have an argument. You lose your temper if something happens that you don't like. You are cross with others, and you behave in a very ugly way.

Paul says when we are jealous or always bickering with others, we are not acting like Christians, but like worldly people. Worldly people don't have the Holy Spirit in their hearts. They don't live according to the Word of God. So one expects them to fight and be jealous. One does not expect this behaviour from Christians. Try to live in peace with all people, and don't begrudge them the good things in their lives.

WWJD
Jesus would live in peace with all people.

"Blessed are the peacemakers ..." (Mt. 5:9)

November 3

Wake up!

"Wake up, O sleeper, rise from the dead, and Christ will shine on you." (Eph. 5:14)

Sleep is good for one. One gets new strength. But if one is spiritually asleep, then it's not a good thing. The Bible says we must not be asleep spiritually, we must be spiritually awake.

This means that we must be on fire for the Lord. One singer says, "Boil for the King." This means we must be diligent, wide awake, and serve the Lord with energy and enthusiasm.

Spiritual sleep is almost like spiritual death. When you sleep you can't do anything. A person who is asleep is not active. There is no sign of real life, like when someone runs or plays or sings or talks. The Lord does not want us to be spiritually dead. He wants us to be alive and lively; others must see that we know the Lord, that we love him and follow him, because our behaviour shows it.

If we are awake and not spiritually asleep, the light of Jesus will be seen clearly in our lives. We usually sleep when it is dark. People who live, live in the daytime. The time we usually work. Let us then live and work in Jesus' light, and serve him zealously.

WWJD
Jesus would help you serve him with enthusiasm.

... always be zealous for ... the Lord. (Prov. 23:17)

November 4

Even more fruitful

" ... every branch that does bear fruit he prunes so that it will be even more fruitful." (Jn. 15:2)

The Lord wants to see fruit in our lives, so that He can be glorified. You and I are like a tree. If one cannot see fruit on a tree, then it is not a fruitful tree. A tree that bears good fruit is the owner's pride and joy. He picks the fruit and enjoys giving some of it to others. Our heavenly Father wants to see fruit on the tree of our lives so that He can be glorified.

The Lord often uses suffering, pain and heartache to teach us, his children, important lessons. In this way He makes us strong in spirit and it helps us to grow spiritually. The Lord is a great gardener and He prunes you and me, so that we can bear more fruit in our lives. A tree is pruned so that it can produce more fruit. It can't be very pleasant, although a tree can't feel anything, but you and I are also pruned at times.

It definitely is not pleasant for us, but God does it so that we can bear more fruit.

The Lord wants to prune all bad things out of our lives, like bad habits, or wrong thoughts, and things we do wrong. Because of God's pruning, we can bear better fruit.

WWJD
Jesus would prune you to bear better fruit.

He (Jesus) must become greater;
I must become less. (Jn. 3:30)

November 5

He will receive me

Though my father and mother forsake me, the Lord will receive me. (Ps. 27:10)

There are many children who are in children's homes. While the parents of some of these children have died, there are also children whose parents are alive, but cannot take care of them. They must feel very alone, not being with their parents. These children are taken care of in children's homes.

Grown-ups also miss their parents. Their parents have either passed away, or they live elsewhere. Sometimes when they feel a little lonely, they long to see their parents again and to sit and talk to them. Loneliness is part of life. We are sometimes lonely because we cannot have our father and mother with us all the time. But the Bible has comfort for us. The Lord promises to take us in his care, and that He will be with us always. After all, his name is also Father. He is not an earthly father, that is true, but He is the heavenly Father who, in Jesus, is with us all the time. He wants to take us in his Father's arms, and He assures us that He will take care of us. Thank the Lord that He, like your father and mother, will take you into his care, and will be with you always. Also today.

WWJD
Jesus will take care of you also.

"If that is how God clothes the grass of the field ...
will He not much more clothe you ... ?" (Mt. 6:30)

November 6

He gives back!

"J will repay you for the years the locusts have eaten ... "
(Joel 2:25)

In the time of the prophet Joel, the Lord sent a swarm of locusts to eat the Israelites' crops. A very difficult time lay ahead
of them. God wanted to teach them a lesson. Yet He promised
that He would give them his blessings again.

The Lord is like that. Often things happen in our lives that
we find very difficult to accept. A family member dies, or our
family goes through a difficult financial crisis. It could be that
your dad has lost his job. The Lord helps his children in times
of hardship. One day in heaven, we will be given the perfect
reward, when everything will be perfect and there will be no
more tears and hurt. The Lord also sometimes rewards us on
earth. He knows what happens in our lives, and gives us wonderful times of happiness and peace and joy, even if we have
our bad patches. The Lord is the great God of heaven and earth
and He will help us when things go wrong. You just put your
trust in the Lord. Leave your life in his hands and know that He
will take care of you.

WWJD
Jesus would take your hurt away.

For the past troubles will be forgotten ... (Is. 65:16)

November 7

Tears

Record my lament; list my tears on your scroll ... (Ps. 56:9)

There is certainly not one person on earth who has not cried. One cries with joy when you are so happy about something that it makes you very emotional. Or heartache can make you cry. Or you can cry because you have been hurt. Pain also makes one cry. And a person can cry if someone has treated you badly or unfairly.

They say it is good to cry. It is never good to bottle up your feelings. It is better to cry about things and get them out of your system, than to keep them inside and pretend that nothing is wrong. Tears help to lighten our load. You must never be ashamed or afraid to cry. Of course one must not cry about every little thing. But if you really hurt it is alright to cry.

Do you remember that Jesus also cried? Jesus cried when He realised that Lazarus was dead. He saw how sad Lazarus' sisters, Mary and Martha, were. He was deeply moved. Because He also loved Lazarus, He cried.

The Bible says that God keeps a record of all his children's tears in a book. One day He will wipe the tears from our eyes, and there will be no more tears (cf. Rev. 21:4).

WWJD
Jesus would cry when He is sad.

... He (Jesus) was deeply moved ... (Jn. 11:33)

November 8

Be caring

... "Where is your brother Abel?" "I don't know," he [Cain] replied. "Am I my brother's keeper?" (Gen. 4:9)

We read the story of Cain and Abel in the Bible. Cain was a crop-farmer and Abel a cattle-farmer. The Lord accepted Abel's offering, but not Cain's. Cain was very angry and jealous. He killed his brother Abel in a field. When God asked Cain where his brother was he gave the Lord a rude answer, and said he was not supposed to look after his brother. What he was in fact saying was that he didn't care about his brother.

People need people, and we must care for others. We cannot pretend that we can get on without one another. We must take care of each other. If we have brothers or sisters in the same family, we are responsible for them in a special way. It is as if the Lord gives one to the other to help and care for him or her. You must encourage one another and be loving and caring, and also show one another in a nice way where he or she goes wrong.

Cain felt nothing for his brother. Actually he wanted him dead. Then he committed a terrible murder. This is not the way to behave. We must not walk around with nasty thoughts towards our brothers and sisters. We must pray for them and love them.

WWJD
Jesus would care for others.

Each of you should not look not only to your own interests, but also to the interests of others. (Phil. 2:4)

November 9

Crouching at your door

" ... sin is crouching at your door; it desires to have you, but you must master it." (Gen. 4:7)

We must realise that as long as we are living on earth sin will always be a problem. Every day brings its share of sin-possibilities. It is as if sin is crouching out there, just waiting to pounce. The minute we are disobedient, sin grabs us.

The Lord told Cain that joy waits for everyone who does what is right. But if you don't, sin is there, waiting to get you into its power. But, the Lord said, you must master sin. This also goes for you and me. Although the possibility of sin is always there, so is the possibility of saying "no". That is often the most difficult thing to do. We must ask the Lord to help us. To master sin is to say "no" to it. Often sin comes in the form of something so inviting that you find it very difficult to say "no". Ask the Lord to help you, and to give you the wisdom to recognize sin when it uses sly ways of getting to you. If we are willing, the Lord will help us to master sin.

WWJD
Jesus would master sin.

 ... "Away from Me, Satan!" (Mt. 4:10)

November 10

One bad apple

He who walks with the wise grows wise, but a companion of fools suffers harm. (Prov. 13:20)

Isn't it interesting that if there is one bad apple in a box, all the other good ones go bad in no time, and before you know it there is not one good apple left in the box.

There is a saying: "He who sleeps with dogs gets up with flees." We are all influenced by one another, and that is why it is important who you talk to, who your friends are, where you visit and play. You are the way your friends are. If your friends have bad habits, it will be easy for you to pick up these habits. Almost like the apples in the box. The Bible tells us if we keep company with wise people and listen to them, we also become wise. If, however, we are with fools all the time, we become just as foolish. You and I want to be wise and do what is right, don't we? Choose Christians for friends, so that thay can have a good influence on you.

A Christian should have Christian friends. You can be friendly with all people, but remember, those who are close to you, are the ones who will influence you. If they love Jesus and know him they will help you serve him even better.

WWJD
Jesus would choose the right friends.

 Blessed is the man who does not walk
in the counsel of the wicked ... (Ps. 1:1)

November 11

Happy to go

I rejoiced with those who said to me, "Let us go to the house of the Lord." (Ps. 122:1)

David is called "a man after God's heart". The Lord loved him very much. Although David made mistakes, he loved the Lord and he showed it. When he made a mistake, he confessed it, and he really tried to do the will of the Lord.

In the Old Testament the Lord lived in the temple. It was called the house of the Lord. David was very pleased when his friends said: Let's go to the house of the Lord. David knew in the house of the Lord, God would talk to him. Today the church is not the only house of the Lord. The Lord now lives in our hearts. God's house is in our bodies. Our bodies are the temple of the Holy Spirit. Wherever we go, God goes with us. Still, we go to church to listen to the Word of God together with other Christians, we ask them how they are, and we encourage and uplift one another. There we pray and sing together to the glory of God.

If you love the Lord, you want to be where He is praised and where his Word is preached. Pray for your congregation and minister and give them your support. Then you will also be happy when someone says to you, "Let's go to church!"

WWJD
Jesus would go to church regularly.

... they found him in the temple ... (Lk. 2:46)

November 12

Ever brighter

The path of righteousness is like the first gleam of dawn, shining ever brighter till the full light of day. (Prov. 4:18)

The life of someone who loves and knows the Lord is different to that of one who does not know him. One way of describing the life of a Christian, is to say it is a light-life. A person who knows the Lord, lives in his light and also has this light in her or his heart.

One of the wonderful things of being a Christian, is that we are lit up by the light of Christ shining ever brighter as we go along. When one accepts Jesus, his light is in your heart. The further we walk the road of life with him, the brighter his light in our hearts and life. At first your life is like the first gleam of dawn in the morning, before sunrise. Later on the sun rises and soon it is bright daylight. Such is the life of a person who lives with the Lord. The longer you live with him, the brighter his light shines in your life.

Let the Lord's sunshine light up your life today.

WWJD
Jesus would let his light shine.

"In the same way, let your light shine before men ... " (Mt. 5:16)

November 13

Are you dressed suitably?

... before me was a great multitude that no one could count ... They were wearing white robes ... (Rev. 7:9)

One must dress to suit the occasion. You wear your uniform to school. When you play sport, you wear sports clothes. When we go to church, we wear church clothes.

Jesus told the parable of a man who held a wedding. Then someone arrived who was not suitably dressed and they threw him out. This is just a story, but Jesus tells it to us so that we know we must be dressed correctly if we want to be with him one day.

What must we wear for the Lord? Not clothes, like a suit or a pretty dress. No, the Bible talks about clean, white clothes. This is an image to say we must be washed clean of sin. In Revelation we read that people standing before the Lord were dressed in white clothes. These are redemption clothes. Only people washed clean from sin, can enter into the presence of the Lord.

When the Lord washes you clean from sin, you will be given clean, white redemption clothes. Then you are dressed correctly. No one will throw you out of heaven. You can enter into the presence of the Lord joyfully.

WWJD
Jesus will dress you correctly to enter heaven.

" ... throw him outside, into the darkness, where there will be weeping ... '" (Mt. 22:13)

November 14

Beautiful love

... love is as strong as death ... (Song 8:6)

Song of Songs is a beautiful book in the Bible. It is a song written about the love between a man and a woman. In this book we read how much the man loves the woman of his dreams, and the woman tells how wonderful the man is that she loves.

Nowadays there are so many love stories on television, or in books, that make true love between a man and a woman so cheap ... Couples fall in love, and the next thing you see, they sleep together, but they are not married. This is not the way the Lord meant it to be. It is a wonderful experience when a man and a woman fall in love. Perhaps you have also fallen in love with someone of the opposite sex, even though you are still very young. Love between a boy and a girl is beautiful. The Lord made it.

Because love is such a strong feeling, the devil can make use of it as well. That is a pity. Often people fall in love, but then they become very jealous. People have even committed murder because of jealousy. Love is a gift from the hand of God. He gives the love between a man and a woman, and He can help you to love in the right way. Ask the Lord now to help you love someone in the right way.

WWJD
Jesus would love in the right way.

 Love ... is not self-seeking ... (1 Cor. 13:4, 5)

November 15

Fishing for Jesus

"Come, follow Me," Jesus said, "and I will make you fishers of men." (Mk. 1:17)

Jesus grew up near the Sea of Galilee. It is a large inland lake. There is a lot of fish in that lake. Even today people still fish in the Sea of Galilee. Jesus often watched fishermen fishing from their boats. Some of the fishermen became his friends and disciples. Simon Peter was a fisherman who decided to follow Jesus.

Jesus uses the image of fishing to tell us how important it is that we catch "people". A fisherman puts bait on a fish-hook, or he lets a net down the side of the boat and pulls the fish in like that. What he catches belongs to him. Jesus taught his disciples to catch "people", so that they can belong to him. How do we catch people for Jesus? We tell them about him. We also tell them how wonderful it is to know him and to follow him, because He is the one who forgives our sins and will let us live in heaven with him. When people hear this, many of them will come to him.

The Lord uses people like you and me to bring others to him, so that they can belong to him. Be a fisher of people today.

WWJD
Jesus would invite people to follow him.

... "Follow Me," He told him, and Matthew got up and followed him. (Mt. 9:9)

November 16

Not empty religion

Even though you bring Me burnt offerings ... I will not accept them. (Amos 5:22)

The Lord does not like it when someone pretends to worship him, but that person's heart is not in it. The Lord does not like religion which is nothing but show. Many people seem to be children of God. They listen to sermons, they sing and look God-fearing. Israel did this.

The Lord speaks through a man named Amos, and tell his people He does not think much of their religion. He says He hates and abhors their religious feasts. He tells them to stop singing him songs, because they are just making a noise (cf. v. 23). Why does the Lord feel so strongly about this? The reason is that they sin such a lot and actually don't love him in the least. It is as if the Lord is saying, "What good is your religion if you are not in a proper relationship with Me?" The Lord does not really care what we do on the outside. He looks into our hearts. He knows if we confess our sins. He knows if we are forgiven. If we serve him thankfully and go to church and sing him songs, He is pleased with us. But He does not like an empty religion.

Work on with the Lord, and see that in your religion you serve him whole-heartedly.

WWJD
Jesus would serve the Lord with his whole life.

... always be zealous for ... the Lord. (Prov. 23:17)

November 17

A father for ever

... He will be called ... Everlasting Father ... (Js. 9:5)

Although we all have fathers, many of us no longer have a mother and father that we can see or visit. Then there are children whose dads are still alive, yet they never see them. Their dads have disappeared, or have decided not to have any contact with their children. Oh, that is really a shame! Other children have the privilege of knowing a father for a long time. They grow up with a father in the house, and later on they get married and become fathers themselves. Now and again they visit their fathers, even if their dads have now become granddads. But grandfathers get older and one day they die. Then their children do not have a father on earth any more.

We have a Father who will always be there. He is the Father of Jesus, and He also becomes our Father when we accept Jesus. Jesus shows us the way to the Father. He introduces us to his Father. His Father becomes your Father and mine. He is a Father that will never disappoint us, who never makes mistakes, who will never turn his back on us, who will never leave us. Jesus saw to it that we have an everlasting Father. He is with you today.

WWJD
In Jesus you will be a child of God the Father.

Everyone who believes that Jesus is
the Christ is born of God ... (1 Jn. 5:1)

November 18

Clouds

Like clouds and wind without rain is a man who boasts of gifts he does not give. (Prov. 25:14)

Farmers depend on rain. If it does not rain, the seed they sow will never sprout. Without rain there is no grass in the fields for sheep and cattle to graze. If it doesn't rain, the world becomes very dry.

Rain comes in the form of clouds. If the wind blows in the right direction, the clouds gather and when they have enough moisture, rain starts falling from the clouds. Not all clouds give rain. Sometimes they are empty.

The Bible says we are sometimes like clouds without rain. They are full of promise, but nothing happens. It is easy to make promises. People say they will do this or that, and then nothing comes of it. People even boast about things they will achieve, and how they will do things for you. Perhaps you have had friends like this: full of promises about what they want to do for you, but it ended just there – with the promise. They are like empty clouds, without any rain.

We must not be like empty clouds. What we say, we must do. People must be able to rely on us. Don't be quick to boast about what you are going to do. It is better to keep quiet and first do it.

WWJD
Jesus would do what He promises.

 "Simply let your 'Yes' be 'Yes,'
and your 'No,' 'No' ... " (Mt. 5:37)

November 19

A cooking pot or pen

On that day "Holy to the Lord" will be inscribed on the bells of the horses, and the cooking pots in the Lord's house will be like the sacred bowls in front of the altar. (Zech. 14:20)

Sometimes we think some things are holier than others. To be holy is to be devoted to the Lord. Perhaps you think the church is holier than your bedroom. But this is not necessarily the case. Wherever the Lord is, there it is holy: in your bedroom, or in the kitchen, or in church or at school.

Zechariah saw a vision in the Old Testament. He saw the words "Holy to the Lord" written on the bells of the horses. Also the cooking pots in the house of the Lord will be sacred or holy. With this vision the Lord was saying that the time has come where all things are equally holy to the Lord. Actually He is saying that all things we use can be instruments to glorify the Lord. Your pen, the pencil you write with, the clothes you wear, your cricket ball, or the CD player in your home can be "holy to the Lord".

Let us make everything we work with every day, holy. Because everything belongs to the Lord.

WWJD
Jesus would use everything to the glory of God.

"See to it that you complete the work you have received in the Lord." (Col. 3:17)

November 20

The elderly

Gray hair is a crown of splendor; it is attained by a righteous life. (Prov. 16:31)

Many children are impatient with old people. Some even make fun of old people because they can't move fast, or because they do things differently.

Do you realise that today's old people were once just as young as you. As the years went by, they got older, and later they started getting weaker. The Bible says the gray hair of old people is like a splendid crown they wear on their heads. Make time to speak to old people. If you still have a grandpa and a granny, make sure you phone them regularly, or write them a letter just to say you love them. Let's pray for all old people who live in a home for the aged.

WWJD
Jesus would treat old people with respect.

Do not rebuke an older man harshly, but exhort him as if he were your father ... with absolute purity. (1 Tim. 5:1, 2)

November 21

His promises

... they will never be silent day or night. You who call on the Lord, give yourselves no rest. (Js. 62:6)

In the Bible the Lord makes a lot of promises to his children. There are many, many promises, so many that there is a promise from the mouth of God for every day of the year. You and I can claim these promises for ourselves.

The Lord promises to be with us, that He will always love us, that He will give us strength, that his Holy Spirit will guide us, and many more promises. Isaiah is now telling us that we must remind the Lord of the promises He made. It's not because the Lord forgets that we have to remind him. It is because you and I sometimes forget about the Lord's promises that we must remember them again, and say them out loud to ourselves and to the Lord. If we do that, we show that we really put our trust in him, and need him. The Lord is pleased when we do that. He doesn't like boastful people who think they can help themselves. You and I must show that the Lord's promises are important to us by claiming them for ourselves.

Every time you are in a difficult situation, think about one of the Lord's promises. Make it your own, in faith. Thank God that his promises are also meant for you.

WWJD
Jesus would trust the Father's promises.

(S)ince you know that you will receive an inheritance (what He promised) from the Lord as a reward. (Col. 3:24)

November 22

Filthy language

But now you must rid yourselves of ... filthy language from your lips. (Col. 3:8)

It is never necessary for a father to teach his child bad language. The child manages all by himself. Most moms and dads have quite a struggle with children who use dirty words they heard somewhere. So many people around us use bad language all the time. Dirty words. Words one does not like hearing. Often bad language is used even in company. This really is a shame.

That which is in your heart, usually comes out of your mouth. If your heart is not clean, it is so much easier to speak dirty words. Swearing is a sign of a heart which has not yet been cleaned well enough. The Lord wants to help us so that our words can be good and clean.

When we give our hearts to the Lord, his Holy Spirit comes to live in our hearts, and He can help us to get our language nice and clean. I know many people who first used very bad language, but when they gave their hearts to the Lord, they felt they did not want to do it any more. I think all Christians have the problem of a dirty word slipping out every now and again. But we say we're sorry straight away, and ask the Lord to help us so that we do not use that dirty word again.

WWJD
Jesus would speak only good words.

Do not let any unwholesome talk come out of your mouths, but only what is helpful for building others up ... (Eph. 4:29)

November 23

Who is right?

All the nations may walk in the name of their gods; we will walk in the name of the Lord our God for ever and ever. (Mic. 4:5)

Many gods are worshipped all over the world. This was true of Bible times and it is true also today. There are many different religions and everyone believes his god is the real one. As Christians we believe in the God of the Bible. He is the Father of Jesus Christ and He gave us his Holy Spirit to stay with us and teach us all about his will.

The question is: Whose god is the real one? As Christians we just know the Bible is correct. Micah said all nations may live in the name of their gods here on earth, but Christians will always live in the name of the Lord our God. Christians say it is not only in this life that we must have a God, and bow down before him, but above all, it is in eternity that we will live with him. It is the Lord God who lives in our hearts.

WWJD
Jesus would serve only the Father.

"Worship the Lord your God and serve him only." (Lk. 4:8)

November 24

When parents divorce

"Is it lawful for a man to divorce his wife for any and every reason?" " ... what God has joined together, let man not separate." (Mt. 19:3, 6)

Nowadays many parents are divorcing one another. Maybe you know someone who is divorced. It could even be that your own mom and dad felt they could no longer stay together, and that they decided to get divorced. It is very sad when this happens. Divorce makes that families can no longer live together in love and harmony. Often children do not know where exactly they fit in – with Dad or with Mom. The Lord does not want people to get divorced.

Often something happens between moms and dads and their marriage break-up and just gets worse and worse. Where there was love at first, there is now growing disagreement. It is so sad. One must first talk about it a lot, seek advice and pray often, before one decides to get divorced.

If people are divorced, the Lord heals the hurt. He can also forgive sins that have been committed. In Jesus we can always start again, make a new beginning. Let's pray for marriages and families, and ask for the Lord's blessing on these.

WWJD
Jesus would pray for every marriage.

Submit to one another out of reverence for Christ. (Eph. 5:21)

November 25

Stone throwing

"If any one of you is without sin, let him be the first to throw a stone at her." (Jn. 8:7)

In this part we read about a married woman who cheated on her husband, and had a relationship with another man. The Bible calls her an adulteress. This woman was caught out, and the church people grabbed hold of her and brought her to Jesus. They wanted to see what Jesus would do. The Old Testament said if anyone committed the sin she had, that person must be stoned. This means that the people picked up stones, or even bricks, and threw them at someone. In this way that person was stoned to death.

Jesus knew that the woman was guilty, but He wanted to forgive her. The Lord wants to forgive us, because He loves us. Then Jesus said that the person who was without sin, could pick up the first stone and throw it at her. No one could do that, because all of them had also known sin in their lives. Perhaps they didn't think their sins were as serious as hers, but they knew they had their faults. Jesus looked at the woman tenderly and told her that He didn't condemn her, but that she should not sin any more.

So we see that you and I cannot throw stones at others, or accuse them, because of all the sin in our own lives. Let's not judge others, but rather pray for them.

WWJD
Jesus would forgive others.

 Forgive as the Lord forgave you. (Col. 3:13)

November 26

Protect his name

"You shall not misuse the name of the Lord your God ... " (Ex. 20:7)

I'm sure you've heard people use the name of the Lord in passing. Not respectfully. They are actually swearing with the name of the Lord. The Bible calls this "misuse of the name of God".

The name of the Lord is holy. The Jews in the Old Testament felt so strongly about the name of the Lord, that they did not say it, not even when they prayed. They were afraid to do it, because to them God was too great and holy. Jesus taught us in the New Testament that we can pray in his name. With the Our Father prayer He taught us that it's alright to talk to the Father.

As a Christian one cringes when you hear how many people use the name of Jesus, or God the Father, just anyhow. It's as if they are putting the name of the Lord on the same level as any ordinary name like Jack or William or Alice. No, God's name is noble and wonderful, and must be used only when we speak of him respectfully. If we hear someone misusing the name of the Lord, we must pray for that person. We must say in a nice way, that we think that name is very special, and that we love that God, because He is the Lord we worship. Ask the Lord to help you so that you will also not misuse his name.

WWJD
Jesus would respect the name of the Father.

 He ... gave glory to God. (Rom. 4:20)

November 27

Nurse the hurt

"But a Samaritan, as he traveled, came where the man was; and when he saw him, he took pity on him. He went to him and bandaged his wounds, pouring on oil and wine." (Lk. 10:33, 34)

Jesus told the story of the good Samaritan. A man went on a journey. On the road robbers attacked him. They took off all his clothes and beat him up until he was lying there, half dead. Then they fled. A few people passed by and saw that he had been hurt, but they pretended not to notice. When the Samaritan saw him, he took pity on him and started taking care of his wounds.

It is so easy to look the other way if there is hurt around you. There are many people in hospitals, or at home, who are in pain. There are also many unhappy people with problems in their marriages, or who have experienced great disappointment. These are all people in need. The Bible says we must not look the other way, but try to help them. Like the Samaritan did. The Samaritan not only bandaged the man's wounds, he also helped him onto his own donkey and took him to an inn, where he paid so that the man could stay there until he was well. This is real love. You and I must do the same with people around us who need help.

WWJD
Jesus would help people in need.

"Blessed are the merciful ..." (Mt. 5:7)

November 28

The church in the house

Greet also the church that meets at their house. (Rom. 16:5)

In the time just after Jesus ascended to heaven, Christian groups were formed, and they met in people's houses. Of course the Christians then were not as many as today. The children of the Lord had good times together, they had their meals together, prayed together and talked about the Lord. They also read the letters Paul and others wrote them. In this way they encouraged one another and their faith was strengthened.

Today there is once again a new movement: people are getting together in smaller groups in people's homes. These are smaller groups of a large congregation, called homecells, who get together regularly to socialize and also worship the Lord together. The members of these small groups get to know one another well, they know about one another's problems, dreams and plans. In this way they can care for each other better, act or speak on someone's behalf, and support one another.

What a privilege to get together openly in one another's homes, to worship the Lord and to praise him. Pray for these groups all over the world. Fortunately we don't have only the church where we can praise God. He is with us in our own homes.

WWJD
Jesus would pray for all Christians.

Holy Father, protect them by the power of your name ... (Jn. 17:11)

November 29

Wonderful friends

Greet Priscilla and Aquila ... (Rom. 16:3)

The Lord gave Paul wonderful Christian friends. Just like you and I, Paul needed close friends to support him and help him. Especially in the letter to the Romans, we read about quite a few of these friends. Shall we name a few?

Priscilla and Aquila were two of Paul's co-workers. They not only made tents with him, they also preached the gospel with him. He says they *"... risked their lives for me"* (v. 4).

Andronicus and Junias were two friends who became Christians before Paul did, and they were in prison with him. There they supported him (cf. v. 7).

Apelles was another good friend of Paul's. Paul says of him that he was *"... tested and approved by Christ"* (v. 10). He was a reliable Christian friend.

Tryphena and Tryphosa were two Christian lady friends. He calls them "hard workers for the Lord" (cf. v. 12).

There are many other names we can list, but it is clear that Paul was very thankful for all these friends that were at his side and helped him to serve the Lord and follow him. You and I should also have friends like these.

WWJD
Jesus would choose friends who also serve the Lord.

"You are my friends if you do what I command." (Jn. 15:14)

November 30

Two ears, one mouth

When words are many, sin is not absent, but he who holds his tongue is wise. (Prov. 10:19)

Someone said, "A person has two ears and only one mouth." This means we must listen twice as much as we speak. Unfortunately the opposite is often true; we talk much more than we listen. If we listen more and speak less, it is quite possible that there will be fewer problems in the world.

Proverbs 10 says if we speak a lot, sin very easily comes to into our speech. It is with all this talking that we sometimes say the wrong thing, or get the wrong idea, and it is then that we hurt others or start spreading rumours, so that things eventually get out of control. This is where sin comes in. No, says Proverbs, you and I must keep count of our words, which means we must speak less and be careful of what we say. Then we are wise, and we leave less room for sin in our speech. Remember that your tongue is the single most important instrument that can cause you to sin. Be careful with it. Ask the Lord to help you speak less and listen more. Ask the Lord, also, that when you do talk, it will be wise words.

WWJD
Jesus would help you to listen.

 He ... wakens my ear to listen ... (Is.50:4)

December 1

Good advice

... He will be called Wonderful Counselor ... (Is. 9:5)

All of us need counselling, because we don't know every-thing! There are many things we don't understand and some-times we need to have things explained to us. This is one rea-son for going to school. Although it is not always fun to be at school, we get good counselling there. Knowledge is good counsel, and it teaches us to do what is right in our lives. It is good to know about all kinds of things, so that we can make the right decisions.

One can have all the knowledge in the world, and still not know the right way to live. We need more than book-learning; we need good counselling. Although we can get good counsel from people, the best counsel there is, comes from the Lord. That is why the Bible calls Jesus "Counselor". He is a wonderful Counselor who can advise you and me about all things in life. The most important counsel He wants to give us, is how to be happy. To choose Jesus and to follow him, is to have a wonderful Counselor. He talks to us in his Word and counsels us in many things. His Holy Spirit also leads us in truth. If we follow the Lord's advice, we should be happy.

WWJD
Jesus would give you the best counsel.

If any of you lacks wisdom, he should ask
God, who gives generously to all ... (Jas. 1:5)

December 2

Nicknames

James ... and his brother John (to them he gave the name ... Sons of Thunder). (Mk., 3:17)

James and John were two disciples that Jesus chose to follow him. We don't know much about them; the Bible says Jesus gave them a nickname. Jesus called them Boanerges, which means "sons of thunder".

It seems that James and John came from a family with quick tempers. They sounded almost like thunder. Thunder is heard when a storm is brewing and it builds up until the storm breaks. Many people are like thunder. They get angry and angrier still, and later they explode like a peal of thunder. Everybody witnesses and experiences their temper. James and John must have acted like this.

John is later mentioned as the disciple that Jesus loved very much and John also loved Jesus. It is John who writes at a later stage, that we must love one another. He mentions it, not once only, but many times in 1, 2 and 3 John. When you give your life to Jesus a miracle takes place: He changes your negative characteristics to positive ones. The sons of thunder later on became the sons of love. Allow the Lord to change you as He wants to.

WWJD
Jesus will make you new.

 ..."I am making everything new." (Rev. 21:5)

December 3

Your name is important

A good name is more desirable than great riches ... (Prov. 22:1)

People know you by your name. Your name is like a picture of you in someone's mind. A name is important, and that is why we must see to it that we do not lose our good name. You get a good name when you do good things. If you have a lovable nature, or you like helping others, people know you as a lovable and helpful person. If you are humble, people know you as a person who does not think too much of yourself ... If you are trustworthy, people know, when your name is mentioned, that they can rely on you.

The same goes for a bad name. If you have become known as a person who does nasty things, and if you always behave in a certain manner, people link the nasty things you do to your name. We all make mistakes, that is true, but if we don't say we are sorry and try to put things right, then people know us only as someone who does nasty things. Then we have a bad name.

The Bible says a good name is worth more than riches. Once you have lost your good name, it is very difficult to get it back again. How lucky we are that the Lord helps us to live in such a way, that even if we do make mistakes, people know we mean well.

WWJD
Jesus would always keep his good name.

A good name is better than fine perfume ... (Ecc. 7:1)

December 4

Do not lose heart

*(E)ach helps the other and says to his brother, "Be strong!"
(Js. 41:6)*

It is easy to give up hope. If things do not work out the way we planned them, we easily just give up. Especially if we have tried something a few times and it still won't work out. Each one of us has, at some stage, given up.

Certain people are wonderful at giving others hope. They motivate people. They tell us about the good qualities we have. They talk to us and build us up and show us they believe in us. These people bring out the best in us. When we are down-hearted, they notice, and do something to lift us out of it.

Perhaps you have seen on television when athletes run the Comrades. It is a long distance to run: almost 90 kilometres. Many runners get tired and feel like giving up. But along the road, there are thousands of people who encourage them and tell them they're doing well, and that they will make it to the end if they just carry on. Also fellow-athletes encourage one another, and all this makes it easier for the runners to complete the distance.

Then, of course, in our lives there is God who helps and encourages us through his Holy Spirit. He fills our hearts with hope and courage. He is there to support us, many times when there is no one to give us hope.

WWJD
Jesus would not let you down.

The ... Lord has given me an instructed tongue,
to know the word that sustains the weary. (Is. 50:4)

December 5

Streams of water

"Whoever believes in Me, as the Scripture has said, streams of living water will flow from within him." (Jn. 7:38)

No plant, animal or human can live without water. Water is absolutely necessary for you and me. If you have ever really been thirsty, you will know how good it feels to drink a glass of cold water. Just think how you enjoy jumping into the cool water of a pool on a hot summer's day. Or even the sea!

Jesus once talked to a sinful woman. She was busy fetching water from a well just outside the town where she lived. Jesus said to her, *"If you knew the gift of God ... you would have asked him and He would have given you living water"* (cf. Jn. 4:10).

Jesus also told her if one drinks from ordinary, earthly water, you will get thirsty again, but if you drink the water that He gives, you will never get thirsty again. The water the Lord gives, becomes like a fountain inside of us. What does Jesus mean? Jesus himself is like water to you and me. If we believe in him, we are fulfilled. Our thirst for sense and meaning in our lives is satisfied. He fills our hearts with his living water. Then we don't want all sorts of other things any more, He has given us fulfilment. Thank the Lord, right now, for his living water. If you are still thirsty, drink from the fountain that is Jesus himself.

WWJD
Jesus will give you living water.

" ...the water I give him will become in him a spring of water ... to eternal life." (Jn. 4:14)

December 6

From lambs to Lamb

" ... Look, the Lamb of God, who takes away the sin of the world!" (Jn. 1:29)

In the Old Testament people brought offerings because they had sinned, and to thank the Lord for what He had done for them. They usually sacrificed a perfect lamb.

The Father sent Jesus to earth to be sacrificed for our sins. In the same way that the lamb in the Old Testament took away sin, Jesus as the Lamb of God, had to take away our sins. Long before Jesus died on the cross, John the Baptist knew in his heart that Jesus would die for our sins. When he saw Jesus coming towards him one day, he said, "There is the Lamb of God who will take away the sins of the world." And he was right, because it is exactly what happened. Later on when Jesus was captured and tortured, and nailed to a cross, He suffered like a lamb for you and me. When his blood flowed and He died, He was the sacrifice for your sins and mine.

Today we do not sacrifice lambs any more, because the Lamb of God, Jesus Christ, was the last and perfect offering. You just need to accept it, and you will also be free of the guilt of sin.

WWJD
Jesus will take also your sin away.

(S)o Christ was sacrificed once to take away the sins of many people ... (Heb. 9:28)

December 7

Eat, drink, watch TV

So whether you eat or drink or whatever you do, do it all for the glory of God. (1 Cor. 10:31)

The Bible tells us that we serve the Lord, not only when we go to church, read our Bibles, or pray. True religion is when we do things to the glory of God, even if no one sees us. We serve him as the king of our lives if we praise him in everything we do.

Paul says whenever we eat, drink, or whatever, everything must be to the glory of God. When is something to the glory of God? When we do it the way Jesus will do it. When we do it in love. When we serve others by doing it. When we do it in such a way that it does not go against the Word and the will of God. Anything we do that is not God's will, is wrong and not to his glory.

The question we must ask ourselves when we watch TV, or eat, or drink, or chat, or visit someone is, "Will Jesus do it this way?" We must remember that the Lord is always with us. Will He always want to be with us wherever we are? Will He like watching what we do, and what will He think of the way we talk? Come, let's make the Lord feel at home with us! Let's do everything to his glory.

WWJD
Jesus would do everything to the glory of God.

... do it all in the name of the Lord Jesus ... (Col. 3:17)

December 8

Jesus with a plus

For this very reason, make every effort to add to your faith ... (2 Pet. 1:5)

Just believing is not good enough. This may sound a bit strange to you. Can't one just believe in the Lord, and all will be fine? Yes, it is true, faith is the most important thing. We must believe in Jesus as our Redeemer. But the Bible tells us do do something more than just believe.

Faith is the beginning of our spiritual life. If we believe in Jesus, we start a new life with him, and He leads us on a new road. As we walk this road with him, He teaches us through his Word, and the Holy Spirit speaks with us deep in our hearts. As we learn new things, our faith grows and becomes richer. Faith is like the foundations of a house. A house cannot stand strong and firm, if the foundations have not been made very strong. Only then can they start building the house. Faith is a strong foundation for you and me. Only then can we start building our faith-home: our lives.

That is why Peter says we must add certain things to our faith. We must work hard to add good qualities: knowledge, self-control, perseverance, love for one another, and love for all people. We must work hard at building our faith through good habits, and by adding all these qualities.

I hope you will do just that today!

WWJD
Jesus would help you live your faith.

... faith without deeds is dead. (Jas. 2:26)

December 9

Dry bones come to life

"I will put my spirit in you and you will live, and I will settle you in your own land." (Ezek. 37:14)

Ezekiel was a minister in the Old Testament. One day the Holy Spirit showed him a vision. A vision is almost like a dream. You see it very clearly in your mind, but it is not really happening so that you see it with your eyes. The Lord used visions to carry important messages across to his servants, so that they could teach people the right way.

At first this vision was not very nice. He saw a valley full of dry dead men's bones; the bones were so dry they were white. The Lord asked Ezekiel if these bones could ever live again. He replied that only God could tell. So the Lord told him the meaning of the vision.

The Lord says his people, the people of Israel, are like dry bones. God will put flesh and muscles on the bones and cover them with skin, and then He will give them a spirit so that they can live again.

Often people are like skeletons. Although they are breathing, they have no real life, no spiritual life. If one does not believe in Jesus and you have not been saved, you are spiritually dead, just like a skeleton. Even Christians can be half-dead spiritually, like the people of Israel. Then we need revival: the Holy Spirit must refill our lives, so that we can do God's will.

WWJD
Jesus will send his spirit so that you can live again.

"And I will put my Spirit in you ... and be careful to keep my laws." (Ezek. 36:27)

December 10

I will, but ...

"I will follow you, Lord; but first let me go back and say goodbye to my family." (Lk. 9:61)

The Lord calls people to follow him. Many say, yes, they want to follow him. They do so with their whole hearts, and that is the right way to do it. Unfortunately there are also those who follow him half-heartedly. They are touched by his words and they are willing to follow him, but they are not really willing to follow him with all their heart. Other things are still more important to them.

One day when Jesus was on his way, someone said to him, ... *"I will follow you wherever you go"* (v. 57). Jesus answered him that it is not always easy to follow the Lord. When Jesus told someone else that he should also follow him, his answer was, ... *"Lord, first let me ... "* (v. 59). He had an excuse: I will follow you later. I must first go and do something. Yet another said he had to go and say goodbye to his family.

The lesson is that we must not follow the Lord if we're not going to do it wholeheartedly. Of course we can go and say goodbye to our families, but Jesus knew this man was just making a poor excuse for not wanting to follow him. Do you perhaps also make excuses for not following the Lord with all your heart? I hope there aren't a lot of "buts" in your life.

WWJD
Jesus would do his Father's will, without making excuses.

"I have brought you glory on earth by completing the work you gave me to do." (Jn. 17:4)

December 11

What makes you happy?

"However, do not rejoice that the spirits submit to you, but rejoice that your names are written in heaven." (Lk. 10:20)

Jesus sent out seventy-two of his followers to every town and place He planned to go. They had to go and preach his peace, they had to heal people, and tell them about the kingdom of God.

When they got back, they said to Jesus, ... *"Lord, even the demons submit to us in your name"* (v. 17). They thought it was wonderful that the name of Jesus was so strong that even the devils listened to them. In those days there were many people who had evil spirits inside them. These demons left the people when they were told to in the name of Jesus.

Jesus' answer to his followers is a bit surprising. He is glad that they saw how wonderful his name and his power is, but they should rather be happy to know their names are written in heaven. To witness miracles and the power of the Lord is important, but it is more important to know that your relationship with God is good, and that your name is written in the book of life.

WWJD
Jesus will write your name in the book of life.

... (no one) will ever enter it ... but only those whose names are written in the Lamb's book of life. (Rev. 21:27)

December 12

Like the dead

When I saw him, I fell at his feet as though dead. (Rev. 1:17)

John was one of Jesus' followers. After the resurrection of Jesus, John preached the gospel of Jesus to many people. He was exiled to Patmos because he preached the Word of God and of Jesus.

One Sunday through the Holy Spirit, John heard a voice speaking to him. Then the Lord appeared to him. It was a miracle! Jesus, in all his glory, was standing in front of John. He wore a long robe with a golden sash around his chest. His hair was as white as snow. His face was like the sun shining in all its brilliance.

Although John loved the Lord, and was on earth with him, he said, *When I saw him, I fell at his feet as though dead ...* (v. 17). He was completely overwhelmed by the supernatural appearance of Jesus. But Jesus looked at him kindly, touched him with his right hand and said, ... *"Do not be afraid. I am the First and the Last. I am the Living One ... "* (v. 17, 18).

One day you will also see Jesus in all his glory. You don't have to be afraid. He will be kind and loving and make you feel at ease with him.

WWJD
Jesus would also make you feel at home with him.

... and I will dwell in the house of the Lord ... (Ps. 23:6)

December 13

His greatest wish

So we make it our goal to please him ... (2 Cor. 5:9)

I wonder what your answer would be if I should ask you what your greatest wish is. Maybe your dream is to have something special, or something so expensive that you cannot afford it. We all have our dreams and goals for our lives.

Paul was an ordinary person like you and me, but when the Lord changed his life, his dreams and goals became new. Yes, he also had his wishes and things he wanted, or wanted to do. He writes that he wanted very much to visit his friends, but then he mentions his most important wish: for his life to please the Lord.

Perhaps it sounds like rather a boring wish, but actually it is a beautiful goal. If you live to please the Lord, you will be happy and will always have peace in your heart. Then there is also the Lord's promise: if we do his will and seek his kingdom, He will give us everything we need. In Psalm 37:4 we read, *Delight yourself in the Lord and He will give you the desires of your heart.* So, we see that Paul is not stupid with this wish to please the Lord. Is it also your wish to do the Lord's will?

WWJD
Jesus will help you make this wish come true.

I want to know Christ ... (Phil. 3:10)

December 14

It was night!

As the sun was setting, Abram fell into a deep sleep, and a thick and dreadful darkness came over him. (Gen. 15:12)

I'm sure you remember that the Lord called Abram from a far-away country, called Ur. Abram was obedient and did what the Lord wanted. The Bible says the Lord was pleased with Abram for doing his will (cf. v. 6). But, we must not think if we follow the Lord nothing will ever go wrong for us.

One night it became dark for Abram; not only outside, but also in his heart. The Bible says fear like a thick and dreadful darkness came over him. Yes, Abram was afraid. He must have wondered about his life and his future. What was going to happen to him in years to come? Often it is also in the dark of night that we start worrying about things that can happen to us.

Just when Abram's fear was becoming too much for him to bear, the Lord started talking to him. The Lord promised that He would be with him, and would help him in everything he did. Sometimes when things are at their darkest, also in our lives, the Lord wants to comfort us and tell us that He is with us, and that He will keep his promises for our lives. Trust him. Like He cared for Abram, He will care for you and me, his children.

WWJD
Jesus will always be with you.

... I will fear no evil, for You are with me ... (Ps. 23:4)

December 15

First make peace

"(L)eave your gift there in front of the altar. First go and be reconciled to your brothers; then come and offer your gift."
(Mt. 5:24)

In Jesus' time people brought gift offerings to the altar to thank the Lord for his goodness and mercy. The Bible calls these thanks-offerings. They also brought other kinds of offerings to ask forgiveness of sins. With these offerings people wanted to make sure that they would always have a good relationship with God.

You and I also bring the Lord offerings. We go to church to worship him. We give money to thank him for taking care of us.

But Jesus tells us, *"So if when you are offering your gift at the altar you there remember that your brother has any [grievance] against you, leave your gift ... first make peace ... "* (v. 23, 24). Jesus tells us that we must first sort out all bad feelings between us and someone else, before our relationship with him can work. Often when we are in God's presence, He reminds us of something in our hearts that we have against another person. Then we must stop praying, the Bible says, and first go and make our peace with that person. Is there someone you need to make peace with? Why not phone him or her right now and say you're sorry. Then you can bring the Lord an offering.

WWJD
Jesus would help you do the right thing.

... the effect of righteousness will be quietness and confidence forever. (Is. 32:17)

December 16

The baby moved

When Elizabeth heard Mary's greeting, the baby leaped in her womb, and Elizabeth was filled with the Holy Spirit. (Lk. 1:41)

Mary was Jesus' mother. After the miracle of Jesus being formed in her body, she decided to visit her family. She came to the town where Elizabeth lived. Elizabeth was also expecting a baby. That baby would later be known as John the Baptist. When Mary moved closer to Elizabeth to greet her another miracle took place: as Mary greeted Elizabeth, the baby moved inside Elizabeth for the first time. The actual words are that the baby leaped or jumped inside her. It was a joyful movement, almost as if the baby inside Elizabeth was pleased that Jesus had come with Mary. At that moment Elizabeth was filled with the Holy Spirit, and she started praising the Lord for the miracle of Jesus' coming birth.

If even an unborn baby could react so wonderfully to the Savior, Jesus, you and I should also be filled with great joy. We must glorify and praise the Lord with our mouths and with everything we do.

WWJD
Jesus would be thankful in everything.

(G)ive thanks in all circumstances ... (1 Thes. 5:18)

December 17

He brings peace

And He will be called ... Prince of Peace. (Js. 9:5)

When Isaiah prophesied that Jesus would be born for you and me, he said that one of his names would be, "Prince of Peace." A prince is the son of a king, and often becomes king himself. But He is not an aggressive king who rules with power and strength. No, He is a prince that brings peace.

Peace is the opposite of war. When people make peace, they are not cross with one another any more, they no longer fight. It is good to live in peace. God wants us to live in peace with him, and this is only possible if Jesus makes us free from sin.

That is why Jesus is our Prince of Peace, because He makes peace with God on our behalf, through the Holy Spirit.

The Lord helps us to live in peace with others. That is why the Bible calls the children of the Lord "peacemakers".

Another important kind of peace is the peace we must have with ourselves. If God accepts us the way we are, we must also accept ourselves.

Thank the Lord that He came to bring peace in our hearts: peace with God, peace with others and peace with ourselves.

WWJD
Jesus would give you peace.

"Peace I leave with you; my peace I give you ..." (Jn. 14:27)

December 18

A wicked king

... he gave orders to kill all the boys ... who were two years old and under ... (Mt. 2:16)

The devil knew that Jesus would be born. He could not stand it, because he knew that if Jesus grew up, He would be the Savior of humankind.

One of the things the devil did to try and put a stop to Jesus' plan of redemption, was to work in the heart of the bad king, Herod. When Herod heard that someone had been born who would become a king, he decided immediately that this child had to be killed. But he did not know where to find him. So he gave orders to kill every baby boy born in and around Bethlehem. Fortunately an angel warned Joseph, so that they could flee with Baby Jesus.

Can you imagine how sad all the mothers and fathers were who lost their baby boys? Herod was very cruel. The devil put him up to this wicked plan. Herod did, however, not manage to kill Jesus, and He grew up to be our Redeemer.

The devil will also try to ruin God's plans for your life, but God is stronger than the devil, and He will protect you. Just put your trust in him.

WWJD
Jesus would feel safe in the hands of his Father.

I will fear no evil, for You are with me ... (Ps. 23:4)

December 19

A small town

... Bethlehem Ephrathah, though you are small ... out of you will come for me one ... (Mic. 5:1)

Long before Jesus was born, it was already prophesied in which town it would happen. The Holy Spirit prophesied through Micah that Jesus would be born in Bethlehem. Bethlehem was a small town and not at all important in the eyes of the people of that region.

Two things about this fact are important. The first is that Jesus was not born in an important place. One would expect that a person as important as Jesus would be born in a palace. He is, after all, the king of the whole world. But Jesus was born in a manger. He was laid down in a crib. Jesus was born in a plain and simple town, because. He was prepared to come to the humblest place on earth, so that even the humblest person could know Jesus is not too good or too important to follow.

The second meaning of Jesus' birth in Bethlehem is that it did not happen by chance. It was predicted long before by Micah. God never makes a mistake. His prophecies always come true.

Praise the Lord because He was prepared to be an ordinary baby for your sake and mine, to be born in an ordinary place, as God had prophesied.

WWJD
Jesus would never think He is better than others.

... whoever exalts himself
will be humbled ... (Mt. 23:12)

December 20

Our strong God

And he will be called ... Mighty God ... (Js. 9:5)

Nobody is as strong and powerful as God, the Father of Jesus Christ. He made the whole world. And He sees that everything is kept up. He is the great, strong, mighty God.

Isaiah prophesied that Jesus would also show the might of his Father. One of Jesus' names is "Mighty God". Jesus came to show God's power when He not only lived on earth and performed many miracles, but also died on the cross and afterwards powerfully rose from the dead. When you and I are afraid, we are comforted by the thought that we have someone with us who is strong, and who can help us. God is always prepared to be with us. Trust in him. He is also your mighty God. Ask him to help you today.

WWJD
Jesus will be with you as the mighty God.

" ... I am with you always, to the very end of the age." (Mt. 28:20)

December 21

The greatest gift

"For God so loved the world that he gave his one and only son ... " (Jn. 3:16)

What is the best present you have ever been given? I'm sure that gift made you very happy. It is always wonderful to receive a gift from someone.

A gift is something we are given. We don't work for it or earn it. A gift is free, someone else pays for it. The best gifts are those we don't expect; someone loves us so much that he or she wants to give us a present. God also gave you and me a gift: his Son, Jesus.

Christmas is that time of year when we give one another presents, because we want to remember that God loved us so much that He gave us the best gift of all gifts. The Lord looked at us and saw that we needed him very much. Someone had to come and help us so that we would not perish in our sins. That is why the Father sent his Son. Everyone who believes in him, will have everlasting life, and there is no gift in heaven or on earth as great as this one.

Thank the Lord right now for the wonderful gift of Jesus. Does it make you happy?

WWJD
Jesus will give you everlasting life.

...the gift of God is eternal life in Jesus Christ our Lord. (Rom. 6:23)

December 22

God likes us

" ... on earth peace to men on whom his favor rests." (Lk. 2:14)

When Jesus was born, an angel appeared to the shepherds near Bethlehem. And the angel said to them, *"Do not be afraid. I bring you good news of great joy that will be for all the people. Today ... a Savior has been born to you ... This will be a sign to you: You will find a baby wrapped in cloths ...* (v. 10-12). Suddenly millions of angels appeared, praising God and singing, *"Glory to God in the highest, and on earth peace to men on whom his favor rests"* (v. 14).

The angels praised the Lord because Jesus would bring peace on earth. Anyone who accepts Jesus as Lord, finds peace because his sins have been forgiven. Peace is the Lord's Christmas gift to us. Why does the Lord do it? Because his favor rests on us. This means that God likes us very much.

He likes people, because He made them. He also knows we are unhappy because the devil tempts us. But because He likes us in any case, He gives us his Son to save us and to make us new. Yes, the Lord loves you and me. That is the Christmas message: God liked us so much that He was prepared to give us his Son.

WWJD
Jesus would give his life for others.

"For God so loved the world that He gave his one and only Son ..." (Jn. 3:16)

December 23

Available

"J am the Lord's servant," Mary answered. "May it be to me as you have said." (Lk. 1:38)

The Lord sent the great angel Gabriel to a young girl who lived in Nazareth. This girl was engaged to Joseph. Her name was Mary. Even today many people are named Mary, because she was such an important person. Yes, you are right, Mary is the mother of Jesus.

The angel came up to Mary and he greeted her. She got such a fright, but the angel told her not to be afraid. He told her that she would fall pregnant and would have a baby boy and that she had to name him Jesus. He went on to say that He will be called the Son of the Most High, and that He will reign as king for ever. Mary was very surprised. She wanted to know how that was possible. He answered that the Holy Spirit would perform a miracle so that Jesus' life would start inside her body. God can do anything; nothing is impossible to him. Then Mary said she was available to God, that He could do with her as He pleased.

How wonderful if you can say to the Lord that you are available, that He can do with you anything He wants to. You can be a wonderful instrument for him to use. Like Mary. Are you available?

WWJD
Jesus would be available.

"Whom shall I send?" ...
"Here am I Send me!" (Is. 6:8)

December 24

Christmas

"Today in the town of David a Savior has been born to you; He is Christ the Lord." (Lk. 2:11)

Today is Christmas Day! It is one of the most wonderful and most important days of the year. This is the day we are happy to get together as families and tell everybody that we love them. We give one another presents and remind each other that Jesus was born on this day.

Today we remember that Jesus was born a little baby in a manger in Bethlehem. He did not stay a baby. Jesus grew up and said He was the Redeemer. He also proved it, because He died on a cross for you and me. There He paid the price for our sins. He is also the Lord, because He rose from the dead: "Lord" means He reigns as king over all the powers of darkness.

I hope you will have a very blessed Christmas and that it will be a wonderful day for you. Praise Jesus, that He was prepared to come to this world as our Savior.

WWJD
Jesus will save you.

... we have redemption through his blood ... (Eph. 1:7)

December 25

Goodwill

Let your gentleness be evident to all. (Phil. 4:5)

The word "gentle" means kind, careful, not rough or violent, merciful, sweet-tempered, willing. The Amplified Bible uses the word "unselfishness" in this verse and explains it as considerateness. All of this means that we are open to others, willing to meet them halfway. A word which is also used in this text is "friendliness". Friendly people are easy-going, they are open, loving and considerate. Oh, how our country needs people like this!

There are many people in our country who don't like one another one bit. They make fun of one another, they talk badly of one another. We have so many different cultures in our country that we sometimes don't know members of another group. This makes that we are not open to them. We are unfriendly towards others and sometimes even afraid of one another. We need goodwill. In one of the languages of our country the word "ubuntu" expresses this feeling of goodwill towards others. It means a good attitude of love and friendliness towards others.

Decide that wherever you go, you will be friendly towards everybody, even if you don't like them. Show friendliness and goodwill to all people.

WWJD
Jesus would be considerate towards all people.

Be devoted to one another
in brotherly love. (Rom. 12:10)

December 26

Marana ta

Come, Lord Jesus. (Rev. 22:20)

I'm sure you also miss someone sometimes. Perhaps it is a grandpa or a grandma, or a very good friend. Maybe you haven't seen them for quite a while, and now you wish you could be with them again. Perhaps you phone them now and then, and say to them, "Please, won't you come and visit!" When we love someone and we like them, we like being with them. When they go away, we long to see them again.

Christians are people who belong to Jesus, and they love the Lord. They would like to see him and be with him. I don't know about you, but I would love being with Jesus one day – not only in faith, but really with him, in his presence. I would like to talk to him and even touch him if I may. The first disciples were very sad when He went up to heaven. They were sad, because they didn't want him to go away from them. In the very last verses of the Bible we find the words, spoken longingly, Come, Lord Jesus! (This is what "Marana ta" means.) And Jesus said that He will definitely come. Perhaps it will be soon. Let us be ready when He comes to fetch us. Until then, our hearts are longing for this day. Tell him now that you are longing to see him, and that it will be wonderful to be with him.

WWJD
Jesus will come again to fetch you.

" ... I will come to you." (Jn. 14:18)

December 27

In heaven ...

The rich man ... died and ... he looked up and saw Abraham ... (Lk. 16:23)

Have you ever wondered what it looks like in heaven, and what we will do there? Heaven feels so far away to us, but maybe it is much nearer than we think.

One of the things that we wonder about, is if we will recognize the people we love on earth, in heaven. The Bible says, yes. When the rich man died, he recognized Abraham. You and I will also recognize our loved ones in heaven. If there is someone in your family who has died and is with Jesus, you will definitely see each other again. Perhaps you will sit and talk under the same tree for ages, because there is no such thing as time in heaven. Isn't it wonderful to know that one day we will be with our loved ones again, in heaven. It seems to me that people will also see one another in hell, but there won't be time for anything good, because of all the pain and suffering. The people in hell will have a very bad time. I hope you belong to the Lord, and that you are on your way to heaven.

WWJD
Jesus will be pleased to see us again.

"Blessed are those who are invited to the wedding supper ..." (Rev. 19:9)

December 28

The court will sit

"The court was seated, and the books were opened." (Dan. 7:10)

The Bible tells us about a very important court which will sit at the end of the world. Everybody will appear before the great white throne of God. There we will all have to account for our lives. This means that we will have to explain why we did all those things that we knew were wrong. God will decide if we are to be punished or not. He will acquit some of us. This means that we will be found not guilty.

All those who do not believe in Jesus Christ will be judged. They will be found guilty of sin. Things people thought no one would ever know about, will now be made known to everyone. What was done in secret, will now be seen by all.

But Jesus is our great Advocate. His blood will cover our sins. Jesus will speak for each one of us who believes in him. We will be acquitted; not because we did not sin, but because Jesus paid for our sins. It is so wonderful to know that you and I will walk out, free, because of Jesus. That is why our relationship with Jesus is so important. Have you asked him yet to forgive your sins? Have you accepted his death on the cross as payment for your sins. He will pronounce you not guilty on Judgement Day. Thank the Lord now because He is good.

WWJD
Jesus will free you at the second coming.

(All) are justified freely by his grace through the redemption that came by Christ Jesus. (Rom. 3:24)

December 29

The trumpet call

"And He will send his angels with a loud trumpet call, and they will gather his elect ... " (Mt. 24:31)

A trumpet is an instrument that makes a very clear sound. It is a difficult instrument to play, but it plays beautiful notes and its sound is really something. In olden times a trumpet call was the sign for a war to start. Also, when important announcements were made, someone blew on a trumpet, so that people knew something important was about to be said.

The Lord says there will be a loud trumpet call on the day Jesus comes back to earth. We know He will come back as He promised. The Bible tells us that when the trumpet sounds, Jesus will appear in the sky, and all the nations of the earth will be dismayed. Everybody will see him come with power and great glory. Then He will send his angels out to gather everyone who loves him and knows him, from all over the world. They will then live with him for ever.

Won't it be absolutely wonderful to see the Lord coming on the clouds? I think people who don't know him will be very scared. You and I must be ready for him when He comes again.

WWJD
Jesus will come again to fetch us.

" ... I will come back and take you to be with Me ... " (Jn. 14:3)

December 30

Ebenezer

He named it Ebenezer, saying, "Thus far has the Lord helped us." (1 Sam. 7:12)

The Israelites were in trouble because the Philistines were making war against them. The Philistines were very strong and powerful. Then Israel decided to get rid of all the heathen gods and serve only the Lord. They got together at Mizpah and confessed their sins. Samuel also pleaded with the Lord for Israel, and the Lord answered his prayers.

The battle against the Philistines was won by a miracle. The Lord sent loud thunder, which threw them into such a panic that they could do nothing against Israel. Then Samuel set up a stone like a monument. He admitted that the Lord helped them.

At the end of this year, we can look back and say the Lord also helped us. He helped us against an enemy that tried to destroy us. He helped and encouraged us with our school work, and in everything we did. There are so many thing to thank the Lord for. Set up a monument for him in your thoughts and in your hearts. Tell your family and your friends, "Up until now, the Lord has helped also me." If we know the Lord was with us during this past year, we can look ahead and know: this same Lord will also be willing to be with me in the new year.

WWJD
Jesus will always be with us.

" ... And surely I am with you always, to the very end of the age." (Mt. 28:20)

December 31